Victimology: A New Focus

Volume I

Theoretical Issues in Victimology

Victimology:
A New Focus

Volume I
Theoretical Issues in Victimology

Edited by
Israel Drapkin and Emilio Viano

Lexington Books
D.C. Heath and Company
Lexington, Massachusetts
Toronto   London

Library of Congress Cataloging in Publication Data

International Symposium on Victimology, 1st, Jerusalem, 1973
    Theoretical issues in victimology.

    (Victimology: a new focus, v. 1)
    Includes primarily papers presented at the symposium.
    1. Victims of crime—Congresses.   I. Drapkin Sendery, Israel,
1905-   ed. II. Viano, Emilio, ed. III. Title.
HV6030.I54 1973 vol. 1   364s [364]   74-14827
ISBN 0-669-95729-1

Published simultaneously in Canada.

Printed in the United States of America.

International Standard Book Number, Vol. I: 0-669-95729-1
International Standard Book Number, Set: 0-669-95778-x

Library of Congress Catalog Card Number: 74-14827

For Beniamin Mendelsohn and Hans Von Hentig,
Pioneers in Victimology.

Contents

Preface

If any single set of books can succeed in making "victimology" professionally respectable and intellectually serious, then the volumes in this series, *Victimology: A New Focus*, will do it. The five volumes of the series, remarkable for the variety and breadth of their content, are: *Theoretical Issues in Victimology*; *Society's Reaction to Victimization*; *Crimes, Victims, and Justice*; *Violence and Its Victims*; and *Exploiters and Exploited: The Dynamics of Victimization.*

While this is not the first publication in the field of victimology, it is a truly comprehensive presentation of the best current work originated in the international scholarly community. Victimology, a relatively new development within the study of crime and deviance, is experiencing a rapid and vigorous development. Although the founders of criminology were well aware of the important role that the criminal-victim relationship plays in the dynamics of crime, it was not until recently that a systematic and sustained effort to study the victims of crime developed. Von Hentig's paper entitled, "Remarks on the Interaction of Perpetrator and Victim" (1941) and his book, *The Criminal and His Victim* (1948); Mendelsohn's paper, "New Bio-psycho-social Horizons: Victimology" (1947); and Ellenberger's study on the psychological relationship between the criminal and his victim (1954) are among the seminal works that spurred research on the subject of the criminal-victim relationship. Since then, many scholars and criminal justice professionals have focused their attention on this dimension of the criminal situation. As a consequence, a respectable body of literature has emerged.

At the same time, practitioners and reformers became interested in restoring to the victim some of the recognition and rights that he had enjoyed in antiquity. Margery Fry, the late English penal reformer, led the movement asking for revival of the victim's importance and for the institution of more effective remedies for victims other than the traditional tort procedure in the civil courts (1955). This movement made some inroads as New Zealand established the first crime compensation tribunal in 1963, followed by England in 1964. In the United States, the first state to acknowledge the need to compensate the victims of crime was California (1965); followed later by New York (1966); Hawaii (1967); Massachusetts (1967); Maryland (1968); Nevada (1969); New Jersey (1971); Alaska (1972); and Washington (1974). Several efforts undertaken at the federal level have been unsuccessful to date.

Other experts have suggested a different approach for the compensation of crime victims: insurance. For example, insurance protection is now reportedly offered in the United States to corporate clients against kidnapping and ransom demands. Meanwhile, other important facets of the victim's situation have come under scrutiny and have spurred people into action. Students and professionals in the criminal justice system have become increasingly aware that a victim of a criminal becomes—more often than not—also the victim of the criminal justice system. Once the victim reports his victimization to the police—the gateway to the criminal justice system—he or she is routinely faced by postponements, delays, reschedulings, and other abuses. All this means loss of earnings, waste of time, frustration, and the painful realization that the system does not live up to its ideals and does not serve its constituency, but instead serves itself and its underlings. As a consequence, many innovative proposals have been advanced, such as the creation of central citizens' complaint and service bureaus; witness coordinators at police stations, courthouses, district attorneys' offices, and defenders' offices; participation of the victim in plea bargaining by prosecutors; reports, at some point, by police to victims on whether they are making progress in investigating and solving their cases; the provision of the services of an ombudsman who would assist the victims of crime by intervening in the crisis, acting as a community facilitator, and referring the victims to the community's and other resources.

This ferment of ideas, research, and reform efforts in the area of victimology has now reached a significant momentum. The First International Symposium on Victimology held in Jerusalem in 1973 gave the area of victimology international recognition as a distinct focus of inquiry within criminology. With the Symposium, victimology has entered its mature stage and will, hopefully, bear fruits from the point of view of theoretical insights, research breakthroughs, and practical implementation.

The major papers in the English language presented and discussed during the Symposium are published in these five volumes. A few other papers, not read in Jerusalem, have also been included because of their relevance to the development of victimology. In this sense, these volumes are an accurate reflection of the current work undertaken by the international community of scholars and professionals on the subject of victims of crime.

The principal aims of the Symposium were to facilitate the exchange of ideas and to stimulate more and improved research in victimology, the potential of which has not yet been well mined. The value of the Symposium for the participants consisted in the pooling of topics, in learning what particular problems interest various people, and then receiving the stimulation of others to pursue problems in one's own work. To date, the field has been one in which individual scholars have contributed as individuals, with little, if any, of the work reflecting the cumulative effort of groups of scholars. These volumes aim at providing new data, theoretical inputs, and analyses that will encourage the building of ideas and the development of intellectual dialogues in the field of victimology. In particular, these volumes seek to contribute to a discourse within the international community of scholars, and to bring together scholars whose paths may not easily cross, in spite of their common interest.

While the papers published in these volumes reflect the wide scope and diversity of pursuits in the field of victimology, they have been organized as follows:

Theoretical Issues in Victimology consists first of all of papers discussing "The Notion of Victimology," that is, the definition of the concept of victim, the locus of victimology in the realm of the social sciences and in relation to criminology, and future directions of development. The second part of the volume, "Victim Typology," debates the issues of victim definition and classification, and their impact on empirical research. In particular, the offender-victim relationship is examined and discussed.

Society's Reaction to Victimization consists first of seven papers on "Prevention and Treatment of Victims of Crime," dealing with the ways and means which society might adopt to come to the aid of victims in distress and also to effectively prevent victimization. Then, a series of papers discuss "Compensation and Restitution to Victims of Crime" as representing the restoration of the social equilibrium in all its aspects, individual and collective, following the disturbance by the criminal act.

Crimes, Victims, and Justice discusses problems related to the treatment of the victim at the hands of the criminal justice system. The case of the falsely accused person and a closer look at the offender as the victim are also examined. Moreover, past and current research being conducted in the area of victimology is described and important methodological questions about victimization surveys are raised.

Violence and Its Victims and *Exploiters and Exploited: The Dynamics of Victimization* pursue the themes developed in the previous volumes by applying them to the analysis of specific situations. The collection of papers in *Violence and Its Victims* is divided in three sections: Homicide and Suicide, Mass Violence and Genocide, and Children's Victimization. The volume *Exploiters and Exploited* addresses the issues of Sex Offenses and Rape, White Collar Crime, Institutional Victimization, Traffic Offenses, and Related Victimization.

We are grateful to the authors of the various papers for granting us permission to publish their contributions. We feel indeed privileged in being able to bring their work to the attention of the international scholarly community for the first time being certain, as we are, that they will be favorably received. We also feel that they will spur further debate, research, and innovative thinking in the area of victimology. At Lexington Books, we would like to thank Mr. Mike McCarroll, Director, and Ms. Barbara Levey, former Editor-in-Chief, for their generous understanding and encouragement; Ms. Shirley End and the production staff for their careful aid in editing and preparing the manuscript for publication; and Ms. Carolyn Hanson for her skillful efforts to bring these volumes to the attention of scholars and of the general public.

References

Ellenberger, H.   "Psychological Relationships between the Criminal and his
1954   Victim." *Revue Internationale de Criminologie et de Police
                  Technique* 2: 103-121.

Mendelsohn, B.   "New Bio-psycho-social Horizons: Victimology." Unpub-
1947   lished communication read to the Roumanian Society of
                  Psychiatry in Bucharest.

Von Hentig, H.   "Remarks on the Interaction of Perpetrator and Victim."
1941   *Journal of the American Institute of Criminal Law and
                  Criminology* 31 (March-April) 303-309.

Von Hentig, H.   *The Criminal and His Victim: Studies in the Socio-biology
1948   of Crime.* New Haven: Yale University Press.

Introduction

*Remarks read by Professor Israel Drapkin, Chairman of the
Organizing Committee, at the Opening Ceremony of the First
International Symposium on Victimology held in Jerusalem
on September 2, 1973.*

The scholars gathered here in Jerusalem today have come with the purpose
of discussing with their Israeli colleagues the basic issues of a topic that is as
old as mankind but comparatively new as a scientific endeavor. We refer, obviously, to "victimology," an expression usually accepted to have been coined in
1947 by Mr. B. Mendelsohn here with us tonight, to whom I should like to pay
respect on behalf of all of us.

From the simple etymological point of view, "victimology" derives from
the Latin word "victima" and the Greek root "logos." "Victima" has two basic
meanings: one implies the living creature sacrificed to a deity, or offered in
performance of a religious rite. The second meaning is that used in criminology
and related fields. It refers to the person suffering, injured or destroyed by the
action of another—which may be due to some uncontrollable quality in himself—in pursuit of an object or purpose, in gratification of a passion, or as a result
of events or circumstances. In other words, "victimology" basically refers to the
study of the victim. It is precisely this plural definition which creates the possibility of studying the subject from quite a number of different, and even antag-
onistic, points of view.

In 1948, the famous German criminologist Hans Von Hentig dealt with the
subject in an extensive way. Since then, a good number of works have come
to the fore, both of a philosophical and a scientific nature. In spite of their
importance, however, they lack a common foundation. Each researcher acted
more or less as a freelancer, without paying too much attention to the personal
points of view of his colleagues working in the same subject. What was lacking
was an international platform on which to interchange ideas and results, to
compare methodology and techniques, and to facilitate coordination and
cooperation in order to try to reach a consensus on basic issues already developed or on matters to be studied in the future. Just this, and nothing else, is
the basic purpose of this First International Symposium on Victimology.

Sir Peter Medawar has properly stressed the point that all advances of
scientific understanding, at every level, begin with a speculative adventure,

and imaginative preconception of what might be true; a preconception which always, and necessarily, goes a little, or even a long way beyond anything in which we have logical or factual authority to believe. The conjecture is then exposed to criticism. Scientific reasoning is therefore, at all levels, an interaction between two episodes of thought, the one imaginative and the other critical; a dialogue, if you like, between the possible and the actual; between proposal and disposal; conjecture and criticism. In this conception of the scientific process, imagination and criticism are integrally combined. Imagination without criticism may burst out into a comic profusion of grandiose and silly notions. Critical reasoning alone is barren.

If some of you might be inclined to believe that the Greek philosophers went too far in their speculative exercises, there are others who are convinced that present-day science pays too much respect to statistical checking and counter-checking. Excessive play with theoretical hypothesis, lacking appropriate critical control, is as dangerous as excessive worship at the altar of statistics, without the benefit of the imaginative mind. It is the adequate blending of these two approaches—the pragmatic and sometimes even distasteful eclecticism—that will bring us nearer to our ultimate and common goal.

In ancient civilizations, the victim of forbidden acts or omissions was always a paramount figure on the stage of the criminal setting. Compensation and "wergeld" were the means by which humanity moved slowly from the practice of private revenge to that of public justice. Then, with state and government taking justice into their own hands, the offender gradually became the central figure of the criminal drama, and the victim was almost entirely forgotten. The last thirty years have witnessed a rebirth in the care for the victim.

Ecclesiastes stresses the fact that for everything there is a season: a time for every purpose and for every work; a time to keep silent and a time to speak. We are convinced that the time has come to speak and to work for the rights of the victim, with the aim of mobilizing public opinion in benefit of this excessively neglected subject.

We are living in a technological and materialistic era, controlled by economic rules, competitive antagonism, and blatant aggressiveness among human beings; a world torn by bitterness and hatred, where the right of force prevails rather than the force of right; a world which seems to forget that violence does not finish with the problems but with the solutions; a world in which honesty is almost considered to be a pathological anomaly; a world which lives dangerously without trying to avoid unnecessary victimization. In this world, all kinds of alienation become the natural and frequent outcome.

Technology, as any other human conquest, has a price to be paid, a price that seems to be a frighteningly high one. The time has come to start thinking of the means to control the dreadful might we have created, and this can only be achieved by returning once more to the eternal moral human values. Let us hope that this modest Symposium may become our common contribution to facilitate the dawn of a new era, where mankind will start again to forgive and to love; an age of hope, brotherhood and peace, dignity and freedom, mutual respect and trust; an era of justice and righteousness.

This is perhaps the most important reason why we have to stop treading the old paths of our prejudices; we have to start daring and risking, leaving part of our own selves on every one of the stepping stones marking the way of our future. If there is a future for our endeavors, it will only be possible if all, or at least some of us, become iconoclasts and destroy those unworthy idols still worshipped by mankind. If this means being called 'extremist', 'revolutionary', 'anti-establishment', 'nonconformist' or any other of the infinite variety of today's slogans—more used than understood—let us not be afraid of it. Like new crusaders, our fight should not be based on religious grounds, but on working for a better future for tomorrow, the world of our children and of our children's children.

The declared purposes of this Symposium can be summarized as follows. We will try, first, to reach an agreement regarding the scope of victimology: should it cope only with victims of crime or should it include all kinds of victims, no matter the source, nature or degree of their victimization? Once this crucial point has been settled, as we hope it will be, agreement on the problems of methodology and other research matters may then be easily arrived at. Secondly, we have to consider the possibilities of establishing a valid typology of victims, an indispensable tool for future developments. Thirdly, it will be necessary to analyze the role of the victim, both in the juridical and judicial settings, in order to improve the present situation as much as possible. Our fourth aim is the analysis of the offender-victim relationship, particularly with regard to the main categories of criminal offense. And, finally, the problem remains of how to improve society's reaction towards victims, be it by means of compensation, insurance, prevention, or treatment.

Besides these five main objectives, it is of the utmost importance to avoid two frequent pitfalls in this slippery field of victimology. On the one extreme, we can overdo the emphasis on the role of the victim and reach the opposite conclusion, namely that the victim is the real criminal and the criminal a mere victim of his victim. On the other extreme, we should abstain from being involved in what could be called the "conspiracy of silence." The vast majority of us acquiesce with silence when the process of victimization starts in the highest echelons of the power structure of our respective societies, no matter what their political flavor is. It is time for us criminologists to become vociferous when government, high-placed authorities, or the so-called "Establishment" victimizes members of the community outside the criminal law framework.

With all this in mind, victimology might be properly shaped here. It will not be an easy task, but it is certainly possible. Every first experience is diffi-cult, sometimes even painful, like all kinds of creative endeavor. We cannot foresee the impact that the guidelines established here might have on the course of immediate and future orientations in this new field. We accept this historical responsibility with a great amount of trepidation, but no fear, and we leave to the social scientist and historian of the future the evaluation of our work here. But on an occasion like this, when an important milestone is reached, there is cause for a common and justifiable pride.

Our personal pride and confidence stems from the fact that this First International Symposium on Victimology takes place here in Israel, the new nation of the Jewish people. We belong to an old people that has been discrim-inated against and persecuted by its fellow men through the ages, for numberless generations, and in spite of all this, or perhaps because of it, we have a deep understanding for all kinds of victim; we never understood nor believed in the existence of the impossible; we have always been in the forefront of change, running away from frozen ideologies; we have been able to sum up the suffer-ings, deceits, and disillusionments of twenty centuries, not in a tremendous failure, but in a resounding success; we are a people who, for the third time in our history, have come back to the land of our biblical ancestors, to rebuild our capital here in Jerusalem, the City of Peace, as the Kings of Israel called it 2500 years ago, and from where we extend to all and every one of you our most cordial Bruchim Ha-Baim, Welcome, Soyez Les Bienvenus, Bienvenida.

We cannot possibly finish these opening remarks without expressing our most sincere gratitude and deepest appreciation for the so many organizations, colleagues, and friends that have contributed so much to the crystallization of our dream: this First International Symposium on Victimology. Without their assistance and stimulation it could never have taken place. We should like to mention the various authorities of the government of Israel; the International Society of Criminology, represented here tonight by its vice president; and the Hebrew University of Jerusalem by its president. They are the sponsors of the Symposium, with the cooperation of the Universities of Tel Aviv and Bar Ilan, the Israel Academy of Sciences and Humanities, and the Van Leer Jerusalem Foundation that have so kindly opened their doors for our meetings. We should also like to express our happiness at having with us here the representa-tives of the Council of Europe; of the International Penal and Penitentiary Foundation; and of the British Council. They have all contributed to the success of this Symposium. Our esteem goes also to the distinguished members of our International Advisory Board, which so much influenced many of our decisions; to the members of our National Organizing Committee, who worked with us from day to day; to the distinguished colleagues who have so unself-ishly accepted the responsibilities of being the chairmen and rapporteurs of the various sections into which this Symposium has been divided; to the members of our Steering Committee; to Mr. Justice Chaim Cohen, who will deliver the opening lecture; and to the academic staff and secretariat of our Institute of Criminology, who so devotedly and anonymously have taken the major part of the organizational burden; to those of you particularly that have come from abroad, despite certain doubts and fears regarding the safety of modern international traveling. To all and every one of you, my personal gratitude for all you have done to make this project possible and successful.

**Part I
The Notion of Victimology**

Introduction to Part I

The studies presented here provide important material to deepen the reader's understanding of the scope and boundaries of the field. Inkeri Anttila discusses what new perspectives victim-centered research has brought into criminology, and what limits and dangers must be taken into consideration. In his paper, Hans Göppinger debates the question facing any criminologist, "Is it meaningful to conduct research on the victim separately?" Zvonimir Separovic pursues this theme by attempting to answer several crucial questions facing victimology as a new discipline. Next, Beniamin Mendelsohn, one of the pioneers in the field, offers his insights, discussing the notion of "victimity;" victim determining environments, the danger milieu, and finally, calling for the establishment of victimological clinics, staffed by interdisciplinary teams.

Stanley Johnston invites the reader to enlarge both the political perspective and the historical time span of ordinary criminology. He endeavors to expand the definition of the concept of victim to include those who suffer from the crimes, from the incompetence and growing irrelevance of national governments.

Milo Tyndel then presents an overview of those cases in which an offense does not necessarily victimize any particular person, the perpetrator being the victim of his own offense, so to speak. He maintains that the perpetuation of these offenses is caused, among other factors, by the law. Therefore, he coins the term "nomogenic diseases" to describe those conditions in whose development and maintenance the law plays a significant role.

Hugo Bedau also analyses the concept of the so-called "victimless" crimes. He concludes, as he makes a critical survey of the works on the subject, that there is great confusion and inconsistency as to the general notion of such crimes and as to how society proceeds in these matters. He further feels that it is irrational and premature to decriminalize conduct on the basis of its victimless nature since the very concept of such crimes has not yet been fully grasped.

For his part, Jeffrey Reiman stresses the fundamental importance for victimology—as a science—to begin with a sound and coherent conceptual foundation. If victimologists are to be successful in adequately defining the concept of victim, then victimology will be spared some of the "definitional crises" which have shaken the field of criminology.

3

1

Victimology: A New Territory in Criminology
Inkeri Anttila

A steadily growing sector of recent research in criminology manifests a concern for investigating the role played by the victims in criminal violations of the law. This kind of research is often regarded as associated with a special *method* for gathering knowledge. The victims are useful because they provide otherwise unavailable information; this information may then be associated with, for example, characteristics of offenders or offences. Victims have for decades been used for such purposes, especially in connection with studies of hidden delinquency. Evidently, this method of research will retain its usefulness even in the future, at least when there are no possibilities of obtaining information from other sources (as in cases where the offender is not caught). Victimological research can thus always be defended on the basis of its general *informational value.*

The concept of victimology is, however, frequently used in a slightly different context. It then refers not only to a particular source of information, but also to the particular type of information as such which is associated with the victim. This type of information could be called *'victim-centered',* and in principle it may be obtained in many different ways, for example, from official statistics, participant observation, or interviews with criminals.

Some Aspects of Victim-Centered Research

What new perspectives are brought into criminology by victim-centered research?

1. Criminologists who focus on characteristics of the individual have obtained a new set of research targets. For decades, the offenders had been in the focus of interest, and much work had been spent on efforts to find out what kind of peculiarities, anomalies, mental illnesses, intelligence or character defects could serve as an explanation of criminality. Now, the same types of questions may be raised with regard to the victims. The scope of individual-centred research was thus enlarged 100 percent, or even more.

2. Victim-centered research has brought a kind of balance to criminological research. Society has always tried to assign the offender a certain societal

Reprinted by special permission from *Scandinavian Studies in Criminology*, vol. 5 (1974), Universitetsforlaget, Oslo. Also, by permission of the author.

role and to keep him in it. This stereotyping of the offender has been effected by looking at him as an outsider, a different kind of person: evil, sick, mentally deviant. The stereotyped victim, on the contrary, has been seen as the innocent party whose miserable fate it was to fall victim to a brutal crime. The new perspective introduced by victimology has, of course, eliminated these stereotypes. In some instances the balance may even have swung too far in the other direction.

New scapegoats are available for explaining criminality. Criminologists have been quick to point out that victims of assault have no one except themselves to blame if they deliberately walk in dark alleys after dark; that young girls actually wanted to be raped if they did not heed the warnings of their mothers; and that the stores deliberately provoke thefts by exhibiting goods in as tempting a way as possible.

Generally, one can say that the earlier stereotypes of 'black and white' have been exchanged for 'grey versus grey'. It is often pointed out that a great part of criminality is concentrated within certain groups and certain areas. Both criminals and victims appear to be odd people, inclined to unlawfulness, provocative and easily provoked. The same individuals may alternatingly or even simultaneously turn up as offenders and victims, while the majority of society's ordinary members are safely outside.

3.   This reorientation—deliberately exaggerated here—has also influenced policy-making. In earlier times, the emphasis was on deterrence designed to influence the motivation of potential criminals: the threat of punishment and the risk of getting caught were considered the primary means of preventing crime. Victim-centered research has pointed to new alternatives. Once the stereotype of the innocent and unsuspecting victim has proved to be false, it has seemed natural to plan measures that are supposed to change the behavior of the victims, rather than that of the offenders. It has become possible to demand that potential victims should use special safety locks, introduce television surveillance in shops and similar technical devices, or insure themselves against burglaries, etc. Speaking the language of criminology: a part of the social costs caused by crime has been transferred from the offenders to potential victims. This new ideology has even brought forth suggestions that the entire costs of criminality could in some cases be placed on the shoulders of the victim: in Scandinavian countries it has been proposed that the owner of a supermarket should not have the right to prosecute the offender in cases of petty shoplifting; and it has been suggested that the banks should themselves accept the responsibility for forged checks. It has been said that the costs of petty offences connected with any particular business could easily be paid by those who profit from that business.

4.   Another new perspective in the field of criminal policy is connected with the determining the gravity of various offences. The general sense of justice, often mentioned as a yardstick, primarily reflects the opinions of the

middle class, while the victims who suffer the damage tend to belong to the lower class. Victim-centered research has indicated that the victim's opinions concerning the gravity of an offence might differ from the opinions of the middle class. If the idea of 'relative loss' is considered, i.e., relative to the life situation of the victim in question, it is definitely necessary to ask the victim himself how he feels. The development of systems for the compensation of victims of crime may well have been influenced by victimological research.

The Limits and Risks of Victim-centered Research

Without any doubt, victim-centered research will continue to be an essential part of criminology. A word of caution may therefore be in order. There are not only advantages but also some limits to be taken into consideration.

1. A real danger is the possibility that interest will simply shift from the individual offender to the individual victim. Research preoccupied with individual characteristics can usually only be effectively used for explaining the *selection process*, i.e., what kind of individuals will be selected as criminals or victims. Variations in the level of criminality remain without explanation. Individual-centered research in its narrowest sense takes into account offender and victim independently. More sophisticated research also considers the interaction process and the general situational factors. But even then, if the problems related to society in general and to the volume of criminality are left aside, the research results tend to be of little importance for decision-making.

2. The growing interest in victim-centered research may lead to over-emphasis on such types of criminal behavior where there is an easily identified individual victim. This implies a concentration of research efforts on traditional types of crimes, such as assaults, larcenies, and sexual offences. Some large groups of crimes seem to be neglected altogether, only because there are no easily identified victims.

The problem of finding a victim depends, as a matter of fact, upon how we view the functioning of the control system. In an abstract sense, every crime has a potential victim. The immediate crime target will, perhaps, not consider himself or herself victimized at all (e.g. when a sex crime against a minor takes place with the victim's consent). The criminalization may then frequently be interpreted so that the real 'victims' are all those persons who feel that the crime violates their taboos or threatens their security. Even the 'crimes without victims', if the popular term is used, have victims: they may, for example, be supposed to cause danger in a society.

The analysis of the victim concept could be taken one step further by viewing the whole society as a victim. Or one could, in a certain sense, consider the criminals as victims. According to the ideology, which stresses the unavoidability of crime in any society, there must always be criminals. They are needed for the purpose of indicating the limits of the specific norms. Criminals, the scapegoats of a society, thus help others to remain law-abiding citizens.

These observations may, I hope, help us to see the limits of victim-centered research. I have, in particular, wanted to point to the dangers of an atomistic mode of thinking, where sometimes only the offenders, sometimes only the victims are the main targets of interest.

It is important to encourage and develop victim-centered research. Let us hope that these efforts will not prevent us from seeing the crime problem in its entirety and in all its complexity.

2

Criminology and Victimology
Hans Göppinger

Sciences with Reference to Criminology and Victimology

When treating the subject of victimology the empirically working criminologist must ask if it is meaningful to conduct research of the victim separately. If one regards as the most important task of empirical criminology not merely the investigation of certain elements drawn from the total of all possible interdependencies, but rather the investigation of the offender in his entire social interdependencies, then it will quickly become clear that the isolation of the victim by performing such investigations will be incomplete, and possibly even incorrect. The present attempted and perhaps partly achieved disconnection between the research subject of criminology and victimology can only be explained if one supposes that many, perhaps the majority, of the scientists who work in criminology are in fact not interested in criminology as a science. Rather, they are interested in one of the sciences in which they are based and which is relevant to criminology. In this paper the contributions which can be made to victimology by the different sciences will be examined.

Criminalistics

If one defines criminalistics (in the broad sense) as the knowledge of technical and tactical facts which are connected with crime and its prevention, i.e., reconnaissance, prosecution, and prevention of crime, then the representative of this specialty will be the most authoritative scientists of victimology. In fact such investigations have always been conducted by real criminalists. They are to be found in the complicated modus-operandi-system which is first concerned with the prosecution of the offender, but also covers intensively the victim. On the other hand their work is often governed by practical constraints. Therefore the practically working criminalist feels that this subject has not yet fully developed into a scientific method.

Jurists

The Penal Law deals not only with the ordering of human behavior but also with the protection of important elements in social life. The potential victim

---

This is a slightly revised version of the original paper.

plays an important role in the abstract definition of crime. But the definition of the victim remains necessarily abstract, as does the definition of crime. The jurist interested not only in dogmatic questions but also in the reality of crime may, when working in victimology, be a pioneer of this science in the same way that he was formerly a pioneer in criminology. Today criminology has become rather irrelevant for such jurists because of its markedly empirical and inter-disciplinary methods. With similar criteria as these (the foundations for a meaningful criminal policy), the jurist will establish facts from the social sphere with or parallel to sociologists. But soon he will also here come to limits similar to those in criminology. In particular the jurist of penal law, who is able to think in exact categories and to apply norms to reality, will at some time note that his investigations of victimology are limited. Assertions, which go further than strict criminalistic interests or statistical control of social criteria can hardly be made by him because of the personalities of the offenders and victims in their social interdependencies.

Sociologists

Insofar as sociologists do not deal with victimology in a pure social policy manner, we owe a good many investigations and statements from the social sphere to them as well as to the jurists. We have a sound knowledge of the formal relations between the offender and the victim of murder or fraud or sexual delinquency. There are investigations of the victim's part in homicide, in sexual and other offences, as well as of certain peculiarities of victims of special offences, for instance alcoholism, age, occupation, or ethnic differences. We know of investigations of the collective victim, of affinity between offender and victim, of the recidive victim, and many others.

Psychiatry

In particular psychiatry deals from time to time with the victim—just as with the offender—when there are thought to be any psychic peculiarities in connection with the crime or some other circumstance. There is, moreover, evidence—in particular from psychologists and social workers—about the characteristics of persons predisposed to become victims. Of course there is no characteristic or biological condition, which may not lead to a predisposition for becoming a victim.

Concerning the harm suffered by the victim one often finds extravagant interpretations connected with a certain idea, especially from female victims of sexual offenses. We do not know of any methodically well carried out empirical investigation on these problems, and persons, who did not come to the psychiatrist because of a "neurosis" but rather were obtained by random selection. We are dubious about extravagant claims because of a study we conducted involving 141 female students (see Göppinger[1] for this and many other questions). The results correspond to those of Renner: more than half of the students had been victims of sexual offences of some kind (including exhibitionism), but only five thought that long lasting psychic consequences remained. Supposing that every victim of a sexual offence would suffer psychic consequences, it would be likely that 50 percent of all women would suffer from "neurosis" purely because of such sexual experiences.

Scientifically Oriented Criminal Policy

If scientifically orientated criminal policy is understood as dealing with reform of criminal law in the broad sense and with law enforcement, then it is necessary that the maker of criminal policy possesses empirically gained evidence about the victim. This is no less important in practical criminal policy where, in the end, the determining policy decisions for the necessary solutions are made.

Results from the research in victimology include important information for both scientifically and practically orientated criminal policy. The information is important not only for law enforcement but also for the prevention of crime at all. Crime prevention is not merely confined to acts proscribed by criminal law, but may include such things as traffic offences, or safety devices against bank robbery, or safety regulations for prevention of accidents in factories. Here, however, the investigation of the victim, which must include the accident-prone person, exceeds the task of conventional victimology.

It is a dubious matter to represent existing concepts of criminal or social policy and accompanying beliefs as the results of empirical research, where there is not more direct empirically gained knowledge. This problem concerns not only victimology but all empirical sciences.

Summary

In summing up there are three points of interest in victimology:

1. *The criminalistic problem.* First of all the criminalist must deal with the problem of the victim of a crime by prosecuting and preventing crime.
2. *The problems of a scientifically and practically orientated criminal policy.* The person concerned with criminal policy needs the empirically investigated knowledge of victimology as a basis for reaching meaningful decisions.

3. *The human problem.* This means on the one hand working out criteria for identifying persons disposed to become victims and on the other developing treatment for people who have been victimized.

A complex conceptualization of a separate science of victimology therefore appears to be of little value. Representatives of each science related to criminology, working both in their own fields as jurists and/or criminalists, sociologists, psychiatrists, psychologists, and in the field of criminology, can deal with the relevant problems much better than a discussion about a new separate science would allow.

Criminologically Relevant Fields of Victimology

The most interesting problem of an empirically and interdisciplinarily orientated criminology, which deals with human and social conditions, with the occurrence, commission, and prevention of crime, and with the treatment of offenders, is apart from the already mentioned relevant sciences, a *specific criminological one, the offender and his social interdependencies.* Now the questions arises if victimology also becomes important for such a direct empirically orientated criminology. For most of the offences (e.g. against property) the victim as an individual is of no special interest to the offender. Often the victim is completely anonymous, and is of no special criminological importance (except perhaps for criminalistic investigations).

Nevertheless there are a few areas of specific criminological interest. They must be investigated together with the offender and his relationships. In this case, there are usually personal relations between the offender and the victim, especially in the case of offences against dependents, personal liberty, and sexual offences.

Exchangeability and Non-Exchangeability of Victim

Here, the concept of exchangeability or non-exchangeability is of great significance. The not-exchangeable victim generally has a specific relationship with the offender, which may cause, support or shape the offence. A man who has never committed a crime may come home from a long journey or captivity as a prisoner of war, find his wife with her lover and kill her. The victim is not exchangeable, the offence is only against *this* victim. There is no danger that the offender will commit such offences further. We call this a jump into criminality (krimineller Übersprung). The crime breaks into the offender's regular social life.

This situation is quite different from that of the more usually encountered criminal, who wants to "do something" and waits for a good opportunity. In this case, the victim is generally exchangeable, even if known to the delinquent. The fact that he knows the victim, however, has nothing to do with this definition. This can be demonstrated in sexual offences when the offender often knows the victim but only in extreme cases is the victim non-exchangeable. In criminological practice the investigation of (non-)exchangeable victims leads to an intensive study of the offender's milieu in order to reach a criminological understanding of the personality of the offender. Besides studying the conditions surrounding the commission of the offence, it is important to analyze the criminological "triad"–"Stellung der Tat im Lebenslängsschnitt" (position of the offence in a person's life); criminological relevant "Konstellationen" (patterns) (kriminovalente bzw. kriminoresistente Konstellationen); "Relevanzbezüge" (relevant bindings). This analysis will provide information about the offender and his social interdependencies. This is the decisive basis for the offender's classification, especially concerning the prognosis. Clues can be gained about the location, leisure time behavior and the "Relevanzbezüge" (relevant bindings) of an offender, when the victim belongs to a certain class of society with which the offender has special relationships leading to the crime (e.g. prostitutes or taxi driver in a corresponding milieu). There may be a murdered prostitute or a robbed taxi driver, who at the same time is a prostitute's protector.

Although some symptoms are quite different, the same statement can be made for membership in a certain ethnic, political, or professional group. More than all assertions (or non-assertions) the choice of the victim can give important hints on the "Wertgefüge" (scale of values) and the "Relevanzbezüge" (relevant bindings) of the offender.

Leisure Time Behavior. Our own Tübingen-Young-Offender-Comparative-Investigation showed that analysis of leisure time behavior is very important for a criminological review of the offender in his social milieu. The relationship between the offender and the victim may be better understood because of the victim's leisure time behavior at the time of the deed. For example, persons frequenting the less desirable sections of a city–the railroad station, bars with a turbulent, fighting reputation, the red-light district, etc.–are more exposed to possible victimization. Usually such analyses of victim and his environment at the time of the offence provide clues not only about the victim's way of life but also about the leisure time behavior and interdependencies of the offender.

Interrelationship of Victim's and Offender's Environments. The mentioned examples show the interrelationships between the environments of the victim and of the offender. They also show and circumscribe the significance of victimology for an empirically and practically orientated criminology. An understanding of the victim's social relationships is not merely added to an understanding of the offender's social relationships. The knowledge of one area often opens the other. Ultimately a very complex criminological approach describing the offender's and the victim's personality is made possible by this method. This is the particular significance of victimology for an empirically and practically orientated criminology. This significance, however, will not only be diminished but may perhaps vanish if victimology is defined not as a part of criminology but as a discipline in itself, apart from criminology.

Notes

1. Hans Göppinger, *Kriminologie*, 2nd ed. (München: Beck-Verlag, 1973), pp. 310, 316, 419.

3

Victimology: A New Approach in the Social Sciences
Zvonimir P. Separovic

Victimology and the Social Sciences

We have to ask ourselves about the concept of victimology not "within criminology," but within the social sciences. Regardless of how we view victimology, as being a branch of learning, or specific doctrine, or science,[1] we have to agree that, according to the name and subject matter of the new discipline, victimology is dealing with the problem of victims. Obviously, our answer on the question about its place within science depends on our definition of the concept of victims. If victims are only those suffering from criminal acts or offenses, victimology will be a part of the crime problem, and consequently, a discipline "within criminology," or as B. Mendelsohn suggested, "a science parallel to it," or "the reverse of criminology."[2]

In our efforts to establish victimology as a new discipline we are still facing these fundamental questions: (1) What is the scope of victimology, (2) Who is the victim; and (3) What is the use of victimology? Besides, creating a new discipline, and we are still at the beginning, poses a twofold problem of determining: (1) the actual usefulness of the model in research and (2) the probable outcome of action based upon it. Finally, since victimology disposes of a great quantity of single data on questions posed within the realm of their reference sciences, there is a question of the relationship between a new discipline and its reference sciences.

Concerning the questions in point, I will confine myself to relatively short comments on some of these problems, in order to answer basic question: What is the scope of victimology?

The Meaning of the Word "Victim"

To answer the question about the concept of victimology, and its scope, we have at first to agree upon the meaning of the word "victim." According to *Webster* we may differentiate the following words and meanings:

Victim—1. a living being sacrificed to some deity or in the performance of a religious rite; 2. someone put to death, tortured, or mulcted by another; a person subjected to oppression, deprivation,

---

This is a slightly revised edition of the original paper.

15

or suffering; 3. someone who suffers death, or injury in undertaking
of his own; 4. someone tricked, duped, or subjected to hardship;
someone badly used or taken advantage of.
Victimhood—the state or condition of being a victim.
Victimization—the act or process of victimizing or the state of being
victimized.
Victimize—1. to make a victim of sacrifice, to slaughter as a sacrificial victim; 2. to subject to deception or fraud; 3. to destroy entirely.
Victimizer—one that victimizes.[3]

So far victimology has been related exclusively to the victim of crime (and/
or victim of offenses). From the legal point of view the victim may be *specific,*
such as a physical or moral person (corporation, state, association), or *nonspecific,* an abstraction (public order, public health, religion),[4] but a criminological
classification of victims is not sufficient, since there are *non-crime victims*, such
as accident victims. There are *actual* and *potential* victims, *known* and *unknown*
(non-reporting) victims, the *simulating* (false) victim, *the victim of an attempted
offense,* the *co-victim,* and some others.[5]
  The word *victim* dramatizes a very real situation in which we find ourselves
and the very real problems which confront us. There is staggering toll of violent
and incidental deaths and sufferings. The deepest human need is to survive, to
live, work, and play together free from hurt. According to Maslow, safety needs
are basic human needs; they refer essentially to the avoidance of pain and physical damage through external forces.[6] But what happens to this crucial need?
In the times in which we live, everybody is exposed to the possibility of a
criminal attack or incident of some kind. It is a problem which, more or less,
crosses all national barriers, faces all nations and whole populations. The problem is that *we are facing everywhere present and possible victimization*, that
we are living in the state or condition of being a victim of one sort or another.
  However, many of the central victim's issues in today's world have thus
far remained relatively unexplored. In particular, the focus of the victimological
approach must be broader, since there are crime and non-crime victims. *We
consider a victim as anyone, physical or moral person, who suffers either as a
result of ruthless design, or accidentally. Accordingly, we have victim of crime
or offense and victim of accident. Victims are those who are killed, injured or
damaged in property.* This concept of the victim and victimization as a social
phenomenon may serve as a point of departure for our theories. This view is
based on the idea that victims of crime, incidents, and accidents have something
in common, that they represent the whole amount of the victimization in a
certain society, that society must take into consideration the whole complex
of victimization as a serious social problem, and, accordingly, undertake a
concerted and concentrated system approach to this problem.
  We find that concepts of victimology so far are mostly too narrow. The

main concern of victimology from the beginning has been the study of the criminal-victim relationship, but the scope of victimology obviously may have wider implication, as there are other victims, such as victims of accidents. Practically all authors think victimology deals only with the crime aspects of social life. This is an important facet, victimology started as a part of criminology, but not the limit of victimology competence.

This is our hope: to deepen and broaden the understanding of the victim in today's world. We think it is of crucial importance, not only for its scientific yield, but for its potential to benefit man's welfare. Our main goal should be to sketch out the conceptual territory and boundaries of the field of victimization more clearly, coherently, and integratively than has been done before. Our aim is to suggest a "focus of convenience" for the field.

Current Theory and Research

We would like to bring into focus a number of points we can make about the current status of theory and research in the field of victimology:

1. There is as yet no single, comprehensive theory of victimology. The founders of victimology, B. Mendelsohn,[7] who originated the idea, and Hans von Hentig,[8] who carried out the first major study in the field, have offered important insight for the understanding of its phenomena, but the area has resisted successful theoretical comprehension. Or, as Schafer sceptically pointed out, "the insistence that this new or, better, revised aspects of crime should be a new science or an independent or separate discipline does not seem to have survived its first sympathetic acceptance."[9]

W.H. Nagel analyzed the boundaries of "criminology" and suggested that if it were redefined as "criminology of relationships," victimology could not be justified as a separate discipline. If criminology could be identified with criminal etiology, victimology would be justified. He stated that the "counting, measuring, weighing, determining and comparing victims" and the "collecting of victimological determinants, factors, associations and correlations" will never achieve any great importance. Instead, he said, "the removal of the conflict situation between criminal and victim should be the goal of criminal policy."[10]

2. Despite its relevance to criminology, safety, and behavioral sciences, the concept of the victim has been treated only tangentially in those fields. In criminology, for instance, we would expect it to play a fundamental role. This does not seem to be the case. Criminologists have been almost exclusively interested in the criminal and his treatment, and only some of them, recently, have shown some interest in the criminal-victim relationship, their reciprocality, roles, and the contribution to the outcome or incident. In safety, especially in the psychological approach to safety, there has been some studies

of personality factors, accident proness, and the like. To sum up, the present state of the scientific study of victims lags woefully behind the other areas of social research. But, despite this pessimistic statement, there are some valuable results of the first victimological studies.

3. Major findings in victimology so far have led to the following: (1) increasing interest in the seriousness of the victim problem; (2) better understanding of the victim's role; (3) creation of victim typologies; and (4) exploration of victim-risks. Research in victimology has been primarily concerned with victims of murder and other assaults, sexual attacks, theft and fraud, and accidents.

Let us direct our attention briefly to the two areas of greatest importance thus far in victimology: the victim's role, and victim-risk.

The *victim's role* may be of a varying nature. A victim can contribute to the offense in many ways. It is a major contention of victimology that the victim may play the role of the major contributor to a crime and accident, to his own demise. In our study the statistical profile of the murder-victim relationship has been analyzed.[11] It was found that the victim precipitated one out of four homicide cases. These findings are similar to those reported by Wolfgang on criminal homicides in Philadelphia,[12] and by others. Amir found that the victim precipitated one out of five rape cases.[13] In many cases, as Wolfgang stated, the victim has most of the major characteristics of an offender. Findings and empirical evidence about the victim's role may contribute to a better understanding of the criminal case. Law enforcement agencies and courts must thoroughly investigate the role of the victim, and some legislative changes seem to be desirable in order to achieve full understanding of the case, to determine whether for instance provocation by victim was sufficient either to reduce or to eliminate culpability altogether.

Victim-risks, or exposure to the risk of victimization, is the most promising field in victimological research and social action. Crime studies have shown that there are certain characteristics, regularities, and typical elements in the victim's personality, his attitude towards the offense and the offender, and the part he played in the offense. Thus, victimology can help predict crime and accidents, or situations which can lead to them. There is a way of predicting that a certain personality in a certain situation could become a victim, at least theoretically. Some institutions and safety agencies are already predicting fatalities that will happen during holidays, weekends, or vacations. Predicting should provide awareness of the situation, better understanding of the contributing factors, which should lead to corrective actions and to preventing situations that could cause death, or injury.[14] This approach is based on the assumption that some types of interactions between human beings are non-random and their results are in fact predictable.

Ellenberger called attention to "victimogen" factors and "future victims," since all individuals have the right to know the dangers to which their occupation social class, or physical condition may expose them. He stressed the importance of crime prevention and practical importance of victim risk.[15]

We believe that victim-risks, or potential of victimization, consists of the following factors: (1) Personal, including biological (age, sex, health—especially mental health) and psychological (aggressiveness, negligence, alienation); (2) Social (society-made victim, immigrants, minorities, occupation, criminal behavior, interpersonal relationship); and (3) situational factors (conflict situations, place and time, etc.). A search should be conducted for these factors or for characteristics of individuals who have been victims, in light of the specific situation in which the incidence occurred. It seems necessary to distinguish between some personal traits, social conditions, and certain situations or circumstances which are more or less likely to lead to victimization. The worst of course is a combination of two or more of these factors. We can explore the possibility of there being a category of "victim proneness."[16] The assumption here would be that individuals "possess" varying amounts of this factor and are more or less crime or accident prone. There may also be a possibility that "site proneness" exists, that is that crimes and other incidents are more likely to occur in some places than in others.[17] The whole system of prevention could then be based on the victim-risks scientific findings.

Some Conclusions

Having thus reviewed some of the major findings in victimology let us consider what can be deduced from these facts. Here are some conclusions:

1. Victimization can be caused by many factors, as it represents a variety of human activities, human interactions, and human maladjustment. This complex human problem has many causes. These causes can be determined and reduced, and remedial action can be taken. But, as far as the victim is concerned questions arise about the feasibility and permissibility for action to be taken.
2. Practically everybody could or may become a victim of crime or an accident.
3. There is no such thing as one uniform type of victim; they differ not only according to the different type of suffering, e.g. life, physical integrity, property, etc., but, within the specific type of incidents, we find broad scope of victimization of a very different nature.
4. People differ very much in their potential for crime or accident risk and these differences represent a continuum of risk from "very bad" to "very good." There are many willing victims.[a]

------

[a]There are those who consciously or subconsciously do things they know will kill or hurt them. Some authorities now believe more men and women die through this "subintentioned" route than by deliberate open suicide: reckless driving, excessive alcohol consumption, drug abuse is suspected. Some are deliberately creating situations in which they will be, very likely, attacked or hurt. Voluntary immolation is an example of self-victimization. Three years ago, Jan Palach, a student, burned himself to death on the main square in Prague in protest against the Soviet occupation of Czechoslovakia.

5. In some instances, it is possible to identify potential victims or victim-prone persons. Victimization proneness means an undue propensity for incidence, an undue incidence or risk potential.
6. Victimization or victim-risk can be studied, and, in some instances, generally predicted by scientific means.

Fundamentally, victimology presupposes that human losses, accidental or criminal, *can* be reduced; and that this can best be accomplished by the application of scientific methods both to the study of the victim problem and to the selection of appropriate remedies. In so doing, victimology may contribute to a better understanding of crime and accident victims—its purpose being not to eulogize the victim, but to offer some explanation of his role and his relationship toward his victimizer.

Victimology asserts that all individuals have the right to know the dangers to which their occupation, social class, or physical condition may expose them.[18] It does not intend to scare, but to talk good sense. Safety or safe living consists as much of knowing how to face danger as of how to avoid it. As Ben Franklin said, "The way to be safe is never to be secure," and there seems to be truth there. Safe living, in general, has been immediately correlated with alertness and intelligence; therefore, we need appropriate education for safe living. Victimological findings are of value in this respect.

Victimology as an Approach to the Human-risk Problem

Justification of victimology as an independent science or discipline, as a branch of learning, or an independent body of knowledge may indeed be a questionable objective, but only the ignorant can oppose or try to devalue the victim's problem. The same may be said about criminology, since even criminology is not so much a science as an association of sciences. There is much to be done to change the prevailing "all embracing" aim of criminology. According to this aim, it is asserted that as a scientific discipline dealing with human behavior, criminology should not be confined to the study of crime in the legal sense. Rather, it is held, it should also deal with any antisocial behavior, whether or not it is defined as a crime. The need now, as Lopez-Rey pointed out, is for a new approach to the control of crime, law enforcement, and the administration of criminal justice. This will necessitate building a new type of criminal justice, a task in which criminology must play an important role.[19] In any case, primacy and importance of criminology and victimology in the sphere of the general crime problem is assured. Both can only break free by broadening their subject matter to include the study of social deviance in general, and victim-risks and victimization as a social problem.

It may be useful to initiate a sophisticated attempt to bring systematic order to an utmost important set of human and social phenomena—victimization, without regard to disciplinary jurisdiction. We all know that studies of these phenomena, although they are the very core of human existence, are scattered all over the map of the behavioral sciences and the humanities. The field of victimology is not even formally recognized as a scientific discipline in its own right, in spite of the above mentioned efforts.

In an attempt to answer what is the scope of victimology, one must try to develop the theoretical base for it. One can easily oppose the classical concept of "victimology" as "the study of the degree and type of participation of the victim in the genesis or development of the offense, and an evaluation of what is just and proper for the victim's welfare,"[20] as too narrow. There is, as yet, no single, comprehensive "conceptual umbrella" for the field of victims' studies today. We need a concept that will take the victim, regardless of the source (agency) of victimization, as its pivotal concern. We need a concept that will or may fill the gap that we see existing between the criminological and "accidentological" approach to the victims. It will be a new, much broader field, with two subfields: the study of the victim of crime and the study of the victim of accidents. Accordingly we should distinguish between victimology in the narrower and victimology in the broader sense.

In a narrower sense, victimology is the empirical, factual study of victims of crime and offenses, and as such is closely related to criminology, and thus may be regarded as a part of the general crime problem. But, what we want to make clear here is that victimology, as we shall use it, includes both, victims of crime and victims of accidents. So, in its broadest sense, victimology is the entire body of knowledge regarding victims, victimization, and the efforts of society to prevent victimization and to preserve the rights of the victim. Thus, it is composed of knowledge drawn from such fields as criminology, safety, law, medicine, psychology, social work, education, and public administration. It includes within its scope the activities of law enforcement agencies, legislative bodies, courts, educational institutions, insurance agencies, and private and public social agencies. It may shed new light on the victimization problem as a total and serious social problem. The final aims of victimology, therefore, are: (1) to analyze the magnitude of the victim's problem; (2) to explain causes of the victimization; and (3) to develop a system of measures to reduce victimization.

Our aim is pragmatic. This means that we desire not only greater scientific attention, but we care about improving the quality of life and safe human living by reducing human suffering, by lessening human risk. Men are everywhere beginning to look toward the social and behavioral sciences as a source of help in creating a better world, to improve the welfare of all men. Victimology includes both research and other scientific approaches, and determination of "victimo-political" principles. The latter is aimed to create educational efforts and other preventive system of measures.

Victimology and its findings give rise to creation of a new, complex approach to the human risk problem, which may be called *safe human living,* or *human-risk problem* (see Figure 3-1). It should be entirely goal oriented toward better protection of individuals. This idea is implicit in some educational programs, and in the literature prepared for them.[21] Its purpose should be to assure, so far as possible, safe human life, primarily safe from violent attack by another human being:

1. By exploring ways to discover latent, potential victims and dangerous situations which lead to death, injury, and property damage;
2. by providing human rights for those who are suffering as a result of an unlawful act or accident;
3. by encouraging people and authorities in their efforts to reduce hazards and to stimulate new program for providing safe living conditions;
4. by providing for research in the field of human safety, including criminological, psychological, and other factors involved, and by developing innovative methods and approaches for dealing with human safety;
5. by providing an effective enforcement program which shall not only

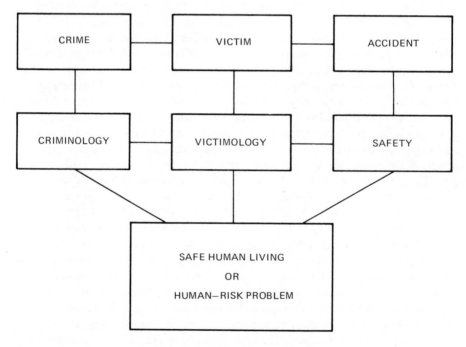

Figure 3-1. Victimology and the Human-Risk Problem.

protect society from offenders' acts by sentencing, punishing, and correction, but also protect actual and potential victims from such acts;

6. by providing for appropriate reporting, which will help achieve such objectives as prevention of future injuries.

Notes

1. Stephen Schafer, *The Victim and His Criminal, A Study in Functional Responsibility* (New York: Random House, 1968), p. 3.
2. B. Mendelsohn, "The Victimology," *Etudes Intern. de Psycho-Sociologie Criminelle* (July-September 1956), pp. 25-26.
3. *Webster Third New International Dictionary*, 2550.
4. E. Abdell Fattah, "Quelques Problemes Poses a la justice penale par la victimologie," *International Annals of Criminology* (2nd se., 1966), pp. 335-61.
5. The list of victim types, as Schafer stated, could be extended but would not serve any purpose. He believes that a typology of criminal-victim relationship along with the patterns of social situations in which they appear might hold more promise. We strongly believe that victim-risks evaluation is the most promising. See: Schafer, *The Victim and His Criminal.*
6. Safety needs refer essentially to the avoidance of pain and physical damage through external forces. See: A.H. Maslow, *The Farther Reaches of Human Nature* (New York: Viking, 1971).
7. B. Mendelsohn, "The Origin of the Doctrine of Victimology," *Excerpta Criminologica* 3, 3 (May-June 1963).
8. Hans v. Hentig, *The Criminal and His Victim: Studies in the Sociology of Crime* (New Haven: Yale University Press, 1948).
9. Schafer, *The Victim and His Criminal*, p. 101.
10. W.H. Nagel, "The Notion of Victimology and Criminology," *Excerpta Criminologica* 3 (May-June 1963).
11. Z. Separovic, "Zrtva krivicnog djela" (The Victim of Criminal Offense), *Zbornik P.F., No. 2, 1962.*
12. Marvin E. Wolfgang, *Studies in Homicide* (New York: Harper and Row, 1967), pp. 72-88 (Victim-Precipitated Criminal Homicide).
13. Menachem Amir, *Patterns of Forcible Rape* (Chicago: University of Chicago Press, 1971).
14. To evaluate and to explore victim-risks may be possible by using appropriate techniques. There is a sense in which it can be said that the methods of science have scarcely yet been applied to human behavior. Personality, character, and temperament factors, as measured by tests, and their relationship to accidents have required considerable attention, particularly with a

view to establishing the reality of accident proneness. Such research is no doubt hindered by the vagueness of test measures and the variability of these factors in an individual over time. There is the recognition, development, and criticism of the strictly statistical finding that actual accident frequencies deviate from expected frequencies and that a relatively small percentage of a population has relatively large percentage of the accidents. See: *The State of the Art of Traffic Safety*, prepared by Arthur D. Little, Inc. (New York: Praeger, 1970) pp. 15, 97-104.

15. H. Ellenberger, "Relation psychologique entre le criminel et la victime," *Revue Int. de Criminologie et de Police Technique* (1954), pp. 103-21.

16. W.C. Reckless, *The Crime Problem* (New York: Appleton-Century Crofts, 1961), p. 24.

17. *The Challenge of Crime in a Free Society*, A report by the President's Commission on Law Enforcement and Administration of Justice (New York: Avon, 1968), p. 136.

18. Ellenberger, "Relation psychologique."

19. Manuel Lopez-Rey, "The All-embracing Conception of Contemporary Criminology," *Criminologica* 5, 3 (1967): 2-9.

20. Leroy G. Schultz, "The Victim-Offender Relationship," in *Violence, Causes & Solutions*, ed. by R. Hartogs and E. Artzt (New York: Dell, 1970), p. 362.

21. Such programs are a part of college education on some campuses in the U.S.A. For instance the School of Public Services, Central Missouri State University, offers a special course, "Psychology of Safety Education and Accident Prevention." Textbook most used is, Stac-Elkow, *Education for Safe Living*, 3rd ed. (Englewood Cliffs, N.J.: Prentice-Hall, 1957).

4

Victimology and the Technical and Social Sciences: A Call for the Establishment of Victimological Clinics

Beniamin Mendelsohn

Victimology in Relation to Criminology. The notion of "victimity"

Today, after twenty-five years of the development of victimology (1947), it seems clearer than ever that its purpose should be to decrease the number of victims in the field to the extent which interests society.

In general there is, at present, a certain amount of confusion about the notions of victimology and criminology. In any case there is no need to reduce the scope of victimology to the victim of crime. Is it possible that a criminologist should declare that criminology deals only with murderers, completely ignoring other criminals? This would certainly be the case of a physician claiming that medicine should be concerned only with cancer and that all other diseases are beyond its range.

One of the new notions introduced by the needs of victimology is "victimity," which seems to me the most original as well as the most important in this field of research of the phenomenology according to which a person becomes a victim. "Victimity" introduces us into an immense "terra incognita" for victimology especially and perhaps for science in general. Even if we suppose the absence of any other argument that could justify the existence of victimology, independent of criminology (without denying, of course, the interdependence between the various branches of science), one can discern already from these perspectives the following details:

1. The "grosso modo" *sense* of victimity, which is (on the face of it) the opposite of the social bio-psychological notion of crime. From a closer examination one observes that in fact the notion of victimity is not identical with the opposite notion of crime, neither by its scope nor by its content. Crime means the noxious behavior of a man, *limited*—from a judicial point of view—only to what the legislator defines (or modifies) as infraction. This definition permits nothing but a restrictive interpretation in order to avoid prejudices against liberty. By victimity one understands a vast sphere. Its socio-biopsychological phenomenology may consist either of the determining the cause of the vulnerability of man, or of the consequences of noxiousness against

This is a slightly revised version of the paper read at the First International Symposium on Victimology. Other versions of the same paper have appeared in the *Revue Internationale de Criminologie et de Police Technique*, no. 2, 1973 and in *The Israel Annals of Psychiatry and Related Disciplines* 11, 3 (1973).

man—whether the noxious or other factors are criminal, and whether or not they are subject to jurisdiction. The limits of victimology are identical with those of victimity, and coincide least of all with those of the interests of society.

2. Suffering is recognized by all as always inseparable from the "victim" notion and, we may add, implicitly from that of victimity. That suffering is one of the characteristics of the victim has been emphasized by Hans Von Hentig as well as by Henry Ellenberger and also by others including myself. In recent years, however, I have reexamined this question. *The victim suffers, but so does the patient.* What is characteristic of the suffering of the victim? How far does the victim suffer as compared with the patient? What are the criteria by which we may differentiate between the suffering of the victim and that of a patient?

Thus one is confronted for the first time with a paramount victimological problem: of which characteristics is the suffering of the victim composed? It is not long since we succeeded in determining the elements which establish, to a large extent, the criteria of this distinction. In order not to deviate from the subject of our present study, we only draw attention to this crucial problem. Our purpose is to prove the necessity of reconsidering the notion of suffering concerning the victim.

3. The facility of socio-psychological contagion of victimity is manifested some times by real and general victimal psychosis, which one can call, we believe, without any risk of disagreement, "victimal epidemics." Its prophylaxis depends very much on the "hygiene of the psychic" in order to succeed in controlling the danger. One of the alarming forms of the epidemics of victimity is, for instance, *the euphory of speed.* The basis of this contagion is, in general, a series of the most diverse socio-psychological factors not less dangerous than the bacteria of contagious diseases, and which tend to spread like a "social victimal psychosis." For instance, the case of traffic accidents, work accidents, many of the vices (narcotics addiction, alcoholism, etc.) or despair (history has examples of surrounded warriors, who had lost all possibility of continuing resistance, and committed suicide en masse); the tradition of the sense of honor (in Japan: Hara-Kiri, or the sacrifice in times of war: Kamikaze); religious fanaticism (the "flagellators" of the thirteenth and fourteenth centuries who whipped themselves in public); the spread of panic in a crowd of people which resembles a movement of a herd of wild animals. Other forms are: imitation and suggestion (the epidemics of suicide in two, in Germany at the end of the eighteenth century, influenced by Goethe's *The Sorrows of Young Werther*); the romantic snobbery of duels between students ("Schlagende Burschenschaft," for instance, in the Germany of pre-World War I); the contagion of cruelty (rebellions, revolutions, captivity, terrorism, etc.); the contracting of professional diseases because of lack of efficient protection in work, etc.

4. As we proceed deeper into the study of victimity, we will necessarily introduce a terminology adequate to us. Thus attention was drawn to the

victimological complex of "endo-tabu," which we try to define here for the first time as "the existing tendency in man to disregard the fact that he might as well fall victim to his own imprudent deeds." This complex belongs to the unconscious—hence to the irrational—and seems to me hereditary, since it is much more prevalent in primitive man. Primitive man, when in danger of becoming a victim, runs to the talisman to which he attributes supernatural powers that guard him from all evil. In these circumstances the individual is dominated by a state of auto-obnubilation of the censorship of reason, which has sometimes a mystic character. By fighting the endo-tabu complex, we may help to reduce the potential of victimity in human society.

5. The problem of victimity is as complex and important as the problems of a patient, or patients, or for that matter, diseases and epidemics. This is the general affliction of society, one of the gravest. The research of victimity, which constitutes the primordial base of victimology, is a severe problem of life. It is inseparable as such, at a certain level of a given civilization.

6. The definition of victimity—in this phase of evolution of victimology— can be indicated essentially by "the whole of the socio-bio-psychological characteristics, common to all victims in general, which society wishes to prevent and fight, no matter what their determinants are (criminals or others)."

The problems of the patient and the victim should be considered in view of the evolution of society. If in past times some diseases were an object of public interest, it was because society was mostly afraid of the danger of contagion. Yet, the primitive society did not attach equal importance to different categories of victims, such as victims of accidents, who in those times were rather rare and of a little interest.

Criminology is concerned with the personality of the criminal and with the problems of crime. The rule is that the active factor in a crime is the criminal. Yet, as an exception altogether, we find that the victim as well has an active role in a crime restrictive only to provocation, legitimate defense, and what is even rarer, under certain aspects, a condition of legal necessity. In view of the rule that the "accessory is bound to share the lot of the principal" (*accessor sequitur suum principale*), the victim of crime belongs as well to criminology as does the delinquent. Consequently, the victim of crime, subject naturally to the problem of crime, is part and parcel of criminology. No matter how distinct the victim of crime may be from all other categories of victims and from their determinants which interest society, the victim remains an integral part of criminology. On the other hand the victim of crime studied with victims of other determinants that are subject to victimity belongs to victimology. This is an analogy between medicine, which has fixed the boundaries of epidemics, and between victimology, which has started to indicate some "real social affliction of victimity" (work and traffic accidents, genocide, pollution, destruction of vital elements of nature, subnutrition, depopulation, overcrowding, etc.). We are using here the word *affliction* in its proper sense for victimology.

From what was discussed above it follows that the object of victimology is of a different nature than that of criminology. Briefly, criminology deals *mainly* with one of the factors that cause suffering, whereas victimology has to deal with the suffering factors themselves. It should be emphasized here that "one" factor that causes suffering corresponds to a number of suffering people. It seems to me that this aspect has not yet sufficiently drawn the attention of scientists, and from all points of view society should take a greater interest in victims, no matter what the cause of the victim's suffering is. Victimology always possesses—apart from any other characteristic—a social characteristic. The limits of victimology should coincide with the interest of society in order to prevent that man become a victim.

Thus, as sociology is dedicated to all problems of societal organization, medicine to all that of diseases, criminology to all that of criminals (regardless of their origin—biological, psychological, sociological, economical, etc.), victimology becomes a science the moment we see as essential all categories of victims and the complex of the problems of victimity without ignoring any of the determinants that interest society. This is the basis of victimology. Questions of criminology should not be called victimology.

If we bear in mind the essence of this concept, we can see why it is that Hans Von Hentig, a man of great merit in this field of research, namely victims of crime, has not come to define or name his work as "victimology." Prof. Von Hentig's concept—independent of other similar concepts—"the specific relation criminal-victim" does not include the notion of victimity. Victimity is a *general phenomenon* characteristic of victims of all determinants, not only of the victim of delinquency. Hence, a new horizon justifies a new term.

Victim Determining Environments

The factors which cause a man to become a victim stem from six types of environments (milieux):

1. The bio-psychological endogenous environment of the victim himself. This can be the only determinant, or one of the determinants, of a victim's behavior, manifested by: negligence, thoughtlessness, forgetfulness, inattention, emotionality, sentimentality, bewilderment, lack of coordination between perception, discernment, decision and muscular reaction (faulty or slow), etc. All that, evidently in situations where every reasonable person should think about his own security, which implies precautionary measures.
2. The natural surrounding milieu, which consists of free, or controlled forces, or such that had already escaped man's supervision.
3. The milieu of changed natural surroundings. This milieu is the outcome of

pollution of the necessary components of life, in the natural environment. Ecology is beginning to arouse public interest, because of the fact that in an industrial society the destruction of the immediate natural surroundings is becoming more and more marked. Efforts are being made to save whatever still seems possible.

4. The social milieu.
   a. Quite often individuals with antisocial tendencies act against the dispositions of the law concerning either man or collectivity and their patrimony.
   b. There are also organizations who engage in antisocial noxious activity and succeed nevertheless to evade the criminal law.
5. The antisocial milieu. Policy of a state or of a party which claims by force the power of a dictatorial, totalitarian or racial government. This kind may lead sometimes even to genocide.
6. The driving milieu. A machine is not dangerous as long as it is still. Once it starts working it becomes dangerous. This milieu is concerned with dangerous industrial or domestic machines in the limited space that they occupy, as well as with vehicles on the roads. This is why we call this milieu a "driving milieu" and not a "mechanical milieu." By driving milieu we mean not only the scope of the movements of the motor, its accessories and the machines, all joined in work, but also the very source of the force. It is evident that in this section the mechanical and electrical engineers have a major role that is rapidly developing. This role is nowadays inseparable of victimology. The engineers can contribute in a decisive manner to preventing accidents, to the therapeutics of victims, and of course to the modernization of research.

The Danger Complex

In order to understand the proportions of the victimity problem, victimology should concentrate on identifying means by which to discover the danger complex in its specific circumstances.

By "danger complex" we mean the whole of the following components: objective, subjective or mixed, permanent or temporary, apparent, hidden or disguised, which cause people to become victims. If the preventive action of discovering the danger complex in time and preventing its action has failed, victimology should try: (1) to reduce to a minimum the victimal noxiousness to the possible extent in the present state of civilization and (2) to prevent that man become a victim again: the victimal recurrence. Thus, while the motoring force incessantly increases its speed, the "human force" remains unchanged, since it cannot exceed the natural limit. Man has almost always the same capacity concerning quickness of perception, discernment, decision and motorial reaction (muscular), with the exception of certain endogenous or exogenous influences. This change provides for more victimity and therefore for more research perspectives and material. At the same time one should bear in mind another change: in general the "danger complex" is progressing rapidly, whereas the means of protection are always lagging behind. This is one of the paradoxes of contemporary civilization. On the one hand, in advanced countries people live in a consuming society where the amount and the quality of goods are constantly increasing. On the other hand, the same goods, if used wrongly, produce further victims such as dead, wounded, invalids, victims of professional diseases, of environmental pollution, of malnutrition, and of genocide, etc. All this is a threat to the very existence of humanity. Thus we have arrived at the heart of the problems to be solved by victimology.

In order to be able to fight the phenomena of victimity, we must realize that in this field the past is completely out of date and that one has to bravely envision the whole as well as the details of the problems that arise. These problems should evidently be studied in their real proportions. First of all, research should take advantage of the possibilities offered by the development of science, technique, means of education, legislation, and of an adequate administration. In the face of the trends of present life, the future of victimology is intimately connected with the technological progress of society. Among other problems, victimology has to be aware that, in the specific condition of the modern world, man spends most of his time at work, including of course the journey involved. The journey by vehicles to the respective work centers is one of the frequent reasons for collisions. Victimology should have a special interest—among others—in traffic and work accidents, and in the condition of industrial hygiene. In this way it can help reduce the loss of human lives, decrease the number of people suffering from industrial diseases, and prevent loss of work-hours as well. Conceived in that way victimology offers to man greater confidence in his security.

With the aid of victimology the victim is no longer viewed as an isolated sporadic phenomenon; victimization is no longer considered to be the result only of the behavior of the criminal. This view does not correspond in any case to the scientific truth. Victimization originates from many determinants, which come from different milieux. Thus, what we call victimity is a general problem that concerns the existence and development of society. Similarly, victimity will exist if it engages in this problem and in its determinants. Thus it will gradually develop its scope, probably as medicine or the studies of engineering.

The sole sector, namely the victim of crime, is not sufficient to constitute victimology, since an elementary condition for research is lacking: the means to compare between different categories of victims and their determinants, between the origin of their suffering and of victimity, etc., as is the case in all diseases and patients of medicine.

We should mention, for reasons of objectivity, that the possibility of founding a science by assembling disparate elements is often denied. It is also denied that it is possible to establish a scientific branch that is concerned with victims of diverse origins. This argument is valid for abstract sciences, but not for those of life, and even less so when the subject is Man.

In fact, life is not subject to the theoretical demands of reason and its needs for homogeneity and logicality. The lack of characteristic uniformity is to be found in other sciences of this sort. Is the distance between a man suffering from a disease caused by bacteriological germs (cholera) and another afflicted by mental illness (schizophrenia) or by a genetic sickness caused by the chromosomes (mongoloidism hemophilia) or because of an endocrine gland (diabetes)—is the distance between them small? Has the difference in the nature of these factors prevented medicine from understanding them? When a new disease appeared, did anyone ever suggest that perhaps it did not belong to medicine? Does criminology not embrace the murderer, the bigamist, the swindler, along with the slanderer, the thief, the counterfeiter, and the contravenient who throws a piece of paper in the street, together with those who commit genocide? They all belong to criminology, although they are not of an homogeneous nature and an enormous distance separates them to such an extent that sometimes the social interest does not exist any more; only the individual's interest remains.

Another objection—yet not so widespread—is that nowadays there is a greater tendency in science for analysis than there is for synthesis. This seems true as long as we consider only part of the characteristic aspects. Actually one should hold to the contrary, namely that analysis applies to certain material and purpose, according to certain criteria (in medicine it applies to the patients, in criminology to criminals, etc.) and explains all the details of a research and study. Why deny to victimology what seems natural for criminology? This should also be the case of victims and victimal diseases. If one accepts only the method of analysis, and yet draws all conclusions, one would then support the fragmentation of criminology according to the categories of criminals. From the separated research on violators—one could have "viology"; from the research on pyromaniacs—one could have "ignology," etc. It hardly can be the real intention of those criminologists who fight against the role of synthesis in science. The purpose of the victimologists' work should not be to establish a science on victims at any price, but to facilitate the process of crystallization of such discipline by gathering the research on victims conducted to date, by researching solutions or looking for preventive measures.

Perspectives of Victimology

During two and a half decades of existence victimology has known success. More than two-hundred works have been published (books and studies published in scientific reviews), in different languages, including sixty-five in Japanese (up to March 1971), and more than seventeen Ph.D. dissertations. But the greatest part of these studies is confined either to certain comments, or to victims of homicide and "infractions contre les moeurs." Hence it is only a beginning. Yet victimology has entered more than thirty-five countries and all continents.

A change is being felt at present in the United States, where Professor Stephen Schafer and Professor Marvin Wolfgang have started an interest in the area of victimology.

At Northeastern University and at the University of Pennsylvania, as well as at The American University and at the University of California at Berkeley, courses in victimology have been introduced for the first time during the last few years.

It is in Japan that victimology has undergone a real development. Victimology provides inputs for all judicial instances, sociology and biology, as well as psychiatry and criminology, and it offers permanent material to the press in everyday matters. Professor Dr. Koichi Miyazawa (Tokyo) founded, some years ago, the first Institute for Victimology in the world. The Institute has more than three-hundred students and is training victimologists, researchers, and professionals. The Institute translates into Japanese all the works on the subject published abroad. There is a specialist team, a library of victimology, and a card-index bibliography of fifty thousand cards. These cards probably contain not only information concerning works in victimology, but also other sources which might interest a researcher of those problems. Moreover, Professor Miyazawa was in Jerusalem in 1969 and suggested the organization there of the First International Congress of Victimology. As a result, a Symposium on Victimology was organized in Jerusalem, by the Hebrew University. This Symposium dealt exclusively with the victim of crime and as a result it actually was a reunion of criminology and not of victimology. Besides, it is regrettable that the program neither contained the subjects nor those categories of crime which cause a vast number of victims, namely those of work and genocide. Finally, no electrical and/or mechanical engineers, who could contribute essentially to the prophylaxis of traffic, domestic and work accidents were invited. Science should always keep a pace with up-to-date requirements of social evolution, in order not to stay behind.

The major problem of victimology is to strive for practical results, which means to save man in danger and from danger. Victimology will become effective and viable, and perhaps even "revolutionary" in the positive sense of the word, only when research will be carried out on the victim himself, and only on him, at the side of the suffering victim's bed, from the moment the physician allows it. Thus will it be possible to determine from the very victimal noxiousness the origin of victimity, to look for means to anticipate cases, to remedy harmful results, and to try to prevent further offenses. This will be the real victimological diagnosis. It is in this manner that one should start the practice of victimology.

The financing of this approach can be arranged more easily than it is thought. In certain countries experiencing a high volume of traffic in their more industrialized regions, special hospital emergency sections have already been established or planned. These sections are furnished with special equipment and are staffed with specialized personnel. These emergency rooms can become *victimological clinics*, once they are staffed with a psychologist, a sociologist, a social worker who will collaborate—as the case may require—with various outside services, like psychiatry, psychoanalysis, endocrinology, etc.

We should understand that the boundaries of victimology should be established in connection with the interest of society in the problems of victims. Thus, we repeat, all the victim's determinants, such as overpopulation, low birthrate, subnutrition, pollution, etc., naturally pertain to the field of victimology (as all diseases pertain to medicine and all criminals to criminology), which gradually establishes its place among the other sciences. One should realize that those questions are closer to the essence of victimology than, for instance, the study of victims of adventures.

This way of facing reality is in conflict with conformism. In the first publication of victimology we showed that we had to undergo two psychointellectual processes in our soul, (1) "The *liberation* from the chains of systems" and (2) "The acceptance of this new aspect of science and *concentration* of our attention on that new way. The past is profoundly anchored in our consciousness and the liberation from social ties requires a constant effort. The law of inertia leaves traces in the domain of psychology as well."[1]

Victimology specifically implies detection of means of research, and elaboration of tests, measures, unique terminology, etc. In order to achieve all this, it is necessary that a group of scientists initiate some action in favor of victimology in the spirit described above. It mainly concerns physicians, sociologists, psychologists, psychiatrists, psychoanalysts, criminologists, and jurists. *There is a need for the first time to enlist the interest and collaboration of electrical and mechanical engineers, ecologists, cyberneticians, demographers, etc.* Some of them will contribute to the knowledge of various categories of victims that interest society, and their causing factor. Others might suggest solutions which only technical sciences are able to provide for prophylaxis, therapeutics, and research possibilities as well. The two categories of scientists may know thoroughly and permanently the data of their partners and thus will arrive at better results. Where would medicine be without the collaboration of electronics in the three above-mentioned fields? Today we already have medical engineers at work.

It should be emphasized that criminology cannot embrace the categories of victims that are not caused by criminals, but society is not less interested in them. Thus, if one cannot deny the existence of other categories of victims, nor the interest of society in them, nor that criminology is unable to deal with subjects of victimology, then the former cannot replace the latter. It follows that they can and should collaborate, having common sectors, but acting separately.

We have here one of the reasons that lead to an elaboration of a science of *independent victimology*—without denying of course the interdependence between the various branches. Professor Koichi Miyazawa (Tokyo) established his position in this fundamental problem in the report presented to the Gesellschaft fuer die Gesamte Kriminologie at its meeting of October 25, 1969 in Saarbrücken: "As far as I am concerned I present the opinion that victimology is a science independent of criminology, which has its own way."[2] Criminology and victimology should not be confused any longer.

As far as victimology is concerned, the victimological clinic is its vital element, which will bring about other realizations of major importance for society. It will open the door to practical victimological researchers. The victimological clinic will have a crucial role for the realistic and natural development of the victimological science and for the victim, as does the hospital for medicine and its patients, and nothing can or will replace it.

Beside this institution, without which it is impossible to conceive how victimology can be useful to society, there are others as well that can bring forth an interesting contribution, that is if they collaborate for initiating the foundation of a victimological clinic. A victimological center should deal with all those other aspects, which by their nature cannot be an object to the activity of a victimological clinic. A victimological society is an additional step of action organized for the benefit of victimology. It could spread the ideas by conferences and reviews. It could organize a card-bibliography and probably gather scientists that have an interest in victimology, in order to facilitate exchange of ideas between victimologists within the country and abroad.

In the present phase it is worthwhile to concentrate on the organizational plan. There is a need to convoke another international congress of victimology, but to invite this time to the meetings specialists of all sciences that may contribute to solve certain problems. In this way contact will be established between those who deal with one category of victims—from the victim of crime to the ecologist and demographer—and between those who may contribute to decrease the number of victims by technical sciences (mechanical and electrical engineers, cyberneticians). The problems of victims are too complicated to be included in one and only the existing science, including criminology; it is evident that they can and should collaborate.

Such a congress should be well prepared and should be a start for establishing contacts through an initiative center, as the symposium will be a preliminary phase. In such a congress work will have to be done by sectors, assembling various branches of science. Conclusions should be discussed after the congress in plenum. In this manner a progress will be achieved, by the way of conceiving the essentials of victimology, by the beginning of a practical victimological activity, and by organizational work.

Notes

1. Beniamin Mendelsohn, "Nouvelle branche de la science bio-psycho-sociale: La Victimologie," *Rev. intern. de criminol. et de police techn.* (Geneve) no. 2/1956, p. 107; idem, *Rev. franc. de psychan.* (Paris) Jan.-Feb. 1958, p. 116.
2. Koichi Miyazawa, "Zum gegenwaertigen Stand der victimologischen Forschung in Japan," Sonderdruck, Heft 9, Stuttgart, 1971.

5

Toward a Supra-National Criminology: The Right and Duty of Victims of National Government to Seek Defence through World Law

Stanley W. Johnston

Victimology is concerned with the victims of crime. In this paper I shall attempt to enlarge the ordinary signification of the word "crime" and thus also the meaning of victimology. I would build particularly on a paper Professor W.H. Nagel delivered at the International Society of Criminology congress at Madrid in 1970,[1] on works of Professor Julius Stone,[2] and on a paper I delivered at the Australian and New Zealand College of Psychiatry congress on aggression in 1970.[3] I want to invite you to enlarge both the political perspective and the historical time span of ordinary criminology, in order to appreciate the changing authority of governments. Supposedly scientific criminologists have tended to accept the authority of national governments uncritically as axiomatic; but we ought to examine that authority along with every other element in the criminal process. We are both unscientific and politically naive to imagine that national law, the standard beginning point of present criminology and crime rates, has always been, or will always remain, fixed and sacrosanct and sovereign. Criminology and victimology must be free to range over the city-state and the feudal state of the past, the nation-state of the present, and the world-state of the future. An independent criminologist will be alert to the possibility of national tyranny, and able and willing to prescribe remedies for the victims of such tyranny.

There are questions such as the following. What is the position of the individual living under a government which is committing war crimes, inciting or harboring hijackers or terrorists, or infringing the human rights of its citizens through racism or through oppressive imprisonment which abandons the objective of conciliatory management? The language of Article 23 of the United Nations *Declaration on the Strengthening of International Security* (1970) invites a supranational criminological analysis. The General Assembly there "resolutely condemns the *criminal* policy of apartheid of the government of South Africa and reaffirms the *legitimacy* of the struggle of the oppressed peoples to attain their human rights and fundamental freedoms and self-determination." General Assembly Resolutions numbered 2189 (1966), 2621 (1970), and 2908 (1972) have referred to "the illegal racist minority regime in Southern Rhodesia"; Resolutions 2189 and 2326 (1967) declared apartheid and all forms of racial discrimination to be a crime against humanity; and Resolution 2621 called on the Security Council for a vigorous application of sanctions against Rhodesia, Portugal, and South Africa. On April 2, 1973, the U.N. Human Rights Commission in Geneva adopted a draft convention making apartheid a

crime against international law, punishable in any signatory country. Countries
which abstained or voted against the convention argued that it would be illusory
since legal machinery to enforce it was lacking in most countries.[4] Again, what
is the position of a person under a government which refuses "to enable the
Human Rights Committee . . . to receive and consider . . . communications from
individuals claiming to be victims of violations of any of the rights set forth"
in the International Covenant on Civil and Political Rights 1966, as provided
for in the Protocol to that Covenant? Or again, in a world where nationalism
is still supreme, can the United Nations provide stateless persons with both
citizenship and any necessary correction?

More fundamentally: While nationalism has never been vaunted so vigor-
ously as during this century, and while there are some countries that have
only recently realized a national identity, are we nevertheless already witnessing the last years of nationalism? With the world as a whole observably
moving this century toward a tangible sense of world order, to the multiplica-
tion of treaties, and to the creation of international and supranational organizations, political sovereignty is already moving beyond the nation-state. With
the advent of nuclear weapons, in particular, it must now be virtually axiomatic
that defence cannot be secured at a national level, or through anything but a
world-state monopoly on the legitimate use of final military and police force.
However, sovereignty is not yet clearly located in the United Nations: we are
in an unsettled transitional period when it is not clearly located anywhere.
Because we lack what John Austin called a determinate human superior,
there is a marked decline in the authority of political and legal institutions
everywhere. The general impression today is that crime is rising and that we
are at greater risk of being a victim of crime. It is possible that a substantial
cause of the increased risk is this decline of sovereignty, of institutional
authority, and of the very validity of law today; that national order no longer
offers the security of effectiveness assumed by the dogmatism of its law
officers and by criminologists; that the law and order which we should aim to
restore will have to be world law and order; that national governments will
never regain their former absolute authority; and that, if they are to recover
any of their former authority and consensus, they will do so only by bending
the knee to supranational law and to the sanctions of supranational criminal
courts.

With the ubiquitously growing demands for international and supranational sanctions since 1945, I believe that criminologists have a useful contribution to make to the analysis of this vexed area of social defence and to
the facilitating of any political transformation that is taking place. For this
session, therefore, I wish to invite the International Society of Criminology
to become a society of international criminology, or rather of supranational
criminology.

1. *Hitherto nationalism has been the baseline*
   of institutional criminology, as of the
   philosophy of law and justice

Changes in social structure during the last few hundred years have
been accompanied by altered conceptions of crime and, hence, of
criminal jurisdiction. Until the late sixteenth century, . . . the
emergent nationstate intervened only incidentally to punish the
criminal. . . . The absence of any notion of state sovereignty at
that time is illustrated by the fact that neither nationality nor
the protection of the state ('the protective principle') were
considered as bases of criminal jurisdiction.[5]

Today, however, the only crime rates we compute are those of crimes committed against national laws. Social defence as so far conceived by criminologists
ignores international crimes and the political background of military defence.
National security police, intelligence and spy systems are taken with great seriousness, on the impossible assumption that they represent absolute ideals. The
world's huge expenditure, upwards of $200,000 million a year, on the military
defence of national political structures distracts attention and resources away
from the prevention of the more immediate and universally deplored crimes of
assault upon person and property, and is itself a provocation to the commission
of just such crimes between and within nations.

When people speak of "the" law today they generally mean national law.
Professor John Rawls describes as "the subject of justice" what he calls "the
basic structure of society," which he conceives "for the time being as a closed
system isolated from other societies."[6] Professor H.L.A. Hart suggests that
nationalism is man's "national environment," that "the minimum content of
natural law" includes national law enforcement as "a natural necessity," but
that "there is neither a similar necessity for supra-national sanctions (desirable
though it may be that international law should be supported by them) nor a
similar prospect of their safe and efficacious use."[7] However, I find it basically
and increasingly inaccurate today to conceive of nationalism (in the sense of
closed systems isolated from other societies) either as existing in fact or as
being for all legal purposes our natural environment. One's sense of national
identity does not require the assertion of national absolutism. Both official
and private movement and communication across borders is no longer exceptional, but is continuous.

Criminology that sees its aim as being only the prevention of crime[8] is
in danger of failing to achieve the status of a scholarly study of all the conditions and circumstances of law enforcement policy. "Out of fear and pride
existing knowledge is denied, insight prevented and possible alternatives

ignored."[9] Government institutes and government-sponsored institutes of
criminology run a particular risk of being identified with the forces of reaction,
as was the Inquisition and the so-called Holy Office of the Roman Catholic
Church. Whether criminology is primarily a study of policy or of any other
part of law enforcement, it inevitably has a political relevance and assumes a
certain political perspective.[10] In arguing that crime is political, Richard
Quinney points out that criminology has a dual task of explaining criminal
behavior as behavior and also of accounting for the definitions by which specific behavior comes to be considered crime. He points out that criminality
is not inherent in behavior but is a property conferred upon individuals by
others in the enactment, enforcement, and administration of the law.[11] I
think we have also to question the creation, authority, and demise of the
norm-delineating institutions themselves. A short-term perspective sees criminology as being concerned with the management of individual instances of
serious, i.e., criminal, social conflict. But a larger, historical perspective will
appreciate the positive contribution which crime and criminals make to the
long-term dialectical development or evolution of laws and political institutions. I would argue that we ought to blend the two perspectives in the daily
administration of criminal justice, so that we never treat a criminal without
paying attention to the lessons he has to teach concerning existing laws and
social organization.

The course both of law enforcement and of law reform will be smoother
if we remain conscious of this dialectic continuously and not only at times
of crisis. In Australia over the last twenty-five years or so, for instance, debate
on capital and corporal punishment has tended to flourish only when someone
was about to be hanged or whipped. During the Second World War and the
recent protests over Vietnam there was widespread questioning of the authority
of national officials. But when the crisis passes we sink back into a slough of
complacency, and there is little demand for preventive planning.

There is a long literature on dissent and civil disobedience, and on the
value of social conflict and deviance.[12] Stone has recently written of the
power and influence of a build-up of individual dissent in dramatically reversing
the tendency of citizen opinion to become enslaved to nationalized versions
of truth and justice, and exemplifying the enduring capacity of the individual
to have his say on the human future, a capacity which bears vitally on the
prospects of peace.[13] I would invite you here specifically to consider the
positive role of crime in subverting that excess of nationalism which is expressed
in the doctrine of national sovereignty.

Oliver Wendell Holmes said that "The life of the law has not been logic, it
has been experience." But logic is a proper test to apply to both the authority
claimed for natural law, and to the destructive retributivism, today allowed to
national law enforcement (though no longer to manorial or church law and not
yet to supranational law). And logic requires us here to distinguish two meanings

attributed to the word "sovereignty."[14] The first is the claim of territorial inviolability and the second is the claim of legislative supremacy. My contention is that, if a nation is to secure the first, it must surrender the second. So far as it makes any sense to speak of the recognition of a claim or right to territorial integrity, to that extent must national legislative supremacy be surrendered to the supranational or extra-national institutions capable of granting that recognition. Hart, Rawls, and Austin are all of one mind in conceiving of sovereignty as being focused on and expressed through an independent or isolated national consciousness and uncoerced national institutions, thus conceiving of national governments as being above all other law, including international law.

The essence of natural law, however, is its universal harmony and consilience.[15] Thus no merely national claim to sovereignty, in the sense of supremacy, can be a principle of natural law, since any such claim must conflict with every other claim to sovereignty (and with the simple claims to humanity of those outside the claimant nation).[16] State A's purported recognition of State B's claim to independent supremacy is a standing contradiction of the independence and supremacy of both states. That each state merely expects that the other is sovereign within its own territory still leaves each state the sole judge of what matters *are* within its own territory, thus producing the fundamental discordance that characterizes the field of law called conflict of laws, or private international law. None of the several claims to absolute national supremacy can be universal; nor can mutual recognition of claims to particular areas of sovereignty be more than an unenforceable agreement on the terms of our present ill-defined world federation. Yet the several divided and conflicting claims to legislative supremacy persist: they are a dangerous fiction, making profits for arms manufacturers and power for brutes, but otherwise making potential victims of us all. Each claim must in fact be opposed by the vast majority of the world's population which is alienated and degraded by any nation's boast of supremacy. No such claim offers a stable basis for scientific criminology, for natural law, for conscientious law enforcement, or for adequate defence.[17] When criminologists succeed in running together the areas of military defence and social defence, we shall have a more adequate basis for law enforcement.

2. *But sovereignty is passing from nations to the United Nations*

While the victims of unrestrained nationalism have numbered more in this century than in any other, this century has also witnessed tangible progress toward institutional expressions of world government. The United Nations is there, and though its powers are still quite unrealised, it had power enough to legitimize the modern State of Israel twenty-five years ago, it has proved a useful forum for rationalizing political dialogue, and it now speaks for all but about three or four hundred million people. On his appointment as Secretary-General of the United Nations in January 1972 Dr. Kurt Waldheim said, perhaps in order to save people from false hopes, that the United Nations is not a world government. But I venture to suggest that the U.N. *is* the institutional expression of world government, albeit weak government. One reason that it is weak is that people too often imagine that the sanctions of a world or supranational government must always amount to war, as in the Korean campaign 1950-1953.[18] It is here that criminologists ought to be able to teach international lawyers subtler ways of penetrating the body politic and isolating key officials, as we daily penetrate the veil of trade unions and commercial corporations, preserving and guiding them as going concerns, and avoiding do-or-die confrontations.

Article 2 of the U.N. Charter speaks of "the sovereign equality of all its members," and provides that nothing in the Charter shall:

> authorize the United Nations to intervene in matters which are essentially within the domestic jurisdiction of any state or shall require the members to submit such matters to settlement under the present Charter; but this principle shall not prejudice the application of enforcement measures under Chapter VIII.

Those matters which are "essentially" within "domestic jurisdiction" are not defined. The use of the adjective "sovereign" there might be interpreted as rhetoric meaning "strict" or "inalienable." Chapter V of the Charter discounts equality by giving the right of veto to the favored permanent members of the Security Council. If those five permanent members have not surrendered much sovereignty, there is no possible reading of the Charter but signifies that the other 127 members have largely surrendered theirs. On paper, that is: for no state has conspicuously sought supranational judgment of its actions, and all stand condemned for breach and contempt of their undertakings under the Charter, particularly Article 43.

The simple growth of organizations, covenants, and treaties regulating the increasing flow of international trade, commerce and intercourse is in effect a transfer of sovereignty from national legislatures.[a] International agreements cover movement by sea, air, and space; postal arrangements and telecommunications, currency, finance and trade; weights and measures, and hopefully soon a more regular calendar. Trade, fiscal and even military decisions and policies are no longer determined solely or even substantially by national legislatures: it is inaccurate and impertinent to pretend today that any nation is still the captain of its fate. But so long as we lack a supranational law and criminology

---

[a]This simple growth is the declared aim of the World Peace Through Law Centre.

the pretence and impertinence are there, and constitute a constant threat to world, national, and personal security.

3.   *With the decline of nationalism, national*
     crime rates are rising, and are not likely
     to fall again

The news media use to carry sensational mention of periodic crime waves, which I believe generally indicate either an insignificant coincidence of a number of major crimes or alternatively a shortage of more important news. The combined result of two recent studies made by the New Zealand Justice Department shows that it is difficult to demonstrate that the rate of violent crime really is rising.[19] However, popular impression is perhaps more important and more influential than statistics; and if press and police reports are to be taken seriously—reports showing something like a 10 percent increase over the previous year in every year for the past half century, and particularly during J. Edgar Hoover's term as director of the F.B.I.—then it makes sense to speak not merely of crime waves, but of a rising tide of crime and violence. The F.B.I.'s *Uniform Crime Reports* (1971) indicate that crime increased by 197 percent from 1960 to 1971.[20] Now it is news if there is any drop in the crime rate. Indeed the expectation of a certain crime rate probably has an unconscious and unrecognized effect on police at the feeding end of the statistical production line, engendering a feeling that figures must be maintained at a particular level, and giving the reporting of cases an artificial importance.[21] Not that artifice is to be deplored, so long as we understand clearly what the artifice really is.

What crime rates are in reality describing in bookkeeping terms is the activities of certain law enforcement agencies; and it is important not to mislead ourselves into thinking that they detachedly measure people's misbehavior. The two have a good deal in common, but are not mirror images of each other. Criminologists write of a "dark figure" of unreported crime.[22] But crime is behavior which is officially incriminated: it is an artifact of a certain political order. The notion of unreported crime is, I believe, a contradiction in terms, and use of the term indicates a delusion as potentially serious and fanatical as the witchhunting delusion of the sixteenth and seventeenth centuries.[23] We do ourselves no credit by whipping ourselves with the paranoid notion of endlessly undiscovered evils which require only bigger police budgets to hunt out. Consider the area of the greatest recording of convictions: road traffic offenses. Every driver knows how unrealistic and unimportant it would be to attempt to estimate the number of unrecorded infringements of the highway code. Or consider the area of the least recording of a crime rate—international crime. Nobody would suggest that there is not serious misbehavior by national officials, yet we calculate no international crime rate because we have no institutions yet competent or authorized to do so.

We compare crime figures over one or two years, or even up to ten years; but, perhaps because we have not dared to believe the figures, or have not really known what they signified, we have failed to make the proper longer comparison. What happens if we extrapolate the rising crime figures over the whole period of fifty years? If you start with a base figure of 1.00 and raise it by 10 percent compound ten times, i.e., for ten years, you get a figure of 2.43; after 20 years the initial one crime a year has become 6.29 crimes a year; after 30 years, 16.28; after 40 years, 42.22; and, at this steady rate of increase, what started off as one crime a year in 1923 has become a staggering 109.51 crimes per annum by 1973. A tide, indeed; a veritable flood tide.

Human nature, of course, has not really deteriorated so much. It is inconceivable that individual psychology, neurology or biology has changed so much in so short a time, and I think we should be confident that mankind is not on a final moral debauch or psychological decline. Misbehavior, in the sense of crudity in social relations, has possibly increased somewhat, so that we are at some greater personal risk of being the victim of criminal injury today than we were half a century ago; but the risk is hardly 110 times greater. If then, individual behavior, willfulness or perversity is not changing in itself, it may be changing in relation to the political structures and institutions that claim to govern and measure that behavior. But the parsimonious interpretation of the figures is that they indicate a substantial change in the political and legal institutions which produce the crime rate, and specifically a rapid decline in the binding efficacy of, in public satisfaction with, and thus in the authority of, national government. Rising crime rates are commonly attributed to urbanization, industrialization, and speed of social change. But I would suggest that a simpler, more radical and more pervasive explanation is this passing of the heyday of nationalism. This is the factor underlying both phenomena: on the one hand it explains the rising official crime rate (which might be seen as a repressive sting in the tail of authorities battling against their own demise); and on the other hand, it explains the disturbance and confusion underlying whatever real increase there is in individuals' suffering criminal injury.

Waves and tides come and go, but when we get a flood tide like this we must expect a good deal of destruction before the flood ebbs. Let us compare today's crime rate with what we might call the European heresy rate of 500 years ago, when nationalism was just beginning to replace feudalism and to overtake the Church order, and Jean Bodin was formulating the doctrine of national sovereignty.[24] Heresy then was a serious, capital crime against a fundamental social order; but still the heresy rate got out of hand. The official reaction was cruel and repressive, but ultimately heresy became theologically more respectable than the Inquisition which had been so fanatically persecuting the heretics.[25] Society held together all right; it was the Inquisition that disappeared, and the Church that lost its authority. If heresy remains a serious matter, it is now matter for resolution through rational debate, not through prosecution as evil. I suggest that when the present tide of lawlessness, violence, and disorder recedes, what we shall see has been destroyed and lost forever will be national sovereignty, the absolutist pretensions of the anarchic nationalism which has recently threatened and still treatens to destroy us all. It will be the passing of an era, the transforming of a civilization.

In short, therefore, the artifice of crime statistics describes a political phenomenon and not a behavioral phenomenon; and what a rising crime rate indicates more surely than anything else is a declining confidence in the institutions of national law and order. We may anticipate that national crime rates will keep on rising until we recognize that nationalism has ceased to be our best ultimate political focus. We may even give up measuring the national crime rate altogether, as we once must have given up measuring the feudal or village crime rate and the heresy rate. It will be unrealistic to expect any substantial decline in recorded national crime rates in the future, for we are set on an unswerving course of violating or fracturing national order, to the extent necessary to re-set political loyalties at a global level. *Pari passu* in that process we shall find ourselves constructing an international crime rate through the formal incriminating of national officials for behavior which may be lawful by the standards of the government which the officials serve, but is unlawful by international standards. Legal or political institutions will emerge to ritualize and manage social conflict, and to transform or subvert institutions which oppose world order and lend themselves to war. A good deal of genuinely law-making groundwork has already been laid for the creation of an international criminal court,[26] and seeds sown whose fructifying presumably awaits further international crises.

4. *Victims of the incompetence of national defence have a right and a duty to seek defence through a more competent law*

Mere pride in national identity is to be distinguished from the anarchistic claim of national sovereignty. "Everyone agrees that it is an essential function of the state to preserve the security of its citizens."[27] And if the safety of the people is the supreme law, then the vaunting of national supremacy is a crime, the government a robber-band (Augustine) and its laws a violence and invalid (Aquinas).[28]

All persons today are victims of that governmental lawlessness, suffering, first, the perpetual state of cold war with its heavy burden of military preparedness and the enervating threat of ungoverned hostilities, and second, the recorded increase in domestic disorder, anomie, alienation, and criminality. These crimes

and wars hurt people as individuals, both directly and indirectly. What then is
to be the attitude of the potential victim of such governmental violence? Hans
von Hentig identified certain psychological attitudes of a victim who precipi-
tates crime as follows:

> apathetic or lethargic;
> submitting or conniving;
> co-operative or contributory; and
> provocative, instigating or soliciting.[29]

The dilemma therefore, is that the official or citizen who remains uncritically
loyal to his national government, in the reasonable hope of sharing the fruits
or spoils of its enterprises, may find himself an accomplice in anarchism, in
the threat or infliction of violence or in governmentally organized crime.
Herbert Marcuse asked:

> How can the individual . . . satisfy his needs without hurting himself,
> without reproducing, through his aspirations and satisfactions, his
> dependence on an exploitative apparatus which, in satisfying his
> needs, perpetuates his servitude?[30]

In discussing the concept of crimes without victims, Edwin Schur remarks
on the difficulty of identifying the victim of a crime against the state, or a crime
against morals.[31] He says that the law may insist that a person is a victim even
where the person is consenting to the forbidden behavior and the "harm" is a
self-harm to a participating individual who makes no complaint. The law stim-
ulates the development of a deviant subculture, the deviant behavior comes to
be elaborated into a role, and the need to act like criminals causes the deviants
"to develop—at the very least—a pronouncedly antisocial outlook." There are
conceptual similarities between the field of decriminalizing victimless abortion,
homosexuality and drug use, and the field of criminalizing, or declaring new
standards, where hitherto people have consented to self-harms because it has
not been politically feasible to prescribe remedies and they have consequently
not seen themselves as victims. The present arrangements of law and order in
the world have assuredly institutionalized national self-images and subcultures
in which people have grown up "to develop—at the very least—a pronouncedly
antisocial outlook," and to accept as normal at a national level "the conditions
of vigilance required on the Indian frontier in the United States, or in the
streets of a fifteenth-century Italian city-state . . . (with) the waste involved
in this diversion of human energies."[32]

While it is wisdom to try to love one's enemy and to practise gratitude in
all circumstances, it is nevertheless generally accepted that one may, and
perhaps should, resist evil.[33] It is regarded as proper, not to condemn, but

certainly to give and receive judgment, appreciation and criticism. One has a right, and to some extent a duty, of self-help or self-defence.[34] Stephen Schafer writes of the victim's "functional responsibility" to avoid and prevent attempts to injure him.[35] The failure to arrest or resist or report a crime may be regarded as criminal complicity in the crime. A person injured by the wrong of another may have a duty to abate or minimize the damage.[37] And an insurance policy may be voided by the contributory negligence of the insured, e.g. by his driving when drunk or leaving a building or car unlocked. The law acts on the principle that prevention is better than compensation.

A public officer, whether civilian or military, has the right and the duty to disobey an unlawful order. If an official, or a private citizen, does not have a *duty* to stop his superior or his government from criminal or careless conduct, he certainly has a moral and democratic right to, even if the right is not yet enforceable in supranational law. While Locke and Rousseau held that protection by the law creates an obligation to obey the law.[37] Hobbes discussed the position of the individual "where there is no protection to be had from the law" or "where the law cannot arrive in time enough to his assistance." "No law can oblige a man to abandon his own preservation," he said, for:

> No man in the Institution of Sovereign Power can be supposed to give away the Right of preserving his own body; for the safety whereof all Sovereignty was ordained . . . The obligation of Subjects to the Sovereign is understood to last as long as, and no longer than the power lasteth by which he is able to protect them. . . When the Sovereign Power ceaseth. . . every one may protect himself by his own power.[38]

The Czechoslovakian leader Thomas Masaryk (1850-1937) said that, "So long as there are martyrs we will continue to have tyrants." Responsible individuals therefore may be driven by reactionary government to express a healthy independence in some criminal form, as with the mass protests in recent years against the Vietnam war and military conscription. The appeal of the dissenters will be to law (world law), but the methods are not likely to be less violent than those of nationalism itself. Edwin Schur holds that, "America is a criminal society by virtue of its involvement in mass violence abroad."[39] America is not alone, however. Consider the reported massacres and expulsions in Uganda under President Idi Amin. We are faced generally today with a lawless world in which every nation is, in Hobbes's terms, in a state of perpetual war with every other nation. Individuals will have to recover an awareness of their own aggressiveness, and thus of the violence they have projected onto and legitimated in national agencies of war and law,[40] in order to withdraw it and to invest world institutions with the authority they need. In 1947 Don Salvador de Madariaga wrote:

> Of the three stages of social nature, man, nation, mankind, it is
> therefore the middle stage which most requires control and restraint.
> For it is the nation which, both towards the individual and towards
> the world society, turns an absolutist face. Towards the individual,
> the nation, once absolutist on the strength of the divine right of
> kings, remains absolutist on the strength of 'the will of the people'.
> Towards the world society, the nation remains absolutist entrenched
> as it is in the doctrine—and practice—of national sovereignty.
>
> The problem first understood as that of 'the rights of man' thus
> reveals itself as one of the proper relations between man, nation
> and world community.[41]

Hart distinguished homosexuality from treason, arguing (against Devlin)
that to legalize homosexuality would modify a moral code but not destroy it,
and assuming that treason or sedition would indeed destroy the whole fabric
of morality and so of society.[42] But it is a matter of degree. This is an age
of treason and sedition, since there is no other clear way to escape from national
military *braggadocio* and to save what is useful in our present moral code. In
the ever-present judgment of history, treason may become as respectable as
heresy. In this context we may increasingly characterize the ineffectiveness,
intransigence, and mere persistence of nationalism as a crimping tyranny.[43]

Even if political change can occur fast enough without the jolting of
conscious political crime, one message of victimology is that the individual
will have to be prepared to act independently of his national government, with
or without its cooperation. In arguing for the rule of law as mankind's most
practical defence, Fernando Fournier wrote:

> In the days before nuclear power, governments could choose between
> the force of arms or the force of law in the settlement of disputes
> between states. Such a choice exists no longer. In the past, efforts
> for peace were considered idealistic but not practical. Men tended
> to accept the inevitability of war as a corollary to a world without
> international control. The future will be marred by violence so long
> as the international community continues without a lawful order,
> an effective system of courts, and enforcement of an international
> system of justice. . . . Not only governments but individuals are
> assuming responsibility for creating a consensus and a structure for
> peaceful order. . . . . governments alone cannot create a foundation
> for peace.[44]

Currently, however, national governments have a monopoly on the force and
the institutions of what is recognized as law, and it is precisely those aggregations

of force which threaten the greatest destruction of peace, order, and good government. The objective then is to find ways of prizing the popularly supported force of law out of the hands of sectional groups which, acknowledging no superior, are a law unto themselves. Very slowly we may come to recognize that one final law, with internal checks and balances, is superior to a multitude of necessarily invalid claims to final law.

The greatest weakness of the United Nations to date has been that it is directed by the representatives of national governments. And, just as there is not much point in talking to a city mayor about national problems, so there is little point in talking to national leaders about global problems. National leaders win office by concentrating their vision and energies on the local scene; and their perspective of defence is likely to remain limited to defence through national institutions. The idea of a standing measured institutionalized defence through global law is alien to them, and we cannot expect that they will take a genuine lead in limiting their own powers. Yet those powers have to be limited in order to implement defence through law and to eliminate war.

5. *Criminologists could describe effective supranational remedies and sanctions to protect the human rights of the victims of national tyranny*

Alvin Toffler observes that the important differences between people are no longer strongly place-related, but that allegiances and commitments are shifting from place-related social structures (city, state, nation or neighborhood) to those (corporation, profession, voluntary association, friendship network) which are mobile, fluid and, for practical purposes, place-less.[45] It is hard for people to reach out from the old security of national order, especially when it may be that, as Georg Schwarzenberger wrote in 1950, "International society still lacks any of the conditions on which the rise of criminal law depends."[46] In the "community and association" terms of Ferdinand Toennies,[47] we are still in the process of moving from (an inevitably loose) association of separate nations towards a true community of mankind.[48] People fear that planetary government will be some great new edifice still more remote and violent than national government.[49] But that can hardly be so. The first achievement of central or unitary government will be to attain that monopoly on the legitimate use of military and police force by which we define and recognize a state,[50] and thus to obviate that military competition which has made anarchistic nationalism (the hallowed *division* of sovereignty which we have hitherto conceived of as the state) so fearfully dangerous. The institutions of world order will introduce certain tensions and fears of their own, it is true; but they will not hold the terror of existing institutions which are committed to ungoverned eccentricity, division, and disorder.

Ideally we shall be able to enlarge the political stature of people from
nationals into humans, as it were, by legislative fiat effectuating the complaints
procedures envisaged by Article 41 and the Protocol to the International Covenant on Civil and Political Rights 1966. By Article 2 of the International Covenant on Economic, Social and Cultural Rights (1966), States Parties to the
Covenant:

> undertake to guarantee that the rights enunciated in the present
> Covenant will be exercised *without discrimination of any kind* as
> to race, colour, sex, language, religion, political or other opinion,
> *national or social origin,* property, birth or other status.

But the operation of these complaints procedures depends upon the good grace
of national governments and no nation has yet been democratic enough actively
to seek for its citizens these rights of appeal against the finality of its own
judgments.

Criminologists are well placed to appraise the defence value of national
institutions and to devise practical procedures whereby individuals who are
diminished by national insularity can appeal to the open judgments of the
world. We are already smoothing this transition by fairly appreciating the
moral and political position of criminals who are generally repudiated from
respectful consideration by the comfortably established authority of governments. With a supranational criminology, however, we could help much more
directly.

Even if the Human Rights appeal or complaints procedure comes into
effect, the Covenants still provide no remedy or sanction other than the moral
pressure of world opinion. And one reason why such opinion has been slow to
crystallize into world law is that the sanctions or sentences we have so far conceived have been so gross that the remedy has seemed worse than the disease.[51]
But sanctions we must have: a law without sanctions is no law at all. Chapter
7 of the U.N. Charter authorizes the Security Council to order "military measures," and also "measures not involving the use of armed force," namely the:

> complete or partial interruption of economic relations and of rail,
> sea, air, postal, telegraphic, radio, and other means of communica-
> tion, and the severance of diplomatic relations.

But neither the Charter nor any other standing instrument of supranational
law conceives of piercing the veil of the body politic and holding key individual
officials responsible, in the manner that national courts daily hold company
and trade union managers accountable. If criminologists could devise sanctions
and remedies calculated to attract local support for any necessary world action
against the crime or other unlawful act of a local leader, we might then be able

to help introduce a system of supranational criminal courts—not just one grand, remote world court, but a whole system whereby the existing structures of national courts are, first, authorized, and then gradually required, to implement the terms of supranational law, as overriding any inconsistent national law. The physical presence of men and buildings in each country will attract popular support beyond the national governments. The International Court of Justice at The Hague, that least active and least innovative of U.N. agencies, could then be wakened out of its somnolence and asked to set up a system of courts to handle appeals from local courts on matters involving supranational law.

Notes

1. W.H. Nagel, "Critical Criminology," *Abstracts on Criminology and Penology,* 11, 1 (1972).
2. Notably Julius Stone, *Power Politics and Human Hopes,* Truman Center for the Advancement of Peace, 1968; and Julius Stone and Robert K. Woetzel, *Toward a Feasible International Criminal Court,* World Peace Through Law Centre, 1970.
3. Stanley W. Johnston, "The Violence of the Continued Claim to National Sovereignty Today," *A.N.Z.J. of Criminol.* 4 (1971): 132-143.
4. Elizabeth Thorneycroft, *Court of International Delinquency;* and "La Prophylaxie du Terrorisme," *Etudes Internationales de Psycho-Sociologie Criminelle,* nos. 20-23, 1972.
5. Lotika Sarkar, "The Proper Law of Crime in International Law," *International and Comparative Law Quarterly* 11 (1962); 446: reprinted in Gerhard O.W. Mueller and Edward M. Wise, *International Criminal Law* (London: Sweet and Maxwell, 1965), pp. 50-76.
6. John Rawls, *A Theory of Justice* (Oxford: Clarendon Press, 1972), p. 8.
7. H.L.A. Hart, *The Concept of Law* (Oxford: Clarendon Press, 1961), pp. 189, 195, and 214.
8. UNESCO, *The University Teaching of the Social Sciences: Criminology,* 1957.
9. Erik Erikson, "Insight and Responsibility," a lecture delivered in South Africa in 1968.
10. Nagel, "Critical Criminology"; W.F. Murphy and J. Tanenhaus, *The Study of Public Law* (New York: Random House, 1972), Chapter 2.
11. Richard Quinney, "Crime in Political Perspective," *American Behavioral Scientist* 8 (1964): 19-22.
12. D.W. Hanson and R.B. Fowler, *Obligation and Dissent: An Introduction to Politics* (Boston: Little Brown, 1971); Morton Grodzins, *The Loyal and the Disloyal: Social Boundaries of Patriotism and Treason* (Cleveland: Meridian 1966); and works by Lewis Coser and Muzafer Sherif.

13. Stone, *Power Politics and Human Hopes*.
14. Stanley I. Benn distinguishes six meanings in "The Uses of 'Sovereignty',"
    Political Studies, 3, (Oxford: Clarendon Press, 1955), p. 109.
15. Thomas Aquinas; G.H. Sabine, *A History of Political Theory,* p. 218;
    A.P. d'Entrèves, *Natural Law: An Historical Survey* (New York: Harper
    and Row, 1965).
16. Hans Kelsen, *General Theory of Law and State,* (Cambridge, Mass.:
    Harvard University Press, 1945), pp. 363-88.
17. Aquinas; d'Entrèves, *Natural Law,* p. 43; Pope John XXIII, *Peace on Earth,*
    1963.
18. Hart, *Concept of Law,* p. 214.
19. *Crime in New Zealand,* 1968, and *Violent Offending,* 1971. See my review
    in *A.N.Z.J. of Criminol.* 5, (1972); 59.
20. F.B.I., *Uniform Crime Reports,* 1971, p. 61. And see *Time,* October 23,
    1972. The F.B.I. reports a drop of 3% in 1972.
21. C.H. Rolph, "Guns and Murder," *New Statesman,* March 10, 1961.
22. *E.g.* E.H. Sutherland and D.R. Cressey, *Principles of Criminology*
    (Philadelphia: J.B. Lippincott, 7th ed.), p. 27.
23. H.R. Trevor-Roper, *The European Witch-Craze* (New York: Harper and
    Row, 1969).
24. Jean Bodin, *De la République, 1577.* New York: McMillan, 1955, (in
    English).
25. H.C. Lea, *A History of the Inquisition of the Middle Ages,* 1887. Reprinted
    in New York: Russell and Russell, 1955.
26. Stone and Woetzel, *Toward a Feasible International Criminal Court.*
27. Anthony Quinton, *Political Philosophy.* New York: Oxford University
    Press, 1967, p. 16. And see the U.S. Declaration of Independence, 1776;
    and Karl Deutsch, *Nationalism and Its Alternatives* (New York: Knopf,
    1969), p. 172.
28. Pope John XXIII, *Peace on Earth,* 1963, paragraphs 51, 61, 65 and 92.
29. Hans von Hentig, *The Criminal and His Victim* (New Haven: Yale University
    Press, 1948). See Jack Gratus, *The Victims* (London: Hutchinson of
    London, 1969), p. 22.
30. Herbert Marcuse, *As Essay on Liberation* (Boston: Beacon Press, 1969), p. 4.
31. Edwin Schur, *Crimes Without Victims* (Englewood Cliffs, N.J.: Prentice-
    Hall, 1965), p. 169-73.
32. E.K. Braybrooke, "The Sociological Jurisprudence of Roscoe Pound,"
    University of Western Australia Law Review 5, (1961): 293.
33. Cf. Matthew 5, 39 with the doctrine of Augustine and Aquinas on the
    just war.
34. Hobbes, *Leviathan,* Chapters 14 and 17; Hart, *Concept of Law,* Chapter 9.
35. Stephen Schafer, *The Victim and His Criminal* (New York: Random House,
    1968), p. 152.

36. *Dee Conservancy Board v. McConnell* (1928) 2 K.B. 159.

37. J.P. Plamenatz, *Consent, Freedom and Political Obligation.* (New York: Oxford University 2nd. ed., 1968), pp. 24-27.

38. *Op. cit.* See Robert-Louis Perret, "Doctrinal Bases for International Penal Jurisdiction," in Stone and Woetzel, *Toward a Feasible International Criminal Court,* pp. 142-55.

39. Edwin Schur, *Our Criminal Society* (Englewood Cliffs, N.J.: Prentice-Hall, 1969), p. 18.

40. Joseph G. Starke, Q.C., *An Introduction to the Science of Peace (Irenology),* (Leyden: A.W. Sijthoff, 1968), pp. 75-79.

41. Salvador de Madariaga, *Human Rights,* a UNESCO Symposium (London: Allan Wingate, 1949), p. 48.

42. H.L.A. Hart, "Immorality and Treason," *The Listener,* July 30, 1959, pp. 162-63.

43. Perret, *Doctrinal Bases,* p. 155. Maurice Latey, *Tyranny: A Study in the Abuse of Power* (London: Penguin, 1972), pp. 20-23 and 33.

44. Fernando Fournier, *World Peace Through Law,* World Peace Through Law Centre, 400 Hill Building, Washington, D.C., U.S.A.

45. Alvin Toffler, *Future Shock* (London, Bodley Head, 1970), pp. 91-92, quoting Professor John Dyckman of the University of Pennsylvania. See also *Man's Wider Loyalties: Limitations of National Sovereignty,* a report by the Wyndham Place Trust, Hutchinson of London, 1970.

46. Georg Schwarzenberger, "The Problems of an International Criminal Law," *Current Legal Problems* 3, (1950): 263. Reprinted in Mueller and Wise, *International Criminal Law.*

47. Ferdinand Toennies, *Gemeinschaft und Gesellschaft,* 1887, translated by Charles P. Loomis, N.Y., 1940.

48. Starke, *An Introduction to the Science of Peace,* p. 39 and Chapter 4.

49. Alex Comfort, *Authority and Delinquency in the Modern State: A Criminological Approach to the Problem of Power* (London: Routledge and Kegan Paul, 1950), p. 75.

50. Quinton, *Political Philosophy,* p. 6.

51. Hart, *The Concept of Law,* p. 214.

6

Offenders Without Victims?
Milo Tyndel

Discussing offenders without victims in a volume on various aspects of victims of offences is bound to appear odd and out of place. However, I shall endeavor to make this presentation fit into the framework of victimology by pointing out that in a great number of cases, the victimless offender in actual fact has a victim, namely himself. Furthermore, I shall present the effects of legislation on the development of legal offenses without victims, in analogy with the undesirable effects of physicians and medicine on their patients.

It goes without saying that the topic of this presentation has nothing to do with those criminal cases in which the person is suspected, or even convicted, of a criminal offence while his victim, e.g. a corpse, is never uncovered. I would like to present an overview of those cases in which an offense does not necessarily victimize any one particular person, the offender being the victim of his own offense, in the last analysis. The perpetration of the offense is caused by psychopathology, by the Law, and more significantly by a combination of these factors.

For this presentation I have chosen three groups of offenders, in a somewhat arbitrary and subjective manner, as I have had personal professional experience with them and have made contributions to the literature on these subjects. I am referring to:

A. The Chronic Drunkenness Offender.
B. The patient with the Munchausen Syndrome.
C. The patient with a Compensation Neurosis.

A. The Chronic Drunkenness Offender

In some countries drunkenness is punishable under a variety of laws, generally describing the offence as being "drunk in a public place," in most instances without providing a precise definition of drunkenness itself. Only some laws include the condition that the offender is "unable to care for his own safety." The chronic drunkenness offender is a person who has been repeatedly arrested and convicted for the same offense, namely being apprehended intoxicated in a public place. The term "chronic drunkenness offender" is used interchangeably with that of the "Chronic Police Case Inebriate," "The Homeless Alcoholic," or "Skid-Row Alcoholic," while the repeated process of arrest, conviction, incarceration, and release is often referred to as the "revolving door."

The question as to what makes a person sink not only to the very bottom of the social ladder, but makes him spend the rest of his life commuting back and forth between skid row and jail, has been raised repeatedly and various answers have been given in the light of the specific interest and viewpoint of the individual researchers and their school of thought. The consensus of opinion was that the chronic drunkenness offender is a sick person from a medical, psychological, and social viewpoint, and that his preoccupation with alcohol is but one of his highly unsuccessful attempts at coping with his problems. Based on a large series of investigated chronic drunkenness offenders, I have come to the conclusion that in virtually every case, psychopathology can be demonstrated and diagnosed. I have formulated a theory based on Freud's ideas on civilization and its discontent, to the effect that the chronic skid-row alcoholic who is liable to become a chronic drunkenness offender is an individual whose passivity interferes to the highest degree with an adequate response to the frustrating experiences caused by the restrictions on the sex drive, and the expression of aggression imposed by civilization. He is using two devices, namely intoxication and isolation, in his attempts to deal with his emotional and social predicament. These processes are facilitated by the conditions of his social level which makes these modes of adaptation more accessible than others.

Just to demonstrate the magnitude of the problem in some countries, I would like to quote the findings of the Task Force on Drunkenness of the U.S.A. President's Commission on Law and Enforcement and Administration of Justice (1967), "Two Million arrests in 1965—one of every three arrested in America—were for the offense of public drunkenness. The great volume of these arrests places an extremely heavy load on the operations of the Criminal Justice System. It burdens Police, clogs lower Criminal Courts, and crowds Penal Institutions throughout the United States." The vast majority of researchers in this field have come to the conclusion that punishing the offender in the majority of cases has no therapeutic effect whatsoever; on the contrary, it serves only to perpetuate the vicious circle in which everybody concerned is moving.

Despite the thorough questioning and research, not sufficient attention has been paid to the most basic question as to why being apprehended in a state of intoxication should be considered an offense, not to be confounded with those criminal offences connected with intoxication and which, of course, should be and actually are, considered separately from the case of public intoxication. Historical studies have shown that the legislation against public drunkenness was an upshot of the puritan outlook and the temperance movements. It is difficult to see how anyone can be genuinely victimized by an inebriated person who is minding his own business, for instance going home, again, I repeat, without disturbing others, committing criminal offenses, or driving a vehicle.

It thus becomes clear that there is no victim to this offence but the offender himself. If not for the law and its enforcement, this person would be regarded as a sick person whose emotional illness is complicated by alcoholism, and he would be treated with either sympathy or rejection according to the personal attitudes of the observer. Hence, it is the Law which creates the serious problem, and to a large extent interferes with a medical, psychological, and social approach to the prevalent condition.

B. The Munchausen Syndrome

The Munchausen Syndrome describes the case of patients who have themselves been admitted on numerous occasions to hospitals, in most instances through the Emergency Department. They fake various diseases and in most instances have acquired the necessary knowledge and experience to deceive even experienced physicians and nursing staff through the proper description of their symptoms, the appropriate behavior, and self-inflicted injuries. They not only submit themselves to various painful medical investigations and surgical operations (some of them even mutilating), but they ask for them in a very insistent manner. Although fortunately not too significant in numbers, patients afflicted with this malingering syndrome may pose various problems, one of them being the psychological issue of the frustrated members of the helping professions.

Although the underlying causes for this strange behavior are to be sought in severe psychopathology, these patients' "acts," namely malingering, must be defined as an offence, classifiable as public mischief or fraud. On the other hand, their offences are not perpetrated against any one victim in particular, but quite obviously and conspicuously against themselves.

My reference to the malingerers presenting the Munchausen Syndrome, a case of genuine malingering, should serve the purpose of contrasting this matter with a great number of pathological cases in which the offence of malingering is less clear-cut.

C. The Traumatic Neurosis

It is not easy to define traumatic neurosis. Perhaps a usable definition is that given by Laughlin (1967), who prefers the term, Neuroses Following Trauma:

The Neuroses following Trauma are a group of emotional illnesses or neurotic reactions having their onset following physical or acute

psychic injury, or both. They are neurotic reactions which have been
attributed to, or which follow a situational traumatic event, or a
series of such events. The resulting emotional or physical consequences
are highly variable in degree and in time of onset. They include a wide
variety of possible emotional responses and neurotic symptoms. These
may be transient or permanent, single or multiple, and may appear
immediately following a traumatic event, or be delayed in their onset.

The number of instances of traumatic neurosis and their significance is
steadily increasing as a consequence of rapid industrialization and mobilization,
but also with the increasing liberalization of compensation legislation in most
parts of the civilized world. More and more professional people in Medicine,
Psychology, the Law, and Social Work, are becoming involved in cases of
traumatic neurosis and particularly in compensation.

According to the psychoanalytic school of thought, the elements of
primary and secondary gain play a highly significant role in the development
and maintenance of traumatic neuroses, and these concepts have been adopted
even by a great number of professionals who are not particularly fond of
psychoanalysis. The primary purpose or gain of the neurotic disorder is seen
in the reduction of emotional conflict and tension through neurotic symptoms.
In contrast to this process, the ego, in "making the best of it," may try to gain
advantages from the external world via the disease, e.g. by eliciting attention
and sympathy, by manipulating other people, and last, but not least, by
receiving monetary compensation. These are some of the secondary gains of
the disease.

In the context of this presentation we shall concentrate on the secondary
gain issue, and particularly on the compensation part of it. In spite of the
existence of a large number of studies on the subject, the now classical description of the mental processes involved, by Fenichel (1945), is still quite apt to
present the problem:

In traumatic neurosis secondary gains play an even more important
role than in the psychoneurosis; these are certain uses the patient
can make of his illness which have nothing to do with the origin of
the neurosis, but which may obtain the utmost practical importance.
The symptoms may acquire secondarily the significance of a demon-
stration of one's own helplessness in order to secure external help
such as was available in childhood. The question how to combat or
to prevent secondary gains, often becomes the main problem in treatment. In cases where neurosis has been precipitated by a comparably
minor incident, the incident itself is often placed in the foreground
by the patient, who in this way succeeds in again repressing the mental
conflicts mobilized by it. Obtaining financial compensation, or fighting

for one, creates a poor atmosphere for psychotherapy, the more so if the compensation brings not only rational advantages, but has acquired the unconscious meaning of love and protecting security as well. Yet anyone who has a psychoanalytical understanding of the neurotic processes will not equate neurosis to simulation and will not repudiate compensation altogether. It may be that there is no fundamental solution of the question how compensations should be handled which would be equally valid for all cases. Perhaps the idea of giving one single compensation at the right time may be the best way out.

Here we are in the midst of a very difficult and controversal problem. Fenichel (1945) rightly advised not to equate neurosis to malingering. On the other hand, the two processes, primary gain through the development of the neurotic condition, and secondary gain, are not only most intimately interwoven but they coexist most of the time, enhance one another, and each of them can be prevalent at a certain point in time, as the psychological and/or practical needs may require. In my own experience with a great number of patients seeking compensation, the secondary gain motives are consciously known to the patient, either in their entirety or at least partially. The pursuit of the secondary gains is thus fostered and perpetuated by unconscious processes, regression and passivity on the one side, and by the compensation motive on the other side. The latter motive in particular, makes the patient perpetrate an offense, namely exaggerating existing symptoms, or even faking new ones. This specific part of the patient's behavior is obviously an offense which, as in the case of the Munchausen Syndrome, can be perceived of as fraud and/or mischief.

In this context, two sets of ideas should be given consideration:

1. The offence is not directed against any one in particular, and no specific victim can be singled out, for in the vast majority of cases, they are large organizations and institutions involved, such as insurance companies, workmen's compensation boards, and the like.

Society has chosen money as the medium to be used as payment for disability following injuries. This often works against the patient's best interests for it tends to discourage early recovery as this lessens the amount of the financial settlement. Whenever compensation plays a significant role in traumatic neurosis which has become chronic, the difficulty of dealing with the problem increases. Unsettled litigation features play a part, but their influence frequently can not be avoided because settlement often awaits the outcome of the illness. Moreover, the logical course of encouraging the patient to resume some kind of employment as an adjunct to his therapy, is often impossible, as litigation, insurance regulations, and union rules interfere. On one hand the patient must maintain his symptoms to collect benefits; on the other hand, payment of benefits awaits the cure of the symptoms. The whole thing is a vicious circle. To quote Fenichel (1945) again:

> . . . the blocking off or decrease in ego functions, characteristic for every traumatic neurosis, created a lasting decrease in perception, judgement, and interest in the external world, a readiness to withdraw from any contact with reality, probably corresponding to a fear of repetition of the trauma. The resulting picture is that of a very restricted personality living a simple life on a low level, comparable to certain psychotics or to certain personalities that have overcome a psychosis with scars in their ego. Early treatment is indicated, before the alterations created by the trauma are imbedded too deeply into the personality.

However, it is only too well known that treatment is either not accepted by the patient or ineffective as long as the compensation issue is not settled. It thus becomes clear that the part of the patient's condition which may be regarded as an offense, namely exaggeration and malingering, may bring a certain financial reward, but on the other hand, the patient-offender himself is victimized by the restrictions imposed on his normal life and by the perpetuation of his condition.

   2. If not for the social legislation protecting the injured person, a great many cases of traumatic neurosis, in the absence of the compensation motive, would have a chance to improve or to be minimized either spontaneously, through the action of homeostasis, or with the help of therapy. Thus the Law, necessary and helpful as it is, creates problems in the sense of fostering and perpetuating a disease and an offense.

Discussion

   The patients referred to in the three preceding sections have a significant feature in common, namely the fact that they are offenders without discernible victims other than themselves. The patients discussed under the headings "The Chronic Drunkenness Offender" and "The Traumatic Neuroses" have another feature in common, namely exaggerated and/or malingering, the first ones totally, the latter ones partially, which again makes them offenders without victims other than themselves. Finally, the chronic drunkenness offenders and the patients exaggerating and/or malingering within the framework of traumatic neurosis have another aspect in common, namely the fact that their conditions are either created or fostered by the Law.

   Of course there is a significant difference between the laws involved in the first case and in the second. In the case of the chronic drunkenness offender, abolishing the law which makes being drunk in a public place as such, without the commission of any punishable offences, would reduce the so-called offender to the person he really is, namely a sick person in need of medical, psychological, and social help. The law could provide for immediate help to the afflicted person and could even make treatment in the long run mandatory. As a matter of fact, more and more legislations have in recent years modified the law concerning the chronic drunkenness offenders, but there is still very much to be done in this respect.

On the other hand, the legislation providing protection and compensation for a person injured at work or in traffic constitutes a highly desirable and progressive step in the right direction. However, it creates psychological problems which enhance and perpetuate emotional illness and lead to the offense of malingering. I have chosen references from the psychiatric literature of decades ago in order to demonstrate that very little changes have taken place ever since. Many professional people involved with patients and claimants belonging to these categories—and there is no need pointing out the magnitude of the problem—unfortunately contribute a great deal to the vicious circle described before. Members of the legal profession and of the insurance industry postpone the settlement of claims and of litigations until such time as the claimant's condition has subsided, and are helped in this respect by physicians who are reluctant to assume the responsibility of advising the settlement in spite of persisting symptoms. The more physicians and specialists of various branches of medicine and surgery are involved, and the more investigations and treatments performed, the less likely will the patient give up his symptoms and the more likely will he develop the tendency to exaggerate, manipulate, and malinger, thus victimizing himself.

The so-called iatrogenic conditions have been well known and accepted in clinical medicine for a long time. The term, iatrogenic disease describes a morbid condition which is due to medical treatment, naturally as an undesirable side effect of the treatment, such as ill effects of various drugs, or an ill-fated approach and behavior on the part of a physician. In analogy to the notion of iatrogenic diseases, *I propose to use the term, nomogenic diseases* (from the Greek *nomos* = law) for those conditions in whose development and/or maintenance the Law plays a significant role. I believe that both the case of the chronic drunkenness offender and of the traumatic neurotic, different though they are, can be used as demonstrative examples of these conditions.

I believe that a close cooperation between various professions, Medicine, Law, Psychology, Social Work, and allied fields, can achieve very much in the long run to undo the damage caused by the Law, and influence the legislatures and the executive powers in various countries to improve the prevailing conditions.

References

Fenichel, O. *The Psychoanalytic Theory of Neurosis.* New York: W.W. Norton and Co., 1945.

Laughlin, H.P. *The Neuroses.* Washington, D.C.: Butterworth, 1967.

Task Force on Drunkenness. The President's Commission on Law Enforcement and Administration of Justice. Washington, D.C.: U.S. Government Printing Office, 1967.

Tyndel, M., and Hoff, H. *Neurose und Invaliditaet.* Wien: Soziale Sicherheit, 1953

Tyndel M. *Die Psychiatrie des Rueckfaelligen Trunkenheitsdelinquenten.* Toronto: Addiction Research Foundation, 1968.

Tyndel, M., and Rutherdale, J. "Munchausen Syndrome and Alcoholism." *Internat. J. of the Addictions,* 8, 1, 1973.

7 Are There Really Crimes Without Victims?
Hugo A. Bedau

I

Early in 1973, according to a report in the *New York Times,*

> The criminal justice section of the New York State Bar Association recommended . . . that all criminal sanctions be removed from a variety of "victimless" crimes, including possession or private use of small quantities of marijuana.
>
> The section . . . was nearly unanimous in its approval of resolutions on prostitution, public intoxication and marijuana use and possession . . .
>
> The section's resolution on marijuana said that the present penalties for possession threatened "the criminal prosecution of a significant portion of our population for engaging in a personal act which poses no demonstratable danger to the public."
>
> The recommendation was for removal of all criminal penalties for "private use and possession of reasonable amounts of marijuana and treating the gifts or profitless transfer of small quantities in a non-criminal manner."
>
> Regarding prostitution, the section recommended repeal of the existing law and adoption of measures similar to the British Streetwalkers Act, which is directed principally against public solicitation. It also recommended non-penal sanctions, such as counseling for first offenders convicted under the proposed law.
>
> The section said criminal penalties for public drunkenness placed "an inappropriate burden on our overtaxed criminal justice system." It recommended "emergency treatment for intoxicated persons in public health facilities and the ending of the processing of these cases through the criminal courts and jails."
>
> (Montgomery 1973)

At the present time, such recommendations as these by the New York State Bar Association are no longer novel. No doubt, if adopted into law, these reforms

A revised version of a paper originally prepared for the Symposium on Victimology. A more extensive version is scheduled to appear in the book (co-authored with Edwin Schur) *Victimless Crimes: Rhetoric or Reality?* Prentice-Hall, forthcoming.

would bring much needed aid to our overextended and understaffed criminal
justice agencies. By expanding the scope of personal freedom under law, these
reforms would respect the rights of various minorities and, for that matter, of
everyone to engage in deviant (atypical, abnormal) conduct. Indeed, "decriminalizing" (removal of criminal penalties for) these activities seems long overdue
if, as the *Times* report describes them, they are truly " 'victimless' crimes."
However, this description, "victimless crimes," should give us pause. Is it really
true that the use of marijuana, the condition of public intoxication, and the
activity of prostitution involve no "victim," and for this reason it is absurd and
wrong to make such things criminal violations, which carry heavy penalties and
lead to millions of arrests each year? In its most general form the issue is
whether there really are crimes without victims. This question naturally leads
to others. If there are crimes which are truly victimless, for what reasons did
they come to be regarded as criminal in the first place? Does a crime become
victimless only when no one at all is injured, or when no person other than the
consenting participants are injured? Should crimes without victims be decrim-
inalized altogether, or should the current severity of the punishments merely
be reduced? On the other hand, if it is arguably false that these activities
have no victims, how did the phrase, "victimless crimes," come to gain the
popularity it currently enjoys?

Thanks to the influential volume, *Crimes Without Victims,* by Edwin Schur,
published in 1965, the connection between law reform on abortion, homosexuality, and drug addiction, and the idea of victimless crime was made explicit
for professional audiences as well as the general public. In the last few years, a
flood of essays and reports has appeared on the themes of overcriminalization
and decriminalization, the coercive enforcement of morals, paternalism, and
victimless crimes (for the most recent list of references, see Geis 1972, p. 255).
Yet anyone who is willing to examine closely these writings is entitled to come
away somewhat dissatisfied. As I hope to show, the scholarly authorities in
criminology have been using a confused concept of victimless crimes. Precisely,
they seem to rely on several distinct and non-coextensive criteria to define this
class of offenses. As a consequence, it is very difficult to draw up a list in any
definite or uniform way of all and only those crimes which are victimless, and
to distinguish them from the crimes which do have victims. Likewise, until
further analysis of the concept of victimless crimes is undertaken, it is impossible
to go through the penal code of any jurisdiction and pick out all and only those
criminal laws which should be revised or repealed because they create victimless
crimes and authorize punishment for them. Yet, surely, these were the false
hopes implicitly created by the notion that we can clarify and organize our
thoughts, and penetrate the jungle of the criminal law, by means of the notion
of "victimless crimes." Now, as I shall try to show, it is possible to construct a
more or less adequate definition of this idea and to make some use of it in
criminal law reform. However, to do this we must rely on some theory or other

of *basic human rights.* In particular, we need to determine which rights-violations deserve absolute *prohibition* by the criminal law, which instead deserve only partial control through *regulation,* and which activities are not rights-violations at all, and therefore must be *tolerated.*

If I am correct, the search for answers to these questions will take us beyond sociology and criminology, and into moral philosophy. Only there can we find the necessary theory of human rights, which in turn sets the conditions for the calculation of the costs which society ought to pay in order to prohibit, regulate, or tolerate conduct of which most people disapprove.

II

Let us begin by noticing the first warning sign of conceptual and theoretical trouble ahead: the authorities do not agree among themselves as to which crimes are victimless. Edwin Schur, as we noted earlier, initially singled out under this rubric only the crimes of abortion, homosexuality, and drug addiction (Schur 1965, p. iii). The criminologist Jerome Skolnick mentioned private fighting and crimes of vice, such as gambling and smoking marijuana (Skolnick 1968, p. 63), as well as abortion, homosexuality (p. 631), and prostitution (p. 632). The jurist Herbert Packer identified fornication, gambling, and narcotic offenses as victimless crimes (Packer 1968, p. 151), but he also mentioned bribery and espionage in this category (p. 267). Norval Morris, criminologist and jurist, cited drunks, addicts, loiterers, vagrants, prostitutes, and gamblers (Morris 1973, p. 11) as persons who commit crimes without victims; he explicitly excluded abortion from his list (p. 62), although in his book with Gordon Hawkins, abortion was equally explicitly included among the crimes which "lack victims" (Morris and Hawkins 1970, pp. 3, 6, 13-15).

One could multiply these lists indefinitely, but even this brief survey shows two things: (1) no two lists of crimes without victims are the same; and this suggests (apart from carelessness or deliberate selectivity by the authors quoted) that (2) the concept of victimless crime does not denote a stable class of offenses at all. One important reason for these two difficulties is that *victimization* is not a simple concept. It is quite possible for a person to fail to victimize someone in a violent or irreparable fashion, and yet to succeed in victimizing someone nonetheless. In order to appreciate the scope of the idea of victimization, it helps to have a brief catalogue of the ways in which one person can victimize another: (i) a person may lose life or limb through another's assault; (ii) a person may be physically harmed, but not irreversibly injured (maimed), by another; (iii) a person may cause another mental anguish, psychological trauma, by assault, threats, or taunts, with crippling or incapacitating results; (iv) a person may be exploited, degraded, manipulated, or debased by another, through isolated acts or established practices; (v) a person may have something imposed upon him, or taken from him, by another and without his own informed consent; (vi) a person may be deprived by another of something of value, e.g., position, status, reputation, influence, affection and esteem of others; and (vii) a person's property or possessions may be lost or damaged through the malicious act of another.

What do all these kinds of victimization have in common? Nothing—at least nothing physical, physiological, or psychological as the common and peculiar effect upon the victimized person. Trivially, we can say that all acts of victimization are acts in which one person does *violence* to another. But doing violence to a person is violating what? (see Shaffer 1971). If we are to make sense of victimization and the violence it involves as a common result of the above kinds of acts, we must say that in each sort of interaction listed above, a person normally (that is, a normal person with an understanding of his own nature and environment) has an *interest* in *not* undergoing the experience, event or interaction in question. In each case, some *injury* would befall him. Furthermore, we can say that society, through its governing agents and officers, has the duty to prevent the injury and protect the interest. Such personal interests which warrant societal protection are usually called *basic human* or *personal rights* (see Melden 1970; Dorsen 1971). The prevailing political and legal theory on which our institutions are professedly built is precisely the protection of such rights of persons. Indeed, from the theories of John Locke in the seventeenth century down to the latest pamphlets of the American Civil Liberties Union, the whole rationale for government is unintelligible apart from the belief that individual persons have rights, and that impartial governmental powers are needed primarily for the implementation and protection of these rights. More needs to be said, of course, about the sources, nature, and possible conflicts of these rights. For the present, however, it suffices to note that we cannot understand the diverse phenomena which involve doing violence to another, victimization and injury, without ultimately appealing to an essential moral doctrine of personal rights. Only in this way can we grasp the common feature of the kinds of victimization there are.

To restate this in terms appropriate to our discussion, we may say that a person has been *victimized* whenever any of his or her *rights* have been *violated* by another; and that whenever a person's rights have been violated through deliberate, malicious acts, he or she has been the *victim of a crime*. (No doubt, a crucial factor in our assessment of such victimization will be the degree to which the victim is judged to have brought the injury on his own head, by provocation, solicitation, enticement or avoidable acquiescence.) To believe, therefore, that one lives in a society where there are crimes without victims is to believe that there are offenses defined by law which involve no malicious or deliberate violation of anyone's rights by another. In order to determine whether this is true, it is necessary to have: (a) a theory (or at least a list) of the basic rights of persons; (b) a subset of these rights which it is appropriate to protect under the criminal law, viz., all those which when violated by deliberate and malicious acts of others cause personal injury; (c) a catalogue or checklist of the criminal offenses in the jurisdiction; and (d) a showing that some of the laws in (c) cannot be coordinated with any of the rights in (b). There, in a nutshell, is the task of criminal law reform organized around the idea of victimless crime, and presented in a way which gives due prominence to the role played by a theory of human or personal rights.

III

Now that we have a better grasp of the idea of victimization and injury, let us return to the prior point of considering the various proferred lists of crimes without victims, to see whether a person can be victimized by any of those activities. It may seem that I am about to belabor the obvious, but if the important first step is to see, as I believe it is, that criminologists do not agree in what they instance as a crime without a victim, then the important second step is to see that, once we understand the idea of victimization, many of these crimes in some instances (and some in most instances) involve a participant who is victimized by it. True, the harmfulness of some of these activities will depend on the age and health of the participant, e.g., fornication, smoking (marijuana or tobacco). In other cases, e.g., prostitution, the relevant question is whether the activity is degrading and whether it is injurious to engage in conduct which is degrading (see Women Endorsing Decriminalization 1973). In a private fight, whether or not anyone is injured depends on what happens, nothing more and nothing less. In some cases, such as espionage, there may be no person injured, even though harm may be inflicted on a government and indirectly upon the society it serves. In the case of bribery, everything depends on what the bribed person has been bribed to do; he may harm others, but not invariably. In gambling, the harm to the gambler may be zero and in any case will vary depending upon his disposable income and other factors. As for drunkenness, public or private, there is little doubt that irreversible physical harm is brought upon the drunk by virtue of the alcohol he has consumed, irrespective of his consent or willingness to become and remain a drunk. The same is less true of drug abuse generally, and not all drug offenses involve narcotic or addictive drugs. The case of abortion is the most problematic, because whether or not anyone is harmed depends on whether the unborn fetus is to count as another person (or a living human being with rights) who is involved in the activity though incapable of consent. Loitering and vagrancy, however, seem to be wholly victimless offenses, even if they easily lead to offenses (trespassing, disturbing the peace) which are not.

This survey teaches us another lesson: nothing uniform about our lists of offenses is revealed when we examine them to see how the chief participant, the "victim," is situated or affected. The participant-as-victim is obviously involved in these activities in a wide variety of different ways. It would be most unfortunate if the new bit of jargon, "crimes without victims," were to cause us to be less sensitive to such facts, and to blur our perception of the ways in which persons can injure themselves and be injured by others. There is some irony in this tendency, since criminologists have in recent years urged that it is important to know precisely who (if anyone) is victimized in any given criminal activity, and to what degree. The implication that there are a whole range of activities commonly made punishable as criminal offenses in which *no one is victimized* is, therefore, unfortunate.

IV

Let us turn now to attempts by criminologists to define the idea of victimless crimes. This requires us to examine the four major features in the offenses we have been discussing that have led criminologists and jurists to say these crimes involve no victims, or—as they sometimes say in qualification—no victims "in the usual sense of the word," or no "direct victims."

Edwin Schur remarks that the offenses he discusses (abortion, homosexuality, drug addition) involve the *consent* of the parties involved to an exchange of prohibited goods or services, and that "the element of consent precludes the existence of a victim—in the usual sense of the word" (Schur 1965, p. v). Let us call this the *consensual participation* feature of victimless crimes. Now it is true, as a general rule, that persons do not knowingly consent to engage in activities which do harm to themselves. But that is true only as a general rule. The problem, of course, is that not all harmful acts are like a gunshot or knife wound: some have a benign facade that conceals the eventual harmful effects on the participant. In the usual sense of the word, "victim," as defined by the typical current dictionary, a person is a victim *whenever* he is harmed or caused to suffer by any of the means discussed earlier (section II). The question of the cause or agency of harm is not at issue; nor are the questions of his consent and permission, his understanding and knowledge, nor the immediacy and proximity of the harm. Whether by virtue of his own act, that of another, or even of an impersonal agency (we do speak of victims of cancer), a person is to be judged a victim of *x* just in case *x* causes him to suffer, harms or injures him. The mere fact that a person consents to engage in a certain activity, without any further qualifications, does not entail that he is never harmed or caused to suffer by what he consents to—as the lives of thousands of alcoholics, addicts, gamblers, and prostitutes testify.

The case of abortion presents obvious and special difficulties. If we are to think of abortion as a crime without a victim, and as an activity in which the participants give their knowing consent, then we must be thinking of the woman who is undergoing the abortion and the abortionist and their presumed relationship. But if abortion (at least at some stages in pregnancy, e.g., during the last trimester) involves killing an unborn, fetal *person,* it is obvious that the activity of abortion proceeds without the consent of one of the parties involved. It is also obvious that since in abortion (or, more strictly, aborticide), one party is killed, abortion always involves a victim, even though it involves no pain or suffering for that victim. If, therefore, abortion is going to be thought of as a victimless crime, then (to borrow from my analysis of the previous section) we must believe that *the fetus has no rights* which abortion violates. That may be so, but it has to be argued (see Feinberg 1973; Hilgers and Horan 1972). Abortion is a special case, however. The other examples suffice to show that, in general, it is not quite true that "the element of consent precludes the existence of a victim—in the usual sense of the word." To put it simply, the class of activities to which all participants consent is not coextensive with the class of activities whose effects never harm or victimize the participants. There is, however, another side to the story and it cannot be neglected. One would expect to encounter severe problems in preventing and deterring any class of acts where the participants in a position to withhold consent nevertheless do not do so. The presence of consent, therefore, bears less on the issue of victimization and more on the issue of enforceability. The legitimate public interest in the latter, however, should not blind us to the former.

This brings us to a second important feature often used to characterize this class of offenses. Jerome Skolnick has written that "by definition, crimes without victims are not reported . . . " (Skolnick 1968, p. 631). Similarly, Morris and Hawkins comment that many "crimes lack victims, in the sense of complainants asking for protection of the criminal law" (Morris and Hawkins 1970, p. 6). Let us call this feature of victimless crimes *the absence of a complainant-participant.* The argument is, presumably, that since both parties are willing participants in the act, e.g., prostitution, the "victim" (the prostitute? her customer?) can be expected not to report the "crime" to the police. This failure to report offenses to the authorities, as many observers have pointed out, leads to various abuses and corruptions in the officials charged with criminal detection, arrest, prosecution, and conviction. Illegal searches and seizures, electronic surveillance, and entrapment, as well as police corruption and demoralization, and even police blackmail of the so-called "victim"—all these thrive on the seemingly futile attempts to enforce criminal penalties against deviance and vice. But we must be careful, and not try to prove too much. Not only so-called victimless crimes go unreported; many activities which indubitably inflict harm upon persons also go unreported by their victims. In the extreme case, it is obviously impossible for a victim of murder (or of any undiscovered crime) to report to the authorities that he or she has been harmed, but no one would argue that murder is a crime without a victim. Gangland extortion, where a store owner may be threatened with severe property damage or personal harm if he reports the crime; embezzlement and employee pilfering, where the employer may find his insurance rates skyrocketing and his customer confidence seriously impaired; sexual assault and rape, where the woman victim is ashamed to submit herself to interrogation by cynical male police officers—these are merely the obvious examples which come to mind where, for quite different reasons, persons who know they have been harmed will not report their victimization to the police. In short, we cannot argue from the fact that an activity is not reported to the police to the conclusion that it involves no victim.

Another problem arises in the notion, expressed typically by Herbert Packer, that victimless crimes are those "offenses that do not result in anyone's *feeling* that he has been injured so as to impel him to bring the offense to the attention of the authorities" (Packer 1968, p. 151, emphasis added). Let us call this the *self-judged harmlessness* of victimless crimes. Packer and others who believe that there is a category of crimes without victims also believe that we should allow the question of whether someone has been victimized by engaging in a certain activity to turn on how he or she "feels" about it at the time. There are at least two obvious objections to such a position. The first is that it tends to blur the general distinction between what a person *feels* (or, more accurately in these cases, what a person believes to be true about himself) and what *is true* about his state or condition. Those who agree with Packer here verge on obliterating the distinction between whether or not a person feels (or believes) that he has not been harmed, and whether or not he has been harmed. We may be inclined to think the generally valid distinction between what seems to be true and what is true has no application in such cases, because where the issue is whether a rational person—informed, conscious, mature—has been harmed by some activity, he can safely be regarded as the final (or at least as a competent) authority. Where a person himself is judging his own condition or status (i.e., asks himself, "Does doing x hurt me when I do it? Do I dislike doing x? Does doing x leave me worse off than not doing x?"), we are inclined to adopt as a general policy that what a person feels in regard to self-harm is a reliable index as to whether he has been harmed. Yet it is not an infallible index, nor is it an irrebuttable presumption of fact. It is not even reliable except on the assumptions already indicated, viz., that the person has an informed, mature grasp of exactly what he is doing, and of what its effects will be upon his life opportunities and capacities, so that it can be said of him that he is not acting in ignorance or otherwise foolishly, carelessly, injuring himself contrary to his opinion at the time.

The second important objection to blurring the general distinction—merely because we have the agent judging his own activities—between feeling unharmed and being unharmed, is that social policy has traditionally reflected our belief that in certain classes of cases society needs to be protected from people who willingly take risks for themselves and others. Laws designed to provide such protection are often confused with "paternalistic legislation," and accordingly are condemned, but this is a mistake (Dworkin 1971). The point can be seen in certain kinds of risk-taking where normal, healthy adults are involved, e.g., operating dangerous machinery. In such cases, we require that the persons engaged in these activities use safety equipment, take rest periods, have regular physical check-ups, etc. We can understand these requirements as paternalistic, but there is a better alternative. They can be understood as attempts to reduce the likelihood of self-injury which are imposed on an unwilling society by persons who are unmindful of the personal risks and social costs involved in serious accidents. In a significant variety of other cases, involving infants, juveniles, the mentally ill or deficient, we readily adopt and defend paternalistic policies because we do not want the law to use as its criterion of criminal harm the self-judgment of the persons involved that they do not "feel" they take unreasonable risks or believe that they have been injured by the activity. But even if we are inclined to let the law use this criterion for the conduct of consenting adults, it may well be in spite of and not because of a belief that the person involved cannot be harmed when he or she feels unharmed. Why we should adopt such legal policies for the conduct of adults remains to be seen.

The fourth and final feature of victimless crimes can be called their *transactional* or *exchange* nature. As Schur puts it, abortion and the other victimless crimes involve "the willing exchange of socially disapproved but widely demanded goods or services" (Schur 1965, p. 8), "the willing exchange, among adults, of strongly demanded but legally proscribed goods or services" (p. 169). There can be no doubt that this aspect is one which is highly relevant to law enforcement and law reform because of the way gambling, prostitution, and drug addiction become sources of vast illicit (and untaxed!) revenues. Their illegality has little effect in reducing the large clientele for these "goods or services." Even so, despite the merits of bringing to bear an unsentimental economic viewpoint on the kinds of offenses under review, much is left out or distorted in this perspective. Prostitution and gambling may well deserve the kind of emphasis this approach yields, but most of the other victimless crimes exhibit a transactional or economic exchange structure, only incidentally, if at all. Homosexuality, for example, essentially involves two or more persons; but unlike prostitution it need have no economic overtones. Narcotic abuse and drug addiction only incidentally involve more than one person; theoretically, a person can manufacture and use illegal and harmful drugs in complete solitude. Abortion does or does not essentially involve an interpersonal relationship, depending on whether one thinks of this act with reference to the unborn fetal person or only with reference to the abortionist and his client-patient. Vagrancy and loitering have no exchange or transactional character at all, and public drunkenness has one only incidentally.

V

We have been examining four different criteria in terms of which criminologists and others have tried to characterize a class of crimes they call "victimless." In order of discussion, the criteria have been: consensual participation, absence of a complainant-participant, self-judged harmlessness, and transaction or exchange. Precisely how criminologists view these four criteria is somewhat unclear. Obviously, the four criteria are not coextensive; therefore none can be treated as a sufficient condition of victimless crimes, unless the others are to be eliminated. The natural step is to treat these criteria so that each is regarded as a necessary condition, and then to combine them as the sufficient condition for the class of victimless crimes. The result is the following definition:

> An activity is a victimless crime if and only if it is prohibited by the criminal code and made subject to penalty or punishment, and involves the exchange or transaction of goods and services among consenting adults who regard themselves as unharmed by the activity and, accordingly, do not willingly inform the authorities of their participation in it.

It is tempting to comment on the interrelation of the four criteria used in this definition. Absence of a complainant-participant appears to be an empirical consequence of consensual participation and self-judged harmlessness. Consensual participation and self-judged harmlessness, however, seem to explain each other, depending on the context. Proper as such abstract conceptual questions are to any rigorous discussion of a definition, let us put aside any further discussion of them here. Instead, let us notice two major difficulties which emerge from this discussion for the theory of victimless crimes.

The first problem is that this definition is quite incapable of subsuming the dozen or so offenses we have seen are to be found on lists of victimless crimes. The definition is too narrow, in that it excludes abortion and vagrancy, public drunkenness and crimes such as bribery and espionage; the lists of victimless crimes with which we began are simply too inclusive. There is no convenient remedy for this. The only alternative is to reject one or more of the four essential characteristics of the concept of victimless crime; such a redefinition of the concept would render it ill-fitted to the actual discussions and issues out of which it originated. It is better to conclude simply that perhaps some activities currently against the law are similar to, but not exactly like, some other activities which truly are victimless crimes.

The second and more interesting consequence is that the idea of harmlessness or victimlessness has a very tenuous relation to the crimes covered by this definition. The presence of the four defining attributes of victimless crimes simply cannot guarantee, either conceptually or empirically, that every such crime is harmless to the participants. We have seen earlier (section II) that there is at best only a loose empirical connection between consensual participation and self-judged harmlessness, on the one hand, and actual harmlessness and non-victimization on the other. It is, therefore, misleading for criminologists and law reformers to argue on behalf of reducing or eliminating the criminal penalties for abortion, prostitution, etc., by implying that these activities are harmless and victimless. About all they can legitimately argue, given the definition of victimless crimes—a definition which does not explicitly or implicitly contain the idea that these activities are always harmless!—is that if any participant is harmed or injured by abortion, prostitution, etc., then he or she has *no ground for criminal complaint* against the other participants. The reason is that more or less informed consent by all parties was a condition of engaging in the activity in the first place, and such consent always bars any subsequent complaint. Not only that. There is the further tacit assumption that if the participants in the activity consent to it and judge themselves unharmed by engaging in it, nobody else can be injured by it, either; and if that is so, society has no right to interfere by prohibiting the activity and subjecting it to penal sanctions.

We have here in these new considerations what in fact is the main thing, from a moral point of view, to be said on behalf of law reform in the area of so-called victimless crimes. We have seen how there is no guarantee that can be given on behalf of the harmlessness of an activity to the participants simply by conceding that the activity is consensual and is judged by the participants to be harmless at the time. Now, we have uncovered a deeper point, one which can perhaps be best expressed by the following argument:

1. Society and government should allow persons to engage in whatever conduct they want to, no matter how deviant or abnormal it may be, so long as (a) they know what they are doing, (b) they consent to it, and (c) no one—at least no one other than the participants—is harmed by it.
2. In activities such as abortion, gambling, public drunkenness, etc., (a) and (b) and (c) are all true.
3. Therefore, abortion, gambling, public drunkenness, etc., are victimless activities and the laws which make them criminal should be repealed.

As we have seen, the sole proof for premise (2) is provided by the judgment of those who engage in the conduct at the time of their involvement. The judgment of disinterested spectators or rueful self-judgment at a later date is presumed to be irrelevant, or at least not decisive. We can see this most clearly if we amplify the point in terms of the notion of rights-violation used in section II to define the notion of victimization. It can be argued that in so-called victimless crimes, even if harm does accrue to one of the participants, he is not really a victim of a crime, because by freely consenting to engage in the illegal activity in the first place, the participant waives any further moral right to declare that his rights have been violated by the harm (it turns out) he has suffered.

VI

One final lesson to be learned from the study of victimless crime is the disturbing inconsistency with which our society proceeds in this area. Why, for example, do we allow persons to gamble with their money, so long as they spend it on some risky ventures (the stock market), but prohibit them if they wish to spend it on others (offtrack betting, the numbers pool)? Why do we license the sale of some personal services (escort services, massage parlors) and not others ("massage parlors," prostitution)? Why do we allow some demonstrably harmful substances to be sold without prescription and merely tax them (tobacco, alcohol) whereas some others (marijuana, cocaine) are unavailable over the counter at all? Why do we rush to pass paternalistic legislation in some areas (the statutory requirements of motor cyclists to wear safety helmets) and ignore it in others (the actual use of automobile safety devices required by law to be installed in new cars)? The list of such paradoxes is endless. The explanation in every case is ideological or historical, not logical or moral. What these paradoxes show is that our society allows victimization through the silence of the law, and that it is extremely difficult and perhaps impossible to find a sound principle or principles which will show that the current pattern of the law is a rational one.

My purpose in this essay has been only partly to attack over-criminalization and the legislation of morality. Rather, it has been to show that the concept of victimless crimes has theoretically unsatisfactory features which make it a less than perfect analytical category in terms of which to assess a variety of political, scientific and moral questions related to the issue of decriminalization. People are, after all, often harmed in such crimes. Persons often give uniformed consent to their own participation in activities, ignorant of the consequences harmful to themselves which in due course will appear. The interest of individuals, in short, both of the participants and of others, may well be violated by many so-called victimless crimes. We can no more conclude from these facts that such conduct must be prohibited by vigorous enforcement of criminal sanctions against perpretrators, regardless of the cost, than we can accept the opposite conclusion, that society must bear these harms and violations of rights in silence. Elsewhere, and in a more constructive vein, I have tried to show that familiar principles of liberal social philosophy, stemming from Mill, give us a much sounder basis for understanding what is wrong with trying to enforce morality through the criminal law (Bedau 1974). We can avoid moralism altogether, and paternalism where it is inappropriate, by relying on a conception of human beings which accords to each of us an inviolable privacy, a freedom from legitimate state interference. And we can leave to sober public discussion and private reflection the difficult question what is to be done with and for those who have engaged in immoral conduct that harms themselves after all.

References

Bedau, H.A. "Victimless Crimes: A Philosophical Approach." In H.A. Bedau and Edwin Schur, *Victimless Crimes: Rhetoric or Reality?* Englewood Cliffs, N.J.: Prentice-Hall, Inc. Forthcoming.

Dorsen, Norman (ed.). *The Rights of Americans: What They Are—What They Should Be.* New York: Pantheon Books, 1971.

Dworkin, Gerald. "Paternalism." In Richard A. Wasserstrom (ed.). *Morality and the Law.* Belmont, Calif.: Wadsworth Publishing Company, 1971, pp. 107-126.

Feinberg, Joel (ed.). *The Problem of Abortion.* Belmont, Calif.: Wadsworth Publishing Company, 1973.

Geis, Gilbert. *Not The Law's Business? An Examination of Homosexuality, Abortion, Prostitution, Narcotics and Gambling in the United States.* Rockville, Md.: National Institute of Mental Health, 1972.

Hilgers, Thomas W. and Dennis J. Horan (eds.). *Abortion and Social Justice.* New York: Sheed and Ward, 1972.

Melden, A.I. (ed.). *Human Rights.* Belmont, Calif.: Wadsworth Publishing Company, 1970.

Montgomery, Paul. "No Penalty Urged in Victimless Crimes." *New York Times,* January 28, 1973, p. 34. Reprinted by permission of *The New York Times.*

Morris, Norval. "Crimes Without Victims: The Law is a Busybody." *New York Times Magazine,* April 1, 1973, pp. 10-11, 58-62.

Morris, Norval and Gordon Hawkins. *The Honest Politician's Guide to Crime Control.* Chicago: University of Chicago Press, 1970.

Packer, Herbert L. *The Limits of the Criminal Sanction.* Stanford, Calif.: Stanford University Press, 1968.

Shaffer, Jerome A. (ed.). *Violence.* New York: David McKay Company, 1971.

Schur, Edwin M. *Crimes Without Victims: Deviant Behavior and Public Policy.* Englewood Cliffs, N.J.: Prentice-Hall, Inc., 1965.

Skolnick, Jerome H. "Coercion to Virtue: The Enforcement of Morals." *Southern California Law Review* 41 (1968): 588-641.

Wasserstrom, Richard A. (ed.). *Morality and the Law.* Belmont, Calif.: Wadsworth Publishing Company, 1971.

Women Endorsing Decriminalization. "Prostitution: A Non-Victim Crime?" *Issues in Criminology* 8 (Fall 1973): 137-62.

8 Victims, Harm, and Justice
Jeffrey H. Reiman

It is undoubtedly a sign of some advancement that a group of scholars should be convened to discuss—among other things— the definition of the concept of the victim while the science of victimology is just being born. Of course, this is the logical order of things—first we define our terms and then we get down to business. Unfortunately the history of a science is hardly ever so logical. Usually observers and recorders and experimenters do their work for a century or two, before philosophers and philosophically minded scientists begin to raise the question: Well, what exactly are we doing?

This is of course the real thrust of the problem of defining concepts. Without clear definitions we don't know exactly what we are doing, or why we are doing it or why it is working, if it is. Without clear definitions we don't know where our work overlaps with that of other inquirers, where unnecessary duplication can be eliminated, where fruitful multi-disciplinary study should be pursued. For these reasons it is a sign of progress and hope that this question is being addressed so early on. The progress lies in the self-conscious attempt to start the science of victimology off on a sound and coherent conceptual foundation. The hope lies in the possibility that if we can clearly and adequately define the concept of victim, then victimology will be able to avoid some of the "definitional crises" which shook criminology because criminologists had never worked out a fully satisfactory definition of crime.

I

A brief look at the "definitional crises" of criminology will shed some light on the parameters of the problem for victimology. Both the classical criminologists and the positivist criminologists of the eighteenth century simply took crime as the behavior for which the criminals in their midst were apprehended and punished. The study of this behavior—its causes, its effects, its prevention—was criminology.

At least three insights, recognized and developed only within the last century, have severely limited the validity of this approach. I call them 'insights' rather than 'discoveries' since it is their very obviousness which makes them so powerful. They are:

1.   the relativity of the criminal law;

2.   the political nature of the criminal justice process; and
3.   the recognition of "white-collar crime" and the normalcy of other
     criminal violations.

All of these insights have been extremely fruitful in inspiring new research
and a new awareness of the actual processes by which acts and actors become
labeled criminal. Indeed, these insights have led to the broadening of the field
of criminology, to the recognition that criminologists cannot be satisfied to study
only what goes on in back alleys or in prisons. What goes on in the corporate
board room and in the state legislature, in the judge's mind and the policeman's,
all contribute to what has recently been called "the social reality of crime"—and
thus they must all also be studied. But none of these valuable results of the new
insights should blind us to the fact that they present questions which strike at
the very heart of criminology as an independent field of study.

To say that criminology is or aspires to be an independent field of study is
not to suggest that it has no need of the findings and methods of other sciences.
If this is what is meant by an independent field of study, then there probably
are no independent fields of study. Chemistry needs physics, and physics needs
mathematics, and mathematics needs logic—yet no one would deny that these
are all independent fields of study. So, too, in the social sciences, economics
and sociology and psychology and political science, all can and have interacted
fruitfully. Here, too, there is no doubt that the interaction is between independent fields of study. To be independent does not mean to be totally cut off
from other areas of inquiry, any more than to be an independent human being
requires overcoming dependence on food and oxygen and the like.

Independence is a relative matter, it comes in degrees of more and less,
and it may ultimately be impossible to determine the exact point at which
anything crosses the line from dependence to independence. However, on questions like this, we must avoid what logicians call "the fallacy of the beard."
How many unshaven hairs must a man have and how long must they be, for us
to say that he has crossed the line from being poorly shaven to having a beard?
The question is of course unanswerable. This should not, however, lead us
simply to throw up our hands and say we don't know the difference between
poorly shaven men and bearded men. Obviously we do. In other words, though
we cannot exactly distinguish some debatable cases, we undoubtedly can
recognize and identify the clear cases on both sides of the line. So too with
independence. Economics and political science, physics and chemistry, are
clear cases of independent fields of scientific inquiry—and we can begin to
indicate the criteria which justify this judgment. Since it is not my purpose
to explore the question of whether criminology or victimology are independent
fields of study, I will go no further than to suggest one of these criteria and
discuss its relevance to the definitional problem.

At the very least, for something to be an independent field of study, it must have a subject matter which is roughly and reasonably delimited from other subject matter areas. Though no man is either purely "economic man" or purely "political man," economic behaviors can be coherently grouped together and delimited from political behaviors, at the cost of some abstraction of course, so that each can afford a fruitful and consistent area of inquiry. So, too, though everything chemical is also physical and vice versa, chemical behaviors can be coherently and reasonably—if roughly—delimited from physical behaviors.

What of criminology? Since our presentation of the definitional problems of criminology is intended as preparatory to addressing those of victimology, the discussion on this point will necessarily be brief and somewhat summary. What is the subject matter which corresponds to the independent field of study known as criminology? The obvious answer, "criminal behavior," is not much help. It simply postpones the problem, because we will have to ask, is "criminal behavior" a subject matter which can be identified, which can be reasonably and coherently delimited from other subject matters?

Let us be clear on the force of this question since it will haunt us when we try to define the concept of victim. The fact that we have a phrase like "criminal behavior" which sounds significant, does not prove that we have delimited even roughly an independent area of scientific inquiry. Think for a minute of two other similar phrases: "human behavior" and "happy behavior." Clearly the first is too broad, and the second too narrow to constitute an independent field of study. This is not an arbitrary judgment. The facets of human behavior are many and unique, the methodologies suitable for studying the psychological facets will not be fruitful for studying the sociological—hence "human behavior" is too broad. It can be delimited from other areas of study like "non-human animal behavior" and "inanimate behavior," but it cannot be reasonably presented as a subject matter for a field of inquiry. On the other hand, "happy behavior" is too narrow. It comprises behavior which might be studied sociologically or psychologically, but in either event by methods applicable to a broader range of behavior. The methods that would yield valuable data on happiness as an emotion would yield data on other psychological events; the methods that would yield insights into happiness as a social phenomena could be fruitfully applied to other forms of emotional events. Thus before we say that "criminal behavior" is the subject matter of criminology, we have to know that criminal behavior is not so broad that it could be divided into several independent fields of study, or so narrow that it could be incorporated as part of some other independent field.

But there are other problems with "criminal behavior." Think now of two other phrases, "mid-month behavior" and "evil behavior." Why not a science which studies "mid-month behavior"? Here is an area which is extremely easy to delimit. While February might present some problems, mid-month behavior is the way people behave from the fourteenth to the sixteenth of each month.

Obviously this fails as a subject matter because, at least until astrology becomes a science, there is no reason to assume that "mid-month behavior" is a phenomenon intrinsically distinct from "end-of-the-month behavior." There is no reasonable principle for lumping together the events of the fourteenth to the sixteenth as a discrete totality. It adds up to no coherent or interesting field of inquiry.

How about a science of "evil behavior"? Now in talking about "evil behavior" we don't mean merely behavior which is thought to be evil—that of course is something else. If there is to be a study of "evil behavior," then it is the study only of that behavior which is certainly evil. Now we don't have to fall completely into value-relativism to see the problems here. I at least am convinced that there is some behavior which is certainly evil. Anyone who holds that it is simply a matter of opinion that Hitler was more evil than St. Francis, simply does not know what evil means. However, though there are several quite clear cases of evil, the gray area, covering acts about which there is reasonable controversy as to their evilness or goodness, is quite wide. As a result, one could not identify a significant area of "evil behavior" without making some controversial value judgments.

What is wrong with basing a science on a controversial value judgment? Well strictly speaking there is probably nothing wrong with it, so long as the value judgment is recognized for what it is. However, there are some good reasons for trying not to base a science on a controversial value-judgment. At least two of these reasons are the following. First, if a science is based on a value judgment then all or many of its important conclusions may only be acceptable *on the condition* that the value judgment be accepted. Thus the more controversial the basic value judgment, the less persuasive the scientific conclusions. Second, in the modern world, science accrues to itself a considerable amount of authority. To say of some statement that it is based on scientific evidence, is to give the man in the street and often even his more sophisticated cousin, a very strong warrant for believing it. Hence, when a science is based on a value judgment, the risk is always present that science will be consciously or unconsciously used in a partisan fashion for the ends of those who subscribe to that value judgment.

Because victimology is the topic of the day, our excursion into the definitional traumas of criminology must be brought to a close. Suffice it to say, that comparing "criminal behavior" with "human behavior," "happy behavior," "mid-month behavior," and "evil behavior," should have suggested several of the problems that must be resolved in trying to establish a science on a clear conceptual foundation. It should also have indicated that the definition of fundamental concepts is by no means a matter for the arbitrary judgment of the scientist. Our analysis thus far has indicated that with regard to the concepts spelling out the subject matter of a science they must be carefully defined so as to cover an area neither too broad nor too narrow to be the subject of an independent field of study; they must delimit an area which forms some reasonable and coherent totality which is worth studying; and as far as is possible they must not incorporate into the science a bias in favor of certain values which might weaken the strength of its conclusions or cause them to tend to support certain social or political forces over others.

This much should enable us to see how the insights into the relativity of the criminal law and into the political nature of the criminal justice process as well as the recognition of "white-collar" crime and the normalcy of other criminal violations, profoundly shook the foundations of traditional criminology. If crime is what is defined as such in the criminal law, and criminal law is relative to the culture in which it is found, then virtually any human behavior *could* be criminal, somewhere. If this is possible, then what unique area of human behavior does "criminal behavior" refer to? Does it simply study any human behaviors, and if so is this not too broad to define a scientific subject matter? Or does it study behavior which deviates from criminal codes, no matter what those codes may be? But isn't this too narrow? Couldn't it better be studied as part of abnormal psychology or of the sociology of deviance? If criminals are the individuals sought, identified, apprehended, and punished by the criminal justice process, and if that process is liable to manipulation by political forces, then criminals are those determined as such by the prevailing political forces. If this is so, then to what extent does "criminal behavior" refer to the acts of those without access to power to manipulate the system? To what extent does this incorporate into criminology the value judgments, indeed the needs and interests, of those with political power? Finally, it seems to be the case that there exists widespread violation of criminal and civil regulations by "respectable" individuals who do not regard themselves as criminals and are neither regarded nor treated as such by society, although their cost to the society exceeds by far the take of robbery and burglary. If this is the case, then what are the common principles which unify "criminal behavior" and set it apart from other areas of behavior as an independent subject matter? If crime is regarded as a willful harm perpetuated on society, then white-collar crime indicates that there is much that is willful and harmful which is not illegal according to the criminal law, or not treated as criminal when it is. If crime is regarded as a deviance from social norms, then white-collar crimes and the normalcy of violations indicates that it may be the one who never commits a crime who is deviant; i.e., that while some crimes (like crimes of violence) may be deviant and committed only by a minority, others (like income tax evasion) are considered quite normal.

We won't take the time to explore the ways in which criminologists have responded to these "definitional crises," since our purpose here has been to elucidate the nature and significance of the definitional problems confronting victimology. It should, however, be clear that if the subject matter of victimology is "the victims of criminal behavior," then victimologists must deal with all of the problems of defining "criminal behavior" *plus* those introduced by the concept of the *victim*. And further that the concept of the victim must be defined in such a way as to avoid the pitfalls sketched out above. That is, victim must be defined so as to cover an area neither too broad nor too narrow to constitute an independent field of study; it must be defined to delimit an area that has some inner coherence and significance as a field of study; and it must be defined in such a way that it does not incorporate value judgments into the science. With these guideposts, we turn now to consideration of the specific problems of defining the concept of the victim.

II

To speak about the victims of a crime is to use the term victim in a more restricted sense, than for instance when we speak of the victims of a flood. In the latter case, we would be referring to any individual harmed in or by the flood. However, by the victims of a crime we do not mean any individual harmed in or by the crime. Suppose gentleman A robs a bank and is killed by a policeman's bullet while escaping. A is harmed as a direct result of the crime, but he is not *a victim of the crime*. He may be a victim of the policeman's bullet, but we would not call him a *victim of the crime*. Suppose B or C rob a bank, and B fires his revolver at the bank guard. Suppose further that the bullet passes through the bank guard and kills C as he is filling his satchel from the bank vault. Now C is a victim of B's shot. Indeed C has been killed by a criminal in the progress of a crime—but he is clearly not a *victim of the crime* in the sense that, say, the bank guard is.

What these examples suggest is that by committing a crime, the criminal disqualifies himself for the title *victim of the crime*. Thus the victim can only be one who is harmed in or by a crime *which he did not set in motion*. The victim is not someone who has initiated the criminal violation. Suppose a policeman comes on the scene to break up a bloody fistfight between two gentlemen, D and E. Both are seriously injured. Who is the victim of the crime? Obviously this cannot be answered without first resolving the question of who set the crime (be it assault and battery or disorderly conduct) in motion. If D attacked E, then E is the victim. If D attacked E because he was duly provoked by E, then D may be the victim. If D and E decided calmly to have it out once and for all, then neither is the victim—since both initiated the crime. If of course, neither assault nor battery nor disorderly conduct are against the criminal law, then in none of the above cases is D or E the victim of the crime—since no crime has taken place.

This is enough to allow us to indicate the questions the victimologist must answer in determining *who is the victim*. He must determine,

a.   If a crime has been committed,

b.   Who has been harmed in or by the crime,

c.   Who has set the crime in motion.

It is condition (a), the determination that a crime has been committed, which opens up for the victimologist the whole Pandora's box of defining "criminal behavior," which has confronted the criminologist. Enough has already been said to indicate the problems here, so we will turn to conditions (b) and (c), since these are unique to the specific problem of determining *who is the victim of the crime,* once it is established that a crime has been committed.

What problems confront the victimologist in trying to determine who is harmed by a crime? The central problem here is to define harm. The alternatives roughly speaking are the following. He can accept the legal definition, and simply say that wherever there is a crime there is *ipso facto* a harm. Or he can attempt to formulate an independent criteria of harm, in terms of which he can determine whether or not a given crime has in fact harmed someone. Both alternatives have difficulties. To take the legal definition means that wherever there is a criminal violation, be it murder or prostitution or income tax evasion, there is *harm* and thus victims. In the case of murder this is obvious. In the case of income tax evasion, there is obviously a harm and a group of victims—i.e., the remaining taxpayers who must pay a little bit more to make up for the evasion. But clearly here the relationship of the victims to the criminal is so attenuated and impersonal, that to lump together in one study the victims of murder and of tax evasion holds the danger of confronting victimology with a subject matter so diverse as to have no particular coherence or unifying rationale.

With the crime of prostitution, of course, the problem becomes even more intricate. If we assume that wherever there is a crime there is a harm and a victim, then in the case of prostitution the harm may be either to the patron, whose active complicity in the crime disqualifies him from the role of victim, or the general public, who are not so disqualified and are thus victimized by the knowledge and indirect effects of the existence of prostitution. From this standpoint of course, there is no such thing as a "victimless crime." Those who hold that prostitution is a victimless crime are simply asserting their view that prostitution ought not to be a crime. Those who believe it ought to be a crime believe that it has victims. They hold that the general public is victimized by prostitution.

At this point of course, victimology appears to be tending in the direction of a field of study with no boundaries. If everyone or almost everyone is the victim of certain crimes, then the study of the victims of crimes is simply the study of the general population. Clearly at this point we have a field too broad to constitute an independent field of study.

This realization may lead the victimologist to the other alternative. That is, he may attempt to erect a criterion of harm which is independent of the law.

Thus he will confine himself to the study of those palpably or demonstrably harmed by criminal behavior. Here some other difficulties arise. First, the problem of relativity. What is a demonstrable or palpable harm? Obviously, if I am a convinced puritan, then the presence of a blasphemer or of someone perverse enough to dance on Saturday evening is a source of much greater pain to me than merely being punched in the nose. We need not elaborate on this further. The problems here are obvious, though probably not insoluble. The more difficult problem arises at the point at which we actually arrive at a criterion of demonstrable harm. Here it becomes obvious that by any definition of demonstrable harm, there are undoubtedly ways in which people can be harmed which do not involve criminal acts. An example might be the promotion and sale of cigarettes. If the victimologist is going to use an independent standard of harm, then what rationale is there for limiting his study to those harmed by criminal acts? Why not simply study those willfully harmed by others in the society? Here the problem is like that presented by "happy behavior," or perhaps even "mid-month behavior." Is there a rationale for carving out a unique area for those harmed *by crimes*? Or should this be a sub-topic in the study of those willfully harmed in general? Clearly from the standpoint of the recipient of harm, pain is pain. It may matter little to him—indeed he may not even know—whether his pain is the result of a criminal act or not. If this is the case, then can "the victims of criminal behavior" really be thought of as a rationally coherent area of study delimited from others?

Let us turn now to the problems of condition (c), determining who has set the crime in motion. The first problem here is the most obvious. Does the victimologist want to commit himself to the view that anyone *really* sets the crime in motion? Does he want to adopt a legal system's view of responsibility, and see the criminal as acting with free and rational will? If he does, then what becomes of the insights into the causes of criminal behavior garnered over the last century? If he doesn't, then is there really an assignable victim? If the victimologist is skeptical about free will and legal notions of responsibility, then *who* is the victim of the crime? Going back to one of our earlier examples, if A (the bankrobber killed while escaping), did not freely embark on the criminal act, then is he not also a victim of the crime? But if so, it would seem that he is a victim in the way that individuals are victims of floods or plagues or natural disasters outside of their control. In other words, if we give up the belief in free will is there any meaningful boundary line between victims of crimes and victims of disease?

The suggestion here is that the determination of the victimologist's field of study appears to be linked to the notion of free will in a way that that of the criminologist is not. The criminologist could take as his field of study the behavior which is legally defined as criminal (i.e., liable to punishment under criminal statutes). He would not necessarily have to commit himself to the legal system's view of free will or responsibility in explaining that behavior.

He could quite consistently view the criminal behavior which the law views as freely chosen, as biologically or psychologically determined. The victimologist does not seem to have this luxurious range of options. Unless he accepts the law's view of freedom and responsibility, he has no good reason for excluding the legally defined criminal from possible candidacy for victim status. Unlike the criminologist, the victimologist cannot accept the legal definition of the object of his study without also accepting the metaphysics of freedom which underlies that legal definition.

To the extent that there is a legal definition of victim, we can take it to be something like the following: the victim of a crime is any individual harmed as a result of a crime, except the criminal responsible for the crime. Now if the victimologist attempts to use this definition without accepting the notion of criminal responsibility, he finds himself with a meaningless distinction on his hands. If he rejects the law's view of freedom, then the crime is an event which "happens" to the individuals involved, and for which no one in particular is responsible. All those who suffer injury as a result of this happening are victims. To single out one person as the legally defined criminal and refuse him the status of victim, while not viewing his crime as a free act, is to act on a difference which doesn't make a difference. It is as if the law could meaningfully determine who among those drowned in a flood were victims of the flood.

The upshot of this is that unless the victimologist is ready to take some position on the issue of free will and of where responsibility for a crime lies, he can neither delimit his field of study from that of the victims of natural events, nor decide whether or not to include the legally defined criminal within the class of victims of crime. Indeed if he takes a view of responsibility at variance with the law's view, he may find—as some victimologists have already found—that some of those legally defined as victims of crimes share responsibility for those crimes. If this is so, it may no longer be meaningful to speak of such individuals as victims—except sardonically.

In any event it should be obvious that the victimologist cannot delimit the class of "victims of crime" without making some metaphysical judgments about freedom and some serious moral judgments about the location of responsibility. In what remains I shall try to indicate some of the dangers laden in judgments of this latter variety. Before doing this, I want to suggest that even labeling the target of the victimologist's study as "victims of crime" already carries a subtle gravitational pull in the direction of the legal exclusion of the criminal from victim status. So as not to bias the outcome of our definitional search, we ought probably to adopt a more neutral label like "victims of a criminal event." This phrase in no way commits us either on the issue of the existence of free will or of the location of criminal responsibility, nor does it beg the question of whether the legally defined criminal or victim are the "real" victims victimology should study.

Recalling our earlier analysis of the concept of victim it should be clear that to answer this question we must determine who—if anyone—set the criminal event in motion. The "real" victims are those individuals harmed as a result of a criminal event which they did not set in motion. Skipping over the metaphysical problem and assuming that someone did "set the criminal event in motion," I wish to argue that we cannot determine who set the criminal event in motion without making a very serious value judgment: *We cannot delimit the proper object of the study of victimology without implicitly taking some moral stand on the justice of the legal system under which a human event is labelled a criminal event.*

In the *Nichomachean Ethics,* Aristotle distinguishes between "distributive justice" and "remedial justice." "Distributive justice" is concerned with the correct principles for distributing the rewards and burdens of social existence. "Remedial justice" is concerned with rectifying violations of "distributive justice." Remedial justice, which has to do with the identification and treatment of criminals, presupposes the establishment of distributive justice which the criminal violates and which must then be remedied. In general we take our legal systems to sustain a valid system of distributive justice, and the criminal law to remedy violations of that system of distributive justice. The remainder of this argument is based on the assumption that some such claim to justice is implicit in a legal system.

But it is possible that a legal system itself is unjust. By a legal system is meant not only the system of laws but also the economic and social system which is *legal,* i.e., which those laws protect and legitimate. Indeed the American treatment of the Indians and the Nazi treatment of the Jews, both under color of law, are examples enough to suggest that the divergence of a legal system from the principles of justice is possible and often clear. *In this case the legal system is itself an unjustified attack on some persons.* If those persons respond to this attack (consciously or unconsciously) by committing an act which is a crime according to the prevailing legal system, then who has *set the crime in motion*? A good argument can be made that the "criminal" is simply reacting to the attack upon him by the legal system—and that he, as much as anyone else harmed, is a potential victim of the criminal event.

At this writing members of the Oglala Sioux Indian tribe have occupied the town of Wounded Knee at the cost of some injuries and in violation of several criminal statutes. They have demanded rectification of violations of treaties between the American government and their tribe. *Who has set this crime in motion?* Obviously this question cannot be answered without first addressing the justice of the legal system which has brought the Oglala Sioux to this pass. If one of the occupying Indians and one of the surrounding federal marshalls were to be killed in the conflict—*who would be the victim of the criminal event*? Clearly we will come up with different answers depending on whether or not we believe that the Indians are responding to a history of unjustified violation of their rights by the American government.

Even if we could agree that some individuals harmed in a criminal event are clearly victims, we cannot determine whether or not the legally defined criminal is entitled to victim status without determining whether or not he set the crime in motion. This is not merely a metaphysical but also a moral question. A crime, being more than physical actions, is set in motion by the unjustified violation of someone's rights. And since a legal system itself might violate someone's rights, we cannot be satisfied with a merely legal determination of the issue.

If we are satisfied with the legal answer, then we have essentially incorporated into our view the value judgment that the prevailing legal system neither sustains nor works any grave injustice. If we believe that the prevailing legal system is unjust, that it either violates or permits violation of rights to which persons are entitled, then those who violate that system may be responding to injustice *and not setting the crime in motion.* Thus, to decide whether or not the legally defined criminal can be a potential candidate for victim, and to determine clearly the proper object of the study of victimology, it is necessary to commit oneself one way or the other on the justice or injustice of the prevailing legal system. In other words the search for a value-free definition of victim may be doomed from the outset.

At this point, let me conclude by apologizing for raising many problems and solving few. Frankly, I must confess that I am rather pessimistic about the chances of victimology actually resolving these problems and providing itself a clear and adequate and value-neutral conceptual framework. There is some value, however, in maintaining clarity about important problems, even when we cannot solve them. And there is some solace after all to be drawn from the fact, mentioned above, that the history of science indicates that a science need not be perfectly logically clear and self-conscious to be fruitful.

Part II
Victims' Typology

Introduction to Part II

In order to identify a common link among the eight papers that follow, they have been gathered under the rubric, "Victims' Typology." These papers represent an important contribution to the development of victimology in that they focus on an essential question, "What is the subject of study?" One of the positive aspects of the Jerusalem Symposium, that is evident in this published material, is that it tended to produce a considerable degree of explicitness about those basic assumptions and general mental models that underlie the scholars' choice in formulating questions and identifying evidence as relevant. Victimology is slowly building its own theoretical framework and its own literature. This process is vital for the development of the discipline. Unless victimologists conceive of their research and theoretical efforts in terms of some such body of established knowledge and ultimately in terms of comparative work, there is not only the risk that information gathered by each scholar will have no comparability to that found by another, but also that the discipline will never advance but, endlessly naive, will retread the same paths, repetitively discovering the same phenomena. Victimology will advance—as any other science—through an integration of planned rationally designed research and theoretical discovery and insight. Since the instruments of this advancement are the victimologists themselves, one should grasp the importance of making as much of their reasoning as possible accessible to other colleagues and professionals, who are interested in further advancing and evaluating it.

The paper by Sung Tai Cho explores the label "criminality" in depth and endeavors to maximize the utility of such classification. A victimization scale is proposed to measure attitudes toward illegal or unjust situations and the distribution of criminality between victim and victimizer.

Robert Silverman critically examines the concept of victim precipitation as it has been defined by various researchers until now. He claims that the existing definitions are vague, unscientific and too broad in scope to be of any meaningful significance. The author offers his own definition of victim precipitation, which he believes will allow for greater consistency in research.

In his paper, Leon Sheleff calls for greater awareness of a tridimensional perspective of the criminal act which would focus on the victim, the criminal, and the bystander. Sheleff suggests that, while the role of the bystander has been largely ignored, much could be profitably investigated from such a perspective.

The most popular typology of property crimes is expressed in terms of the

"professional-syndicated" dualism. J.A. Mack criticizes it as linguistically confusing and proposes a substitute dualism, "predatory-parasitical." He then
proceeds to construct a typology on the basis of the role of the victim in the
different modes of crime.

Landau's study examines the perception of the victim on the part of four
types of offenders: offenders against the person, against property, guilty of
fraud and forgery, or guilty of sex crimes. The findings of the study reveal a
distinct profile of victim perception as well as other characteristic features
in each group of offenders.

Joachim Weber states in his paper that the psychiatric-psychological
exploration of the offender should be complemented by that of the victim as
well. He examines the attempts made to instrumentalize the assumed relationship between offender and victim and to quantify it. He also describes the
practical and test-related methodological difficulties accompanying such testing
as the Semantic Differential Scale, the Giessen Test Profile Analysis, the Rating
Test, and the TAT Matching Procedure. While useful in exploring the phenomenon of the conscious or unconscious attraction between those special "partners," the criminal and his victim, these tests cannot, in Weber's opinion, replace
a precise examination of the biography of the criminal and of the victim, or the
use of other approved psychodiagnostical tests.

In their different and original paper, Joel and Champion Teutsch consider
the victim and the victimizer as inseparable components of an interpersonal
functional unit occupying the same unified field based upon consciousness
factors. The dynamics responsible for the process of victimization have been
found by the authors to have their basis not in psychology, but in physics as
formulated by Newton, Einstein, and others and as translated into Human
Physics. Consequently, they conclude, the reign of law, first discovered by
Kepler to apply to nature, extends also to man.

The paper by Arthur Lapan concerns the victim in contemporary drama
and novel, particularly in Kafka, Ionesco, and Beckett. In these "presentations," the victim tends to be the subject and central character. His victimization is presented in two ways: either as ultimately meaningful, as in Brecht,
or as ultimately meaningless, as in Kafka and Ionesco. Where victimization
is seen as meaningful, it is a literature of social resistance; where it is seen as
meaningless, the plays and novels *as symbols* negate it by presenting it as
absurd, and frequently comic.

Criminality, Victim, and Victimizer
Sung Tai Cho

The interest in differentiating, classifying, and segregating the victim and victimizer has maintained uncontested, undiminished, and unceasing attention and popularity since time immemorial. Irrespective of the ulterior motive for such an interest, many devices and systems have been attempted, applied, and utilized.

Classificatory placement of individuals through labeling is not without ill effects, unintended and unrecognized. Such placement is often accompanied by a degradation ceremony and the stigmatization of the labeled. A taxonomic scheme frequently transforms the labeled (victimizer), with full complement of permanent "deviant" status assigned and rigid and restricted activities, into a hopelessly incorrigible deviant.[a] Self-fulfilling and other prophecies are then quite probably the result. The original taxonomic scheme becomes a justification for assuming, creating, and adding "pivotal" deviant status and confusing the status with permanent and unchanging personal quality of the labeled.[b]

On the other hand, the classificatory placement of individuals has its utility. Social protection can be insured and justice may be gained in systematically treating the victim and victimizer through the medium of a classification system differentiating the victim and victimizer. It may even help individually rehabilitate the victimizer and restore the victim.

It is our hope to minimize the ill effects and maximize the utility of this classification endeavor. In order to do so, we have to consider several vital questions. The first set of questions pertains to the nature of criminality: Is it a real entity? If so, is it a person's trait? Or is it a result of labeling? The second set of questions deals with measurement: Is it measurable? If so, how is it measured? The third set of questions relates the nature of the measurement of criminality: Is criminality behavior, potential behavior, verbal behavior, or attitude? Is it an individual quality as a part of personality; if so, is it a fixed trait, constantly changing or an ontogenic part of personality as an individual system?

This research note is primarily based on a report entitled *Criminal Victimization Study: A Report of a Regional Survey,* completed for the Toledo Metropolitan Area Council of Governments, Toledo, Ohio, U.S.A., April 1972.

[a]The labeling of the victim is designed for the confirmation of the victimizer and the attitude toward the victim is ambiguous and ambivalent.

[b]This assumption, often hidden, directly contradicts correctional and rehabilitative aims of the criminal justice administration. We suggest that this value conflict should be eliminated before any meaningful normalization of the labeled is expected.

Presumably, the victim-victimizer distinction is based on the behaviorial set observed in connection with the victimization incidence; potential behavior is inferred from earlier behavior and this premise is present in the way an ex-con is treated; verbal behavior, in connection with potential behavior and attitude, has been a most popular and economical measurement, and inferences about known behavior (through attribution or imputation of motive of the victimizer) and potential behavior (prediction based on postdiction) is made from verbal behavior and/or attitude measurement.

Closely related to the third set of questions is: Is criminality an exclusive trait of the victimizer? Is it the pivotal or total trait? Is it transmittable, genetically or culturally? Is criminality additive, subtractive, transferrable, or coextensive with anti- or non-criminality? Is criminality coextensive with criminal behavior or is it a determinant of criminal behavior? Is criminality a result of interaction with punitive others after the victimizer is known and processed? Does criminality emerge from the assigned criminal status and role expectations?

It should be a bewildering experience to recognize these questions and to answer them all. The above considerations are offered here only to call the reader's attention to this essential but quite dangerous and delicate part of the criminal justice administration. In lieu of answering all the questions posed thus far, we shall offer and explicate our assumptions about criminality.

It should be apparent by now that (1) the difference, if any, between the victim and victimizer is most probably overstressed and/or overestimated; while similarity is understressed and/or underestimated; (2) a quick and easy answer to victimization from the standpoint of the victimizer quality is sought while the victimizer quality tends to be regarded as the key determinant of victimization; (3) a simplistic trait instead of a complex totality of interaction between the victim and victimizer is sought to explain victimization in general and to justify action taken in regard to the victimizer; (4) a low level differentiation is made among the act, actor, and attitude, attribute and power position of the victimizer, hence labeling is often justified resulting in the tendency described in (3); (5) the victimizer trait, once identified by whatever means, tends to be applied to the labeled, therefore known, victimizers, much more so than to others including victims and general population, and this tends to perpetuate the mysterious victimizer quality; (6) even the reason, intention or motivation for the victimizer is prepared through victimization source attribution and other imputation so that the criminal proceeding appears to be more like a ritual wherein the suspected victimizer is tried for the label, status, and trait; (7) the law is not necessarily written for or from the standpoint of a human being who is fallible, and thus certainly is not written for or from the perspective of "bad" man; (8) the quality of act, good or bad, is ascriptive and prescriptive more than descriptive and empirical so that the judgment on the victimizer as to victimization is not on a par with explanation of the behavior from survival adaptation, both biologic and symbolic; (9) many respectable others ignore and deny that they too are fallible and functioning like the victimizer as species qualified as *Homo volens* (the striving man), *Homo sapiens* (the thinking man), and *Homo mechanicus* (the reactive man).

On the basis of the above generalizations, we shall present our own view. Crime is a mode of adaptation and criminal behavior is an adaptive behavior. Criminal adaptation may be made for adventure, defensive, and offensive reasons. The meaning and availability of a criminal mode of adaptation are found in the situation in which others are found. The victimizer chooses the prescribed mode in interpersonal interaction with others and can formally be declared a criminal upon detection. Others' reaction, especially labeling, can and usually does crystalize and stabilize the criminal status.

Criminality is a behavioral tendency inferred from the act, but also from verbalized behavior and/or attitude, which may or may not be paired with the act.

Criminal mode found within the interactional situation is differentially meaningful and available to the actor. The freedom of choice is relative to the actor-other transaction and the action-reaction nexus. Criminal mode can be made meaningful and available by others and the criminal actor can help others to make such a contribution. In this sense, crime is learned from others and is interactional in nature.

The victim and victimizer interact directly by sharing the same arena, or indirectly by symbolic relationship. The differentiation of the victim and victimizer on the basis of criminality should result from the assessment of victimization incidence, relationship, roles, and risks. Victim and victimizer proneness is primarily a positional indicator of "criminality" rather than an individual trait. Moreover, risk differential is partly role behavior and partly positional variable. For example, the fact that males between the ages of twenty and twenty-nine possess the highest known victimizer and victim risk, should mean that they show categorical role behavior and positional risk in such a way as to constitute a high level of victimization.

Victimization is an emergent in interpersonal interaction and situation. As adaptation need changes so does victimization; as situation changes victimization changes; as situation changes so does adaptation need. The human drama found in the interactional situation unfolds victimization: motivational analysis deals with individualistic quality, interactional analysis handles the interpersonal as well as intrapersonal transaction, and organizational analysis stresses the interactional set and institutional setting.

The victim and victimizer should be understood in terms of victimization incidence and relationship. Both "affinity" and "propinquity" factors should be considered for the differentials in participation, commitment, and involvement in victimization. Though not intended for creating an impression that the victim and victimizer are "guilty by association," we are suggesting that the interaction and relationship should be explored rather than assumed, and that guilt should be understood objectively rather than assumed to be a hallmark of the victimizer.

Criminality inferred from verbalized attitude is found in the victim and victimizer positions. Whether the occupants of these positions have more, or less, or the same amount of criminality is not known unless and until we clearly understand the nature of these positions in concrete and specific victimization incidence.[c] Is criminality independent of positional implication, that is, is criminality a part of victimizer position so that the victimizer *gains* criminality, or criminality drives the victimizer into the position? It appears that the ex post facto reconstruction of victimization interaction is at best an approximation from which criminality of the victimizer is determined. It is not clear if the criminal trial is none other than confirmation of the fit between the criminality of the suspect and the victimizer position, thus leaving the question of criminality as an independent factor relatively untouched. Criminal career or recidivism on the part of the known victimizers misleads many into believing that the victimizers have been "criminally inclined" all along and it is fortunate to detect the victimizer. However, it is quite possible that these recidivists are merely reacting back to punitive others thus fulfilling self- and other prophecies. This is a matter of a "criminal mode of adaption" made most meaningful and available to these career criminals: this is a case of "secondary deviance," a defensive and reactive crime.

Studies of the distribution of criminality among the victim and victimizer, and population have been one-sided. As an alternative, we offer a victimization scale. Criminality scales measure attitudinal expression of negativism toward pro-social values, norms, institutions, and individuals while this particular victimization scale is designed to measure the attitude toward "unjust" or "illegal" situations.

In order to cross-validate, we compared the Mylonas law scale measuring the degree of negativism expressed toward law and legal institutions and our own victimization scale.[d]

We expect that a high score (negativism) in the criminality level index should be expressed in a high score (positivism) in the victimization scale.

The samples for this validation study were students at the University of

---

[c]Victimization is most probably a culmination of the interpersonal interaction between the victim and victimizer.

[d]The present writer, in his cross-cultural analysis of a criminality index, found that the prisoners in Greece, Korea, Ohio, and West Pakistan invariably showed extremely high negativism toward law and legal institutions while the laborers in these countries invariably showed low or no negativism. The difference between two groups, prisoners and laborers, was statistically significant at the 0.001 level for the majority of the cases. See Sung T. Cho, "A Cross-cultural Analysis of the Criminality Level Index," Ph.D. dissertation, *The Ohio State University, 1967.*

Toledo and Wayne State University. We codified and analyzed 75 cases out of 450 collected for our preliminary investigation. Our partial test indicated somewhat statistically significant relationship between criminality score and victimization score.[e] There was built-in control of relevant variables through matching that is, the same individuals took these two tests.[f]

Since the samples were not known to be either victims or victimizers, criminality score amounts to the measured level of attitude toward law and legal institutions (societal reaction level) by undifferentiated groups whose attitudinal expression should be compared to the general population.

Table 9-1 shows eight average scores on the 24 Mylonas law items collected from the aforementioned cross-cultural study of criminal level.

Our student sample has a mean score of 2.73, which can be ranked ninth if compared with the above criterion groups. This mean score places the student sample within "non-criminal" (or non-victimizer) sector.

The students showed a mean score of 4.71 on the victimization scale, and this can be ranked sixth if compared with the inner city residents (5.30), females (5.12), total (5.08), males (4.94), victims (4.92), and suburbanites (4.81), ranked 1, 2, 3, 4, and 5 respectively. The students' goal placed them on a "liberal" side.[g]

Table 9-1

| | Prisoners | | Laborers | |
	Mean Score	Rank	Mean Score	Rank
Greek	3.57	1	2.82	7
Korean	3.40	3	2.85	5
Ohio	2.84	6	2.23	8
W. Pakistani	3.56	2	3.06	4

[e] X^2 (Chi) = 9.96   df = 9-1=8   .30 < (P) >   .20

[f] The known offender population in Ohio is being observed for a simultaneous measurement of criminality level index Victimization Scale Scores.

[g] It needs to be emphasized that the victimization scale measures the attitude toward the victimization situation while the type of interpretation is being measured. In short, the respondent sizes up the victimization situation and simultaneous measurement is made on the respondent. It also needs to be noted that a low score on the victimization scale is a partial indicator of ideological position found on a continuum, anarchist-revolutionary-radical-liberal conservative-reactionary-vigilante-anarchist. Their interrelationship is not known as yet; for example, liberalism does not mean high victimization risk; nor does vigilante status free the individual from victimizing others. Lastly, we might add that criminality level measured by the criminality level index should also be examined for its relationship to the ideological position, for it measures the reaction against the criminal justice administration. For example, the prisoners may have been actually reacting against their tormentors and rejectors.

Now we are ready to consider some of the interpretations for the low relationship between criminality and victimization scores. First, there may actually be minimal difference between the victim and victimizer, and this difference may also be small between the victimizer and others in the general population. But this position is yet to be empirically tested. The second interpretation is that these scales are coterminous in the sense that they measure similar aspects of societal reaction; hence, the expectation of opposite characteristics measurable by these scales should be radically modified. The third view is that both criminality and victimization scales do not measure the behavioral tendency toward or away from victimization as such, but that they measure the ideological position relative to law, legal institutions, and victimization; the ideological position may or may not have a direct relationship to the victim and victimizer risk.

Our coup de grâce on this issue of criminality (differentiating victim and victimizer) will come in a form of a modified strategy for future verification. The cross-validation should continuously be made with provisions that: (1) both criminality and victimization scales are regarded as measures of societal reaction formed by different sectors; (2) both measures contain ideological positions taken by divergent criterion groups; and (3) external validation of these scales be made with specific reference to the patterns and reasons for different societal reaction formed by divergent criterion groups—why they feel the way they do in the interactional (the action-reaction nexus and network), sense.

More specifically, then, we propose to administer these scales to various groups based on demographic variables (age, sex, income, occupation, education, religion, political affiliation, etc.), and, at the same time, these groups divided further into the victim, victimizer, and residual categories. Eventually, the within-group variation is to be compared with the between-group difference. For example, average criminality and victimization scores for a general college sample are compared for specific sub-categories within this sample such as known victims, victimizers, and so on. The relative variance is a good indicator for the relative ideological position as well as victimization position for this criterion group.

10 Victim Precipitation: An Examination of the Concept
Robert A. Silverman

Introduction

Mannheim has suggested that

> ... the distinction between criminal and victim, which in former
> days appeared as clear-cut as black and white, actually often becomes
> vague and blurred in individual cases. The longer and the more deeply
> the actions of the persons involved are scrutinized, the more doubt-
> ful will it occasionally be who is to blame for the tragic outcome.
> (1965: 672)

Studies of victim-offender relationships have been undertaken to examine
such statements. One tool that has been used to examine a particular type of
victim-offender relationship is known as victim-precipitation (VP). This
concept deals with the case in which the victim has had something to do with
his own victimization.[a] The VP concept has played an important role in the
development of victimology and has been used with some success both theoretically and empirically. The purpose of this paper is to critically examine
victim-precipitation as it has so far been employed in criminological theory
and research, and to offer some suggestions concerning future uses of the
concept.

It will be argued that the VP concept has become confused and, as a
result, has lost much of its utility as an explanatory and empirical tool, and
that its empirical use has been predicated on disparate and often incompatible
operational definitions.

Theoretical Uses

The concept of victim-precipitation (though not necessarily the term) has
been with us since the early days of victimology. Hans von Hentig first suggested

---

The author wishes to thank R. Jay Turner for a critical reading of a draft of this
paper.

[a]This statement is made in a very vague way because of the great range of definitions of the concept. No precise definition can account for all of the meanings that have
been attributed to the concept.

the mutuality of the victim-offender relationship in a paper entitled "Some Remarks on the Interaction of Perpetrator and Victim" (1940), and later expanded the notion in *The Criminal and his Victim* (1948). He suggests that "... the victim shapes and moulds the criminal" (1948: 384) and that ultimately the "victim may assume the role of determinant ..." in the criminal event. In writing of similar cases Ellenberger referred to the 'penal couple' (1954).

Walter Reckless suggests a victim-doer-victim model in which

> ... (T)he victim initiates the interaction. He sends the signals that the receiver (doer) decodes.
>
> In this model, one should assume that the victim generates the criminal behavior in the doer; for he has triggered the doer... (I)t is suspected that a large percentage of murder victims initiated the action which led to assault and death, almost as if they wanted to commit suicide (death wish) and could not ..." (1967: 142)

E.A. Fattah has described the VP situation in the following way:

> ... (T)he provocative victim plays a definite role in the etiology of crime, either by inciting the criminal to commit it or by creating or fostering a situation likely to lead to crime. This type of victim can be said to 'provoke' the crime by his own actions ... (1967: 167)

Fattah further distinguishes between those that directly provoke the attack (the active type) and those who indirectly provoke the attack (the passive type). He also offers a sub-category that he names the 'precipitating' victim to illustrate those cases in which the victim was the first to show a weapon or use physical force (1967: 167).[b]

In discussing *victim-induced criminality,* M. Fooner states that

> ... studies suggest that where ... a person has not acted with reasonable self-protective behavior in handling his money, jewelry, or other valuables and has become the victim of robbery, he cannot be considered an innocent victim—he has ... created a "temptation-opportunity" situation, giving the criminal incentive and help.
>
> In popular parlance "he has himself to blame." (1966: 1080)

The concept of VP has been used in many discussions of victim-offender relationships besides those mentioned above.[c] Concerning the uses of the

---

[b]This is similar to Wolfgang's operational definition (1966).

[c]See for instance: Holyst 1964; Morris 1964, 1966; Wolfgang 1966; Amir 1967; Schultz 1968; Schafer 1968; Mulvihill et al. 1969; Silverman 1971.

concept in such discussions, Henry Sand warns researchers as follows:

> . . . Albeit seems reasonable, superficially, to take as equivalent in
> spirit the notion of victim-facilitated, victim induced, victim preci-
> pitated and victim provoked victimization . . . to do so without
> caution obscures some fundamental aspects of the victim-offender
> relationships in victim-precipitated crime . . . (1970: 25)

Despite Sands warning, there seems to be reason to argue that these various concepts, if not wholly equivalent, are at least closely related on a theoretical level.

At this level the idea is very broad in scope, taking into account victim
behavior that ranges from the obviously culpable to behavior that hardly seems
to implicate the victim at all. We can probably all agree that if I pull a knife on
someone and make threatening gestures and I am subsequently killed, then I
have contributed to my own demise and therefore share some of the responsibility with the offender. But could every researcher agree with Morris and Blom-
Cooper (1964) when they suggest that leaving goods on the front seat of a car is
asking to have them stolen? Or could we fully accept the notion of LeRoy
Schultz (1968) when he suggests that victims must exercise reasonable caution
in not becoming a victim or they share the responsibility? Steven Schafer puts
this issue into a game-like framework in saying that victims know that they
are supposed to do their best not to become victims.[d]

I have suggested elsewhere that if we take this line of reasoning to its logical
extreme we find that we are all somewhat responsible for our own victimization
simply because we exist (1971). Quinney and Schafer have both stated that
victims are necessary for crime, hence in a way all victims are somewhat responsible. But if this is the case then criminologists should be pursuing the subject
of degree of responsibility rather than the simple fact of responsibility.

Even if we do not go as far as the logical extreme we can still see some
pretty strange results from the use of VP in its broad form. For instance, for
a pretty girl to avoid claims of responsibility in the act of rape she would be
expected to ugly-up and dress down. How could we check to see if a man were
really prudent in protecting his material possessions—is one lock per door
enough or are special locks required? We could go on with such constructs,
but more would serve no purpose.

One problem that has been emerging through this discussion is that the
notion of VP seems to be culture-, time- and place-bound. This problem will
be taken up after an examination of the operational definitions that have been
used to explore the VP concept.

---

[d]See his discussion of functional responsibility (1968).

Selected Operational Definitions and Findings

In his study of homicide in Philadelphia (1958), Wolfgang used the following definition in the case of victim precipitated homicide. ". . . The role of the victim is characterized by his having been the first in the homicide drama to use physical force directed against the subsequent slayer" (Wolfgang 1966: 252). Wolfgang found that 26 percent of the Philadelphia cases involved VP. Using the same definition Hepburn and Voss (1968: 507) found that 38 percent of the Chicago homicides that they investigated involved VP, while Mulvihill et al. found 22 percent VP homicide cases in their seventeenth city survey (1969: 226).[e]

In the case of homicide, as long as our data are complete, most researchers would find it relatively easy to apply Wolfgang's definition. Of all the operational definitions examined in this paper, this one is the clearest. Even here, however, there will be certain situations that will require some interpretation on the part of coders in order to determine VP. It should be noted that while this definition is clear, it takes into account the narrowest range of victim behavior of any of the definitions.

In *Patterns of Forcible Rape* Amir uses the following working definition of VP cases:

> . . . rape situations in which the victim actually, or so it was deemed, agreed to sexual relations but retracted before the actual act or did not react strongly enough when the suggestion was made by the offender(s). The term also applies to cases in risky situations marred with sexuality, especially when she uses what could be interpreted as indecency in language and gestures, or constitutes what could be taken as an invitation to sexual relations. (1971: 266)

Amir found that 19 percent of his cases involved VP while Mulvihill et al. found 4 percent VP in the case of rape (when they used Amir's definition) (1966: 228).

Amir's definition of VP rape cannot be easily used in replication studies. Elements that involve 'risky situations' or situations in which language is interpreted as indecent or as an invitation to sexual relations are difficult to use. Whose perception should be used—the offenders, the victims, the police reporters or the researchers? This part of the operational definition is not readily operationalized.

Mulvihill et al. found that 14 percent of the aggravated assaults examined in the seventeen city survey were VP when the following definition was used:

---

[e]Hepburn and Voss do not state that they use the same definition as Wolfgang, but given their other methodology it seems a reasonable assumption.

". . . the victim was first to use either physical force or insinuating language gestures, etc. against the attacker" (1969: 227). Mulvihill's formulation for aggravated assault indicates that the victim is the first to have used physical force, insinuating language, gestures, etc., against the attacker. Personally I would find the "etc." difficult to use in a replication. Would my etc. be the same as yours or theirs?

Normandeau makes the following statement about VP robbery:

> . . . The concept is less applicable to robbery because the confronta-
> tion of the victim with the offender usually only occurs at the time
> of the offence itself. However, precipitation at a distance is possible
> in cases of unreasonable self-protective behavior in handling money
> or goods. Some victims are "careless" and imprudent and create
> "temptation-opportunity" situations. Although our sources are
> highly unreliable about such data, we found about 11 percent of
> careless or victim precipitated robberies. (1968: 11)[f]

Mulvihill et al. used the same definition and found 11 percent VP for armed robbery and 6 percent VP for unarmed robbery (1969: 226).

In terms of replication, the 'temptation-opportunity' concept and the notion of carelessness suffer from the same problems as those definitions discussed above. What constitutes reasonable care? What constitutes flagrant violation of the norm that suggests that a victim must exercise reasonable care in his affairs? (Schafer 1968: 152).

In his study of the victim's role in homicide in Poland, Holyst uses a rather broad definition of VP. Any situation in which the provocative action of the victim played an important part in the perpetrator's decision to act is VP homicide.[g] Also included in his definition is the component of prudence on the part of the victim. Using this definition Holyst found ". . . in as many as 238 cases (49%) of the total it was the provocative behavior of the victim that had a decisive importance in the origin of the homicide" (1964: 325).

It seems that Holyst's definition is so broad that it would impede researchers from reproducing his results. My definition of VP in *Victims of Delinquency* (1971) can be faulted for the same deficiency. Like Holyst I used a rather broad definition of VP in which both verbal and physical provo-cation were deemed sufficient to call an event victim-precipitated. In analyzing face-to-face events (those events where victim and offender have at least visual

---

[f]This is for armed and unarmed robbery.

[g]I am restricted in my interpretations of Holyst's work because I do not have the original source, but rather I am working from the excerpt cited in the bibliography. It is unclear from this source whether a synonym for VP is actually used in the study.

contact) I found 29, or 19 percent, of those cases for which information was available were victim precipitated (1971: 118).

Although I had the opportunity to analyze VP in cases that did not involve a face-to-face situation, I declined from such analysis because I found it almost impossible to apply my own operational definition of VP to those cases.[h]

Though there are other studies that have used the VP concept, those cited above shall serve for illustrative purposes. As they have been used in research thus far there are problems of reliability inherent in the application of these operational definitions.

The first of these problems involves the ease with which the studies might be replicated. As I have pointed out several times, the definitions used do not lend themselves to repeated use. Amir, Normandeau, and Silverman have all expressed an uneasiness with their own definitions but all were able to apply them in the research situation. Amir states that given the nature of the reports that he used, he sometimes had to rely on his own interpretations. Normandeau suggests that his sources were highly unreliable about data that might indicate a temptation-opportunity situation. I suggested that with the exception of violent crimes there is no precise definition of VP (1971: 119). I am now willing to go further and suggest that with the exception of homicide there is no adequate operational definition of VP; that the measures used in the past (above) have been highly unreliable from a methodological point of view because they are highly dependent on a researchers interpretation rather than on a fixed criteria.

It is clear that almost any coding situation will require some interpretation on the part of coders. The implication for most of the studies cited is that the latitude of interpretation is too great for replication, hence results will probably be unreliable.

It may be argued that if consistent definitions and coding procedures were used then comparisons made of like geographical areas should result in similar findings. The reader is reminded that the findings of the studies cited above do not show such consistency. For instance, the homicide studies found 26 percent, 22 percent, and 38 percent VP. (Wolfgang 1966; Hepburn and Voss 1968; Mulvihill et al. 1969, respectively). The two rape studies found 19 percent (Amir) and 4 percent (Mulvihill et al.) VP rape while using the same definition. Other comparisons show similar discrepancies.

This evidence is, of course, not enough to prove unreliability, but it is an indicator of possible discrepancies in the use of the operational definitions.

---

[h]In the *Victims of Delinquency* study, 2 out of 146 cases that were not face-to-face in nature were considered to be VP. (These crimes usually involve burglary or larceny from individuals rather than commercial establishments.) In these cases the theft and/or damage is usually done in reprisal for some precipitating action.

Depending on the conceptual definition of VP, cultural differences in the perception of VP might account for variations in findings. If this problem does exist it could affect all of the comparisons made above and would have particularily severe consequences in the Violence Commission study (Mulvihill et al.) in which the results were based on combined data from seventeen U.S. cities. The problem of cultural variation is pursued below.

Reexamination of Victim Precipitation

In questioning the reliability of the operational definitions I am also (in this case) questioning the internal validity of those definitions. That is; I have suggested that the operational definitions do not correspond to the nominal definitions of the concept (Zetterberg 1954: 36). At least part of the reason for this is that no one has ever really examined the implications of VP in enough depth to allow for a cogent nominal definition. When I examined discussions of VP I was left with a feeling that VP involves an important part of the analysis of victim-offender relationships and that this particular relationship occurs when the victim contributes to the offence by initiating some kind of action that the offender takes as a cue to act. After examining the operational definitions I am not left with any more clear ideas of what constitutes VP. Very simply, an examination of operational definitions has not brought me any closer to a coherent conceptual definition.

This conceptualization (sic) is not adequate. It leaves far too much to the imagination of investigators. For instance, it does not take into account the definers of VP. Defining victim-precipitation is very much an issue of perspective. The naive girl who wears micro-mini skirts while trying to be fashionable is not aware that she is precipitating action in potential offenders. But according to some of the authors discussed above she shares in the responsibility for an act against her even though from her perspective she is not doing anything improper.

Further, VP is obviously not defined the same in a small town as in a large urban area. In a small town it may be quite normal to leave a house unlocked at times when no occupants are present. Not so in a large urban area. In a small town it may not be considered provocation to leave your house doors unlocked when you are out. But certainly in the large urban area this is precipitation. As pointed out by Tony Poveda, the residents of the small town he analysed felt that ". . . you could leave your keys in the car all night, and not lock your door at night. There was no need to worry" (1972: 148). If one wishes to incorporate Schafer's notion of a norm that dictates prudent behavior on the part of victims (Schafer 1968: 152) into a conceptual definition, then care must be taken to specify the cultural context of norm. Clearly the norms involving VP from the victims perspective vary in different sized cities. Such differentiation may have very practical implications in victim compensation proceedings. In the same crime situation but different geographical setting, one victim could be declared completely innocent (rural) while another is declared to have shared the responsibility.

Even in less dramatic examples we can see the problem of the definer entering into a classification of VP. In the case of violence the offender may interpret certain words of gestures as provocative, while the victim does not. The immigrant who is not familiar with the symbolic meaning of all local gestures or words may precipitate violence while performing very ordinary (for him/her) actions. The offender perceives the act as precipitating while the victim does not.

One variable that has a tendency to creep into such discussions is the motive of the victim.[1] This is really a social-psychological variable that should be excluded from our discussion. The girl in the micro-mini skirt didn't mean to provoke, but she did. The immigrant who misinterprets cues didn't mean to provoke, but he did. The fellow who leaves keys in his car didn't mean for this to be a temptation-opportunity situation, but it is. Some psychologists might try to convince us that these people really *wanted* to be victims for some imagined reasons, but that is not a good enough explanation for our purposes. It seems to me that the 'victimization wish' is a legitimate area of exploration but that it will be more fruitful if it is kept separate from VP.

The offender is the one who really consciously or unconsciously interprets events that are precipitating. Thus far in research it has been the researcher who has been doing the interpretation with little or no regard for the offenders actual perception. I suggest to the reader that what is often being measured in previous research is a researchers notion of what would constitute a provokative act if he (the researcher) were a potential offender. If this is the case then of course we can claim that previous work suffers from a lack of reliability because researchers perceptions of provokative acts will differ and they will not be able to replicate each others perceptions.

The crux of the problem lies in the fact that researchers have been basing their working definitions on a different or at least a vague nominal definition. This is a common problem in both sociology and criminology and in the interests of precision it is desirable to formulate a nominal definition that will provide a common base for future research. Below I offer a tentative nominal definition of victim precipitation. I agree with Matza when he suggests that ". . . a nominal definition is one that is not too outlandish, one that will facilitate and not hamper meaningful discourse." (Matza 1969: 10) I have tried to keep that in mind in formulating the definition and I hope that it will stimulate meaningful discourse which results in a conceptual basis for criminological research that involves victim precipitation.

---

[1]See above, p. 100, the reference to Reckless and the death wish. (1967: 142)

Victim precipitation occurs when the offender's action in committing or beginning to commit a crime is initiated after and directly related to, an action (be it physical or verbal, conscious or unconscious) on the part of the victim. The offender perceives the victims behavior as a facilitating action (including temptation, invitation) to the commission of the crime. The action of the victim might be said to have triggered the offenders behavior.

In terms of a nominal definition the suggested definition stipulates the importance of the offenders perception in the precipitating situation. At the same time it allows for extensive discussion of such elements as victim provocation, victim contribution, victim proness (see Wolfgang's discussion, 1967), and even 'victimization wishes'. Finally any theorist will still have to take into account the mutuality of the victim-offender relationship which is involved in victim-precipitation.

The main contribution of this definition should come in the form of offering a common base from which research might proceed. In terms of such research there are obvious problems that remain. Operationalizing from the given definition will still cause some difficulties. However, the components that should be included in an operational definition should be more clear than has been the case.

It has been suggested to me that the way in which one might ensure reliability is to stay as close as possible to observable acts in formulating one's operational definitions. The problem with this suggestion is that it corresponds to one of the errors of internal validity delimited by Zetterberg (1954: 38) in which the nominal definition is greater in scope than the indicator of it. While researchers rarely attain the ideal of a perfect fit of a nominal and operational definition, I feel that with some care researchers should be able to get closer to that ideal than this suggestion allows.

I suspect that in actual use the victim-precipitation notion will be broken down into its analytic components. It will take empirical research to test adequate indicators of each of the component parts.[j]

While I have (for the most part) concentrated on the theoretical and research implications of VP in this paper, I should like to close with a note on the practical implications of this topic. As the notion of victim compensation becomes more widely accepted, VP theory and research will become more important in the formulation of victim compensation laws. The role of the victim in the crime often plays a central role in legal arguments concerning the culpability of the offender (witness rape proceedings, for instance).

----

[j]Such components are suggested by Wolfgang (1967: 181) and Fattah (1967: 167). Sand has suggested that sub-parts of the victim precipitation concept are likely to be used. He also suggested one possible way of quantifying the parts (1970: 26).

Precision in theoretical understanding of the concept and in research techniques is required of criminologists before we can offer adequate input into such legal formulations.

References

Amir, M. "Victim Precipitated Forcible Rape." *Journal of Criminal Law, Criminology and Police Science* 58, 4 (1967): 493-502.

Amir, M. *Patterns in Forcible Rape.* Chicago: University of Chicago Press, 1971.

Ellenberger, H. "Relations Psychologiques Entre La Criminel et La Victime". *Revue Internationale de Criminologie et de Police Technique* 8, 1 (January-March 1954): 103-121.

Fattah, E.A. "Towards a Criminological Classification of Victims." *The International Journal of Criminal Police,* No. 209, 1967.

Fooner, M. "Victim-Induced Criminality." *Science* 155, 3740 (September 2, 1966): 1080-83.

Hentig, H. von. "Remarks on the Interaction of Perpetrator and Victim." *Journal of Criminal Law and Criminology* 31 (September-October 1940): 303-9.

Hentig, H. von. *The Criminal and His Victim.* New Haven: Yale University Press, 1948.

Hepburn, J. and H. Voss. "Patterns of Criminal Homicide: A Comparison of Chicago and Philadelphia." *Journal of Criminal Law, Criminology and Police Science* 59, 4 (1968): 499-508.

Holyst, B. "The Victims Role in Homicide" (Rola ofiary w genezie Zabojstwa). Lodz Panstwo i Prawo (Warsaw) 19/1, pp. 746-55. Excerpted in *Excerpta Criminologica* 5 (1964): 325-26.

Macdonald, J.D. *Rape: Offenders and Their Victims.* Springfield: Charles C. Thomas, 1971.

Mannheim, Hermann. *Comparative Criminology.* Boston: Houghton Mifflin Company, 1965.

Matza, David. *Becoming Deviant.* Englewood Cliffs, New Jersey: Prentice-Hall Inc., 1969.

Morris, A. "What About the Victims of Crime." *Correctional Research*; Bull. 16 (November 1966): 1-11.

Morris, T. and L. Blom-Cooper. "Victimology" A Calendar of Murder: Criminal Homicide in England Since 1957." (Chapter 7). London: Michael Joseph Ltd., 1969. Reprinted in Wolfgang, M. (ed.) *Studies in Homicide*, New York, Harper and Row, 1967.

Mulvihill, D. and M. Tumin with L. Curtis. *Crimes of Violence.* Washington: National Commission on the Causes and Prevention of Violence, 1969.

Normandeau, A. "Patterns in Robbery." *Criminologica* (November 1968): 2-15.

Poveda, T.G. "The Fear of Crime in a Small Town." *Crime and Delinquency* (April 1972): 147-53.

Quinney, R. "Who is the Victim." *Criminology* 10, 3 (November 1972).

Reckless, W. *The Crime Problem*. New York: Appleton-Century-Crofts, 1967.

Sand, H. "The Victim and His Students." Unpublished manuscript, University of Pennsylvania, 1970.

Schafer, S. *The Victim and His Criminal*. New York: Random House, 1968.

Schultz, L. "The Victim-Offender Relationship." *Crime and Delinquency* 14, 2 (1968): 135-41.

Silverman, R.A. "Victims of Delinquency." Ph.D. dissertation, University of Pennsylvania, 1971.

Voss, H. and J. Hepburn. "Patterns in Criminal Homicide in Chicago." *Journal of Criminal Law, Criminology and Police Science* 59, 4 (1968): 499-508.

Wolfgang, M.E. *Patterns in Criminal Homicide*. New York: Science Editions, 1966.

Wolfgang, M.E. *Analytical Categories for Research in Victimization*. Germany: Kriminologische Wegzeichen, 1967.

Zetterberg, Hans L. *On Theory and Verification in Sociology*. New York: The Tressler Press, 1954.

11 The Criminal Triad: Bystander, Victim, and Criminal

Leon Sheleff (Shaskolsky)

The concept of victimology has provided a useful framework out of which a host of ideas, theoretical approaches, and research projects have been developed dealing with the interactive nature of the criminal act. The early suppositions and hypotheses of such pioneers as von Hentig, Mendelsohn, and Ellenberger have been substantiated in many areas of criminological work,[1] testifying to the validity of their insightful contention that knowledge of the victim is, in many instances, an essential prerequisite for a full understanding of the crime and the criminal.

Yet the penal couple does not exhaust all the interactive possibilities ensconced in the criminal act. The criminal scene may be inhabited by others whose presence can—and often does—contribute to the manner in which the criminal act is carried out. Bystanders to a crime may affect the conduct of the primary parties to the act; they may provide encouragement for the criminal or deter him in his intent, they may offer aid to the victim or ignore (or even take pleasure in) his plight. Just as factors such as the personal qualities of the victim (carelessness, greed, etc.), his transitory emotional state (excited, drunk, etc.), the social categories to which he belongs (old, young, etc.) or the nature of the prior contacts between him and the criminal (provocative action, lengthy feud, etc.) may be the decisive factor in the criminal act, so the bystander, by his presence at the scene, by his perception of the act, by his own reaction to it, may be a decisive factor in determining whether or not the criminal act will be initiated, persisted in and/or consummated.

It may well be that in expanding the focus from the two-dimensional interaction of the penal couple to the tri-dimensional perspective of the criminal triad it will be possible to formulate a framework which will provide useful leads for the research and theoretical considerations of academicians as well as practical ideas for those involved in policy-making. It is the purpose of this paper to explore a number of areas which might be investigated from a bystander perspective.

Until recently criminological—and victimological—investigations have, with few exceptions, ignored almost completely the effect that a bystander may have on a criminal act; yet there are signs that the role of the bystander is beginning

The author wishes to thank Professors Walter Reckless and Simon Dinitz of the Ohio State University for their valuable suggestions when some of the ideas related to the innocent bystander were in the initial stage of formulation.

to be given consideration. Pecar, in particular, has drawn attention to the etiological impact of a third party (the *involved bystander*) in prompting the criminal to embark on the crime.[2] In contrast, my own work in this area has revolved around the social, legal, and moral dilemmas confronting the casual and unwitting witness of a crime, referred to as the *innocent bystander*.[3] A few years ago, a symposium dealing mainly with the legal and philosophical aspects of the problem used the New Testament concept of the Good Samaritan as the rubric for analysis.[4]

In addition to these preliminary theoretical musings, some pioneering research has also been carried out by a number of social psychologists seeking to find the factors which influence the bystander in his decision as to whether to act. Most notable contributions in this area have been the extended series of research studies by Latané and Darley, who have analysed the circumstantial factors which in a particular stressful situation determine the passivity of what they term the *unresponsive bystander*,[5] the report of a 1968 conference on altruism and helping behavior,[6] Kaufman's experiments on what he terms the *unconcerned bystander*,[7] and Milgram's research findings, which show the degree to which people, in particular situations, are capable of ignoring the plight of strangers in distress and their pleas for assistance.[8]

While these laboratory and contrived real-life situations are the source of much valid information, a large part of our knowledge of the bystander must still be gleaned from press reports with the clear danger that only the most exceptional and sensational instances of bystander reaction are recorded—both the case of cruel passivity in the face of a stranger's plight, and heroism in going to the aid of a fellow-being in distress. Yet, of the bulk of bystander reaction we have little or no knowledge. We do not know to what extent the *proximity of third parties* is relevant in determining whether a family quarrel will peter out or reach explosive proportions, whether a youth will be tempted to vandalize someone else's property, whether an unlocked car will tempt a passer-by to go for a joy-ride, whether a hurrying motorist will attempt to beat a red light, whether a kleptomaniac will attempt to steal in a shop or a pyromaniac attempt to light a fire, whether a policeman will accept a bribe or whether a confidence man will accost a potential prey.

Within the area of criminology and the behavioral sciences in general we need to come to terms with the meaning—for crime and for social life—of a host of instances of bystander behavior which are reported only in press and anecdotal accounts. As an example—what is the deeper social significance of the following magazine report:

> . . . three men were indicated on numerous counts for terrorizing
> East Side (New York) restaurants whose owners would not submit
> to their extortion demands . . . the extortionists had repeatedly
> invaded the resisting restaurants during the dinner hour, shooting

off guns, breaking windows, and throwing glasses, plates, and, in at least one instance, a bottle filled with gasoline. The police had no knowledge of these events for over a year because the owners were afraid to complain and *the customers simply didn't; when things got messy, they moved on to eat elsewhere.*"[9]   (Emphasis added)

Just as organized crime finds its base in the desire of 'victims' for the services that organized crime can offer (drugs, loans, gambling), so it flourishes under conditions such as those outlined where no bystander even bothered to put through an anonymous call to the police relating what had happened.

On the other hand, within the legal system, the bystander has always been a critical variable; it is his presumed objective evidence—in identifying the criminal, in reconstructing the crime, in verifying or contradicting the evidence of the parties—that is often the key factor in determining the outcome of a case.[10]   Indeed, in certain instances, generally involving sexual crimes, the corroboratory evidence of a bystander is essential in order to sustain the complainant's version; where no such evidence is forthcoming the judge—despite his own personal conviction that the complainant is telling the truth—is obliged to dismiss the case.[11]

Substantively, also, certain crimes may incorporate a third party in the very definition of the crime. For example, one of the elements in the crime of defamation may be publication to third parties. For as long as the calumnious statement is not brought to the attention of third parties, no crime is committed.[12]

Yet within the framework of criminology the bystander role has been largely ignored. Even theories based on interactive perspectives have for the most part confined their analysis to the criminal-victim dyad, partly indeed the result of victimological considerations, more generally because of a lack of appreciation of the bystander role. Even where there is acknowledgment of the bystander role, theoretical or practical considerations may dictate that the analysis focus more specifically only on the principal actors. Thus, Shoham and his coworkers, in attempting to build a model of the cycles of interaction in violence point out that, " . . . many violent situations involve more than the principal actors. Observers, both participant and non-participant, often play a part, even to the extent of an all-out brawl." However, since their theoretical model is based on " . . . the conception of violence as a dyadic type of interaction between ego and alter," the study " . . . confines itself to an examination of the dyadic interaction. . . . "[13]

The most pertinent statement on the etiological role of the bystander in crime may be found in some of the original presentations of Pecar, who has drawn attention to the varied ways in which a bystander may bear part of the responsibility, perhaps even the major responsibility, for the commission of a crime. Discussing an empirical study of murder carried out in Yugoslavia, Pecar enumerates the various ways in which a third party may be involved in the dynamics of a criminal act, and concludes that, "The third party may contribute a decisive share towards the crime, . . . may indeed be chiefly responsible for it. . . . " In most instances the involved bystander is "closely associated with one or even both members of the (penal) couple." This trait draws attention to the fact that often " . . . they are themselves interested, more or less, in the conflict, its development and outcome. Infrequently, however, they are direct or *total* causers of the conflict or the central figure in the encounter. They most frequently remain in the background or even unnoticed, unexposed to moral condemnation and stigmatization."[14]

Drawing on examples from his study of murder, Pecar shows how a bystander perspective might easily divulge seemingly irrelevant factors, which may nevertheless be crucial for a full understanding of the etiology of the crime.[15] It seems clear that a theoretical perspective of this nature opens up new areas for fertile research which might well provide additional leads into the causative factors making for various criminal acts. Studies such as those of patterns in crime as carried out in Philadelphia by Wolfgang on murder and Amir on forcible rape[16] could usefully search out additional aspects of the mosaic of the criminal scene by focusing not only on the criminal and victim (and these studies have made a significant contribution to proving the relevance of victimology), but also on any possible bystanders and their role in the commission of the crime.

Whereas Pecar has accentuated the role of the bystander in fomenting the criminal act, a no less significant aspect of the bystander role might be the contribution to the prevention of crime. Here research procedures would perhaps be more complicated. Attempts would have to be made to determine the extent to which the presence of bystanders—their numbers, their composition, their demeanor—could undermine a criminal intent and frustrate a criminal act. For instance, to what extent would a potential shoplifter be frustrated in his intention by the numbers of fellow-shoppers, by their glances toward him, or by his knowledge of how they had acted in similar situations in the past (turned a blind eye, remonstrated with the potential thief, physically intervened by arresting him, or quietly reported the incident to the management).[17] To what extent do a few civic-minded citizens, who, at risk to themselves, attempt to prevent a particular bank robbery, have an impact on other potential robbers making them less inclined to practice this mode of criminal activity?

One of the most significant aspects of bystander impact on crime is obviously in the area of the milder forms of crimes against the person—assault and battery. Here, perhaps more than in most other criminal activity, the presence of bystanders, may be critical—acting either to calm the passions or as catalytic agents in inflaming them. Similarly, driving violations may be significantly affected by the knowledge that a concerned and activitistic citizenry cooperates with the police in reporting infractions. In Israel, a scheme of this nature has been attempted by actually providing a number of drivers with semi-official duties of reporting traffic violations. Unfortunately, the scheme has not proven too successful—perhaps partly because of the fact that too little is known of what makes for active bystander response, or, for that matter, for the impact such response has on the potential violator. Perhaps, too, analyses of road accidents might benefit from an awareness that most accidents take place within a total situation that embraces more than just the parties to the accident. Many accidents are possibly caused by prior negligence on the part of other road users, whose role is subsequently ignored by police and judicial authorities as well as by researchers.

Beyond this, the total environment within which the action takes place may be relevant. Where, for instance, the overall value system is attuned to a sub-culture of violence, the effect of bystander presence or participation would often tend to be in the direction of escalation. On the other hand, Jacobs, in her perceptive analysis of interaction in everyday urban life, has pointed out how the gestalt of certain social situations may be conducive to combatting criminal activity.[18] She outlines the hidden assumptions of social life which make the difference between the fear of the isolated individual in a teeming anonymous city and the preservation of safety in neighborhoods where trust of neighbors and strangers is an implicit concomitant of everyday social intercourse. Her description of the "uses of sidewalks" accentuates how the situational aspect is always overladen by an ongoing social environment. "The bedrock attitude of a successful city district is that a person must feel personally safe and secure on the street among all these strangers."[19] This can only be achieved when it is realized that the public peace of cities "is not kept primarily by the police, necessary as police are. It is kept primarily by an intricate, almost unconscious network of voluntary controls and standards among the people themselves, and, enforced by the people themselves."[20] Jacobs claims that the more a street is in constant pedestrian use, the more likely it is that safety will be assured. She describes a number of instances where, in well-used streets in which such controls do exist and such an atmosphere does prevail, the users of the streets are far more likely to go to the aid of someone in distress. The shopkeepers and shoppers, local inhabitants and strangers—all serve as the eyes and ears, ever watchful, ever prepared to come to the aid of a person in distress.

Similarly, Japan, under the Tokugawa administration, maintained a system of policing achieved by citizens watching each other, particularly through the five-family groups (known as "gonim-gumi"),[21] while Sjoberg, discussing pre-industrial cities, states that "the wards, the guilds, and various ethnic groups, religious organizations, and extended families all assist the governmental agencies in maintaining order on the local level."[22]

Part of the work of Latané and Darley has been devoted to this ecological dimension of the bystander problem. For the most part their work has centered around the situational aspects of the stressful incident, and sought to determine the extent to which one bystander is influenced by the reaction of other bystanders. Among their most noteworthy findings is that the inaction of others may have a contagious effect on the bystander, that the presence of others at the scene may diminish the possibility of action since the feelings of responsibility and subsequent shame will be diffused, and that often bystander indifference is a consequence of incorrect perception of the act (e.g. where an assault is perceived as a family quarrel).[23]

However only in a few isolated cases have they used an artificially contrived situation involving crime; it is more than likely that there are specific features about the nature of a criminal act that are liable to differentiate it, in terms of the bystander response, from other stressful situations. Thus the flood of altruism often evidenced at the sight of a natural disaster is generally a consequence of unique factors related to social aspects of a disaster and does not necessarily provide a precedent for anticipating similar other-oriented behavior in a crime situation.[24] Indeed Latané and Darley themselves point out that different influences may be operative when the stressful situation involves a crime.

> A villain represents a danger not only to the victim, but to anybody who is rash enough to interfere with him. A single individual may be reluctant to tangle with a villain. If it comes to physical violence, his odds are at best equal. At worst, the villain will be armed and vicious. Undeterred from crime he may be undeterred from physical violence as well.[25]

Yet for most crimes, fear of violence or retaliation by the criminal is only one of several considerations that may affect the nature of the bystander response. Often the sheer inconvenience of reporting a crime with its involvement in the subsequent stages of law enforcement and administration of justice, may serve to deter potential bystanders from intervention. Sellin enumerated several factors inhibiting bystander reaction, including the desire to avoid annoyance and publicity, the inconvenience of being subpoenaed to give evidence in court, and the negative overall public attitude toward certain crimes.[26]

At another level, a short vignette by Saul Bellow in his book, *Mr. Sammler's Planet*, gives indication of the way bureaucratic apathy may dissipate the good intentions of a citizen intent on displaying prosocial behavior aimed at combatting crime. Wishing to report a pickpocket whom he had observed on a number of occasions at 'work' on a bus, Sammler gets involved in a frustrating phone conversation with an anonymous policeman at the other end of the line.

> — I wish to report a pickpocket on the Riverside bus —
> — O.K. —
> — Sir? —
> — O.K., I said O.K., report —

— A Negro, about six feet tall, about two hundred pounds,
about thirty-five years old, very good-looking, very well
dressed —
— O.K. —
— I thought I should call in —
— O.K.
— Are you going to do anything? —
— We're supposed to, aren't we? What's your name? —
— Arthur Sammler —
— All right, Art. Where do you live? —
— Dear Sir, I will tell you, but I am asking you what you intend
to do about this man —
— What do you think we should do? —
— Arrest him —
— We have to catch him first —
— You should put a man on the bus —
— We haven't got a man to put on the bus. There are lots of
buses, Art, and not enough men. Lots of conventions, banquets,
and so on we have to cover, Art. V.I.P.'s and Brass. There are
lots of ladies shopping at Lord and Taylor, Bonwit's, and Sak's,
leaving purses on chairs while they go to feel the goods —
— I understand. You don't have the personnel, and there are
priorities, political pressures. But I could point out the man —
— Some other time —
— You don't want him pointed out? —
— Sure, but we have a waiting list —
— I have to get on *your* list —
— That's right. . . —

— — — — — —

— Let me make sure I understand you, officer—mister detective.
This man is going to rob more people, but you aren't going
to do anything about it. Is that right?—
It was right — confirmed by silence, though no ordinary silence.
Mr. Sammler said, 'Good-bye, sir.'[27]

An interactive perspective would posit further factors which, in any particular instance, might be relevant, and which would stress the nature of the
relations between the members of the criminal triad. To what extent, for
instance, does the bystander sense a connection of any sort between himself
and the penal couple? With which of the two does he identify? Are there any
points of identity between him and the criminal and the victim, or any other
points of meaningful social contact between himself and either of them? To
what extent would a common racial, class, ethnic, national, professional, sex

or age relationship between the bystander and/or the victim affect the considerations and actions of the bystander?[28]

To a certain extent the victim himself plays a social role *qua* victim which may override all other social factors. Lerner, in a perceptive analysis of the victim, has suggested that in the case of people imbued with a sense of justice, they are also equipped with a blanket defense mechanism in which the demand of the victim are offset by seeing him as receiving no more than his just desserts. In Lerner's language "All the world loathes a loser,"[29] and accordingly tries to apportion to him the blame for his predicament, whether of social circumstances in general, or of a particular crime. Just as the criminal is obliged to deny the victim by using what Sykes and Matza call techniques of neutralization,[30] or what, in a similar vein, Redl and Wineman refer to as "tax evasion of guilt feelings,"[31] so the bystander has his own processes of rationalization by which he can deny the claims made on him as a bystander. As Ryan has noted in a larger social context, the easiest way to justify inaction in social affairs is to "blame the victim."[32]

A major factor causing bystander inaction is the incorrect perception by the bystander of the true nature of the act that he is witnessing. Latané and Darley have laid great stress on this factor in their research, claiming that many instances of supposed apathy or even callousness on the part of the bystander may be no more than a result of his inability to interpret correctly the nature of the scene unfolding before him.[33] Indeed a recent research project investigating the role of the bystander in a contrived real-life shoplifting situation revealed the interesting serendipitous finding that the vast majority of shoppers were not even aware that a theft had taken place despite the efforts of the researchers to ensure that their 'theft' would be conspicuously performed and easily discernible.[34]

While Latané and Darley emphasize chiefly the circumstances surrounding the stressful situation, they tend to overlook the fact that the way in which people perceive events is generally a consequence of a total social environment. Indeed it is probably specifically when there may be doubt as to the true nature of an event, that the overall environment may well be decisive in determining the way it will be perceived. The more people sense a basic alienation, the less likely they are to see the dangers confronting a stranger; the more they sense bonds of empathy, the more likely they are to be attuned to and aware of underlying nuances in a social situation which pose potential dangers, as Jacobs has tried to show. Admittedly such a hypothesis would be difficult to research. Yet there may be fruitful research possibilities in attempting cross-cultural research in this area. A replication, for instance, of the Latané-Darley experiments in other societies might yield interesting insights into the larger social relationships of different types of societies.

In this context particular attention should be given to the role that the law can play in fostering the kind of climate that might be conducive to pro-social behavior aimed at preventing crime and aiding the victim. Indeed the ongoing debate as to the connection between law and morality might well incorporate, as Honore has suggested, the question of the degree to which it would be desirable for the law to intervene in encouraging people to behave in an altruistic and moral manner.[35]

Just as wide-ranging interest in victimology has served to rekindle interest in such time-honored problems as compensation for the victim, so, it is to be hoped, focus on the role of the innocent bystander may help to pinpoint the need for clearer rules and procedures for bystander reaction to crime (and other stressful situations) and for clarification of society's overall attitude to the bystander. In many instances the bystander responding positively and actively to frustrate a crime may find society showing as little regard for any adverse effects he might suffer (actual injury to himself or civil action against him) as many modern societies still show towards the victim. The growing modern movement to ensure adequate compensation for the victim might accordingly well be expanded to involve clear legislative rules as to the provision of compensation for the active bystander, as well as immunity for claims arising out of his action. In this regard the common law systems seem to have been more remiss in allowing lacunae, since the continental systems generally seem more aware of the need for rules of this type; though there has been a discernible change in the Anglo-American approach in recent years, which gives evidence of a greater willingness to countenance support for the active and concerned bystander.[36] At the same time the continental systems of law have also been more willing to attempt to enforce pro-social behavior through the medium of criminal sanctions. Except for occasional specific rules such as rendering aid to a policeman at his request and the little-used crime of misprision, i.e., failure to report a crime of which a person has knowledge, the common law approach makes little demand upon the bystander.[37]

In sociological terms, however, we have almost no knowledge of the manner in which such laws have an impact on the behavior of bystanders. This seems to be an unexplored area that could profitably be the subject of much intriguing and valuable research. In addition, we do not know to what extent the offer of rewards has an impact on the willingness of people to respond to the plight of a victim. There is clearly a need to investigate whether it is desirable for society to encourage bystander involvement in crime enforcement. Indeed certain laws can only be enforced when 'bystanders' in the broadest meaning of the term are offered direct rewards, often in the form of sharing with the state in the financial penalty imposed on the culprit, e.g., rewards to those who act as informers for contraventions of the income tax laws.

Indeed, there are many other "crimes without *direct* victims" (to adopt Schur's phrase)[38] where only active participation on the part of the public

can result in the culprits being apprehended. The area of pollution of the
environment is probably the outstanding example of such crimes. Here the
damage is usually indirect and long term—only the vigilance of concerned
bystanders can really ensure that the authorities are able to enforce the laws.
An interesting example of how the law might reward concerned bystanders
is an environmental law in the United States dating back to 1899 (the Rivers
and Harbors Act, known generally as the Refuse Act since it deals with
refuse thrown into rivers and harbors), which provides that people giving information as to contraventions of the act may, at the direction of the court, be
entitled to half of the fine imposed on the culprit.[39] Although the act lay
practically dormant for over half a century, it was resuscitated recently in the
light of growing concerns for the environment. When the particular paragraph
providing for a share in the fine was given publicity it led to a spate of reports
to the authorities of violations of the act. It would seem that here too there
is a need for research to determine to what degree the battle against crimes
without direct victims, particularly in the area of the environment, could be
fought by greater encouragement of bystanders through a system of adequate
rewards. On the other hand there are other areas of crime control in which
too zealous a response could create more problems than the original crime.
Recently a report for the United Nations Congress of the Prevention of Crime
and the Treatment of Offenders drew attention to the fact that in certain
countries citizens often took the law into their own hands with bystander
involvement occasionally including the use of such illegal and antisocial means
as lynching or vigilante groups.[40] In some instances, of course, vigilante groups
work in conjunction, either overtly or covertly, with the police.[41] On the
other hand, the police are often wary of too zealous a response by the public.
In addition the whole problem of police informers and the use of agents provocateurs is an area of legal enforcement which, while attracting deep analysis
by jurists, both in court decisions and academic treatises,[42] has been almost
completely ignored by criminologists. Related to these issues is the complex
and delicate problem of the blood-feud which still persists in residual form
in many countries, especially in the Middle East area, for example among the
Arabs of Israel. This is an interesting phenomenon deeply interwoven into
the whole social fabric of life in terms of the *gemeinschaft* values that still
characterize the web of human relations within the extended family
system—yet it has been given only minimal treatment in criminological, or
for that matter anthropological and sociological, writings.[43] Indeed an analysis,
in historic and comparative terms, of the roles of the victim and the bystander
(sometimes, as in the case of a family feud, not even directly present at the
scene), would serve to accentuate the close connection between these two
roles. Thus, for instance, Schafer's analysis of the "history of the victim"[44]
becomes to an extent the history of bystander involvement, e.g., the development from blood revenge to composition and compensation (which, broadly

speaking, deals with different forms of bystander response). Even more clearly, the role of the bystander emerges in terms of the attempt to make the community responsible for preventing crime—through the systems in English legal history, for instance, of the hundreds and the tithing, and the frank-pledge system, the watch and ward and the hue and cry; in all of which clear obligations were placed on citizens to respond actively and immediately to frustrate crime, aid the victim, and apprehend the criminal.[45]

Thus, while victimology has focused the need for legal reform mainly on the question of compensation for the victim, the problem of legal reform to accommodate the various problems related to the innocent bystander seems far more complex and far more wide-ranging. Without wishing to advance any specific solutions I would suggest that the various questions to be decided in relation to the bystander involve the following issues:[46]

1. Should the bystander be legally obliged to act, taking into account factors such as the degree of danger confronting the victim and the nature of the offense?
2. Should the bystander be obliged to act subject to the degree of danger or inconvenience which he would encounter, and subject to his capacity to be effective?
3. Should the obligation to intervene in a crime situation be applicable only to a direct witness of the plight of the victim or to anyone who has knowledge of the act?
4. Should responsibility devolve automatically on every bystander or should there be a limitation or responsibility where there are several bystanders and there is justifiable reason to believe that others may no less effectively succeed in averting the danger to the victim?
5. What should be the nature of the obligation devolving on the bystander, with varying possibilities ranging from the need for personal intervention to contacting the necessary authorities?
6. Should failure to comply with the obligation involve any kinds of sanctions?
7. Where the bystander, in the course of fulfilling his obligation to render aid to the victim, inadvertently causes harm—to the victim, or the criminal, or to another bystander—should immunity be provided against civil claims, subject to determining the degree of negligence?
8. Where a claim is not allowed against the bystander, should provision be made for a claim to be submitted to a governmental authority?
9. Where the bystander suffers harm or incurs expenses, should he be entitled to claim compensation—from the victim, or the criminal, or from a public authority?

I would suggest that many of the issues outlined here cannot be finally resolved until more knowledge is available as to the impact of such rules on human behavior and till more thought and discussion have been given to the social aspects. It would seem that we are still at a very initial stage in our analysis and understanding of the bystander role. Perhaps extra impetus could be given for research in this area if it was acknowledged as a recognized sub-area for study within the field of criminology—thus it might be advisable for the *Abstracts of Criminology* to provide a separate section dealing with the innocent bystander (at present the few articles in this area are indexed under the sub-section—the victim). In a parallel field it might be noted that a sudden burgeoning of studies of disaster research in the late 1950s and 1960s led to a fund of diverse knowledge being made available, which Barton finally integrated into a meaningful theoretical framework.[47]

But beyond the academic and practical issues related to the innocent bystander, I would suggest that we are dealing with an issue which, though peripheral to society, nevertheless touches on the very essence of a society—its nature and the quality of its life. The President's Commission on Crime and Law Enforcement, in an original piece of research, related how knowledge of a rising crime rate affected people's everyday behavior—their willingness to go out at night, the pressures of them to change their place of residence, their attitudes to strangers.[48]

Indeed, in a larger sense, given the interdependent, open, massmedia-oriented world of today, we are all bystanders of the events of our society. There is no escape in the final analysis from the role of bystander. What we need then, is greater awareness of the meaning and implications of this role—in moral, social, legal, and practical terms.

Notes

1. Hans von Hentig, *The Criminal and His Victim—Studies in the Sociobiology of Crime* (New Haven: Yale University Press, 1948); B. Mendelsohn, "The Origin of the Doctrine of Victimology," *Excerpta Criminologica* 3 (1963): 239-41; Henri Ellenberger, "Relation Psychologiqyes entre le criminel et la victime," *Revue Internationale de Criminologie et de Police Technique,* 1954, pp. 103-121.

2. Janez Pecar, "Involved Bystanders: Examination of a Neglected Aspect of Criminology and Victimology," *International Journal of Contemporary Society* 9 (1972): 81. See also Janez Pecar, "Involved Bystanders—Victimological Aspects," *Rev. Kriminalist. Kriminol,* Vol. 22, pp. 172-84, as indexed in *Abstracts in Criminology* 12 (1972): 76.

3. Leon Sheleff (Shaskolsky), "The Innocent Bystander: Socio-Level Aspects," in *Israel Studies in Criminology,* Vol. 2, edited by Shlomo Shoham (Jerusalem, Jerusalem Academic Press, 1972/3), pp. 197-229; Leon Shaskolsky, "The Innocent Bystander and Crime," *Federal Probation* 34 (1970): 44-48.

4. James M. Ratcliffe (ed.), *The Good Samaritan and the Law: The Morality – and the Problems – of Aiding Those in Peril* (New York: Anchor Books, Doubleday, 1966).

5. See particularly Bibb Latané and John M. Darley, *The Unresponsive Bystander: Why Doesn't He Help?* (New York, Appleton-Century-Crofts, 1970).

6. See Jacqueline R. Macaulay and Leonard Berkowitz (eds.), *Altruism and Helping Behavior: Social Psychological Studies of Some Antecedents and Consequences* (New York, Academic Press, 1970).

7. Harry Kaufman, "The Unconcerned Bystander," in *Proceedings of the Annual Convention of the American Psychological Association,* 1968.

8. Stanley Milgram, "Some Conditions of Obedience and Disobedience to Authority," *Human Relations* 18 (1965): 57-75.

9. *The New Yorker,* January 27, 1973, p. 21. This particular quote is a mere random sample of the type of item that can frequently be found in the press.

10. This problem in itself is deserving of much more serious study than it has hitherto been given. The legal rules of evidence are not always attuned to ensuring that the psychological factors of perception, memory, recall, and powers of description of the witness (i.e., the innocent bystander) will be adequately dealt with. For an excellent analysis of this question by a lawyer, see James Marshall, *Law and Psychology in Conflict* (Indianapolis, Bobbs-Merrill, 1966).

11. See, for example, J.F. Archbold, *Criminal Pleading, Evidence and Practice,* 37th ed. by Butler and Garcia (London: Sweet and Maxwell, 1966), p. 494.

12. See, for example, J.W.C. Turner, *Russell on Crime* (12th ed.) (London: Stevens and Sons, 1964), p. 781.

13. Shlomo Shoham, Sara Ben-David, Rivka Vadmani, Joseph Atar, and Suzanne Fleming, "The Cycles of Interaction in Violence," in *Israel Studies in Criminology, op. cit.,* p. 72

14. Pecar, "Involved Bystanders," p. 85.

15. Pecar gives several examples taken from a study, *Criminal Homicides in Slovenia,* to show how an involved bystander can contribute to, or even create, the conditions leading to the crime. For example: "Two married couples, sharing a flat, were quarrelling because of the children and about the cleaning of the flat's conveniences. The quarrels *were instigated* particularly and also caused by the *victim's wife and the offender's wife.*" See Pecar, "Involved Bystanders," p. 84, in which he relates several other similar incidents.

16. Marvin E. Wolfgang, *Patterns in Criminal Homicide* (Philadelphia: University of Pennsylvania Press, 1958); Menachem Amir, *Patterns of Forcible Rape* (Chicago: University of Chicago Press, 1971).

17. For an original and interesting research report dealing with shoplifting, see

Donald P. Hartmann, Donna M. Gelfand, Brent Page, and Patrice Walder, "Rates of Bystander Observation and Reporting of Contrived Shoplifting Incidents," *Criminology: An Interdisciplinary Journal* 10 (1972): 247-67.

18. Jane Jacobs, *The Death and Life of Great American Cities* (New York, Vintage Books, 1961).

19. Ibid., p. 30.

20. Ibid., pp. 31-32.

21. See B. J. George, Jr., "The Impact of the Past Upon the Rights of the Accused in Japan," *American Journal of Comparative Law* 14 (1966): 673.

22. Gideon Sjoberg, *The Pre-Industrial City* (New York, The Free Press, 1960), p. 246.

23. Latané and Darley, *Unresponsive Bystander*.

24. For an analysis of the differences between a natural disaster and a crime situation, see Leon Shaskolsky, "Volunteerism in Disaster Situations," Paper No. 5, 1967, Disaster Research Center, Dept. of Sociology, The Ohio State University.

25. Latané and Darley, *Unresponsive Bystanders*, p. 69.

26. Thorsten Sellin, *Research Memorandum on Crime in the Depression* (New York: Science Research Council, 1937), pp. 69-70.

27. Saul Bellow, *Mr. Sammler's Planet* (London: Penguin, 1971), p. 12-13.

28. See Shaskolsky, "The Innocent Bystander and Crime," "Volunteerism," p. 48. In a related context see Harry Kaufmann and A. Marcus, "Aggression as a function of similarity between aggressor and victim," *Perceptual and Motor Skills* 20 (1965): 1013-20.

29. Melvin J. Lerner, "All the World Loathes a Loser," *Psychology Today*, June 1971, p. 51.

30. Gresham M. Sykes and David Matza, "Techniques of Neutralization: A Theory of Delinquency," *American Sociological Review* 22 (1957): 664-70.

31. Fritz Redl and David Wineman, *Children Who Hate: The Disorganization and Breakdown of Behavior Controls* (Glencoe: The Free Press, 1951), pp. 145-56.

32. William Ryan, *Blaming the Victim* (New York: Vintage Books, 1972).

33. Latané and Darley, *Unresponsive Bystander*. See especially Chapter 9, "Motivation and Perception in Emergencies."

34. Hartmann et al., "Rates of Bystander Observation," p. 255, where they indicate that "only 28% of the exposed shoppers observed the staged incident despite our precise cueing, multiple stagings and attention-attracting procedures."

35. Antony M. Honore, "Law, Morals and Rescue," in Ratcliffe, *Good Samaritan*, pp. 225-42.

36. See Allen Linden, "Rescuers and Good Samaritans," *The Modern Law Review* 31 (1971): 241.

37. Aleksander W. Rudzinski, "The Duty to Rescue: A Comparative Analysis," in Ratcliffe, *Good Samaritan,* pp. 91-134.

38. Edwin M. Schur, *Crime Without Victims: Deviant Behavior and Public Policy* (Englewood Cliffs, N.J.: Prentice-Hall, 1965). It seems to me that the concept of "crime without *direct* victims" might have potential significance in terms of the criminal law—for much of the awareness of new social problems, such as the environment, relates to a gradual insidious victimization of society in general, without any direct, immediate damage being felt. Thus, while there may be an overreach of the criminal law in crime without victims, there may conversely be a weakness of the criminal law in not being able to cope with "crimes without direct victims."

39. Sec. 13 of Rivers and Harbors Act, 1899. For an analysis of the law and its manner of application see Rodgers, "Industrial Water Pollution and the Refuse Act: A Second Chance for Water Quality," *University of Pennsylvania Law Review* 119 (1971): 761. See also, Leon Sheleff (Shaskolsky), "Tradition and Innovation in Legal Approaches to the Environment," paper presented at the 1st International Conference of the Society of Engineering Science, Israel, 1972.

40. See *International Review of Criminal Policy*, No. 27, 1969, p. 66. See also R.E.S. Tanner, *Three Studies in East African Criminology,* Uppsala, 1970.

41. See Gary T. Marx and Dane Archer, "The Urban Vigilante," *Psychology Today,* January 1973, p. 45.

42. See for instance, J. McClean, "Informers and Agent Provocateurs," *Criminal Law Review,* 1969, p. 527; *Note,* "The Serpent Beguiled Me and I Did Eat," *Yale Law Journal* 74 (1965): 942.

43. See, for example, the articles in Paul Bohannan (ed.), *Law and Warfare—Studies in the Anthropology of Conflict* (New York: American Museum, 1967): by Margaret Hasluck, "The Albanian Blood Feud," pp. 381-409; and Rafael Karsten, "Blood Revenge and War Among the Jibaro Indians of Eastern Ecuador," pp. 303-327.

44. Stephen Schafer, *The Victim and His Criminal* (New York: Random House, 1968), Chapter 1, "The History of the Victim."

45. See Alan Harding, *A Social History of English Law* (Baltimore: Penguin, 1966).

46. For a fuller discussion of these issues see Leon Shaskolsky, "The Role of the Bystander in the Prevention of Crime," master's thesis, Ohio State University, 1967.

47. Allen Barton, *Communities in Distress: A Sociological Analysis of Collective Stress Situations* (Garden City, N.Y.: Doubleday, 1969).

48. *The Challenge of Crime in a Free Society,* A Report by the President's Commission on Law Enforcement and Administration of Justice, pp. 50-53.

12 A Victim-Role Typology of Rational-Economic Property Crimes

John A. Mack

This paper sketches a limited criminal typology using as its differentiating and classifying factor the role of the victim. As the writer has argued elsewhere, all effective criminal typologies are limited typologies.[a] This one is doubly limited. It falls within the rubric of property crime, and more precisely property crime involving some degree of organization. It is limited also to rational crime (rational in Max Weber's sense of the word), economic crime, crime in which the primary motivation of the participants is economic gain.

This essay in typology developed out of a rather different proposal, suggested by the Council of Europe, to report on the present state of our knowledge of "professional" and "organized crime." An early recommendation by the research team was that the two terms be scrapped. The reasons for this are given in a recently published paper (Mack 1973) and are briefly referred to below. The main point of the discussion for our present purposes was that we held the U.S. President's Commission, and the principal U.S. textbooks, to be right in distinguishing "professional" and "organized" crime as two distinct forms of crime,[b] and probably right in assuming, as they appear to assume, that the two categories

---

[a]Most of the criminal typologies extant have two defects. They are typologies of offenders, usually detected and incarcerated offenders, and usually over-emphasize the part played by pathological criminals, a group which largely overlaps with pathological non-criminals. The second and much greater defect is inherent in the historical drive to make criminology a science of the kind in which the phenomena under study can be systematically classified *without remainder*. This leads to the belief . . . that because all crimes are socially and juristically defined as such, all criminals have something in common as a matter of sociological fact. This explains those frequent attempts, like that of Clinard and Quinney, to produce a *complete* classification of types of crime. The typologies discussed here work very differently. They separate out, from the enormous diversity of situations and types of activity which involve the liability of incarceration for certain of the persons concerned, this or that limited sector which gives evidence of a high degree of homogeneity. The general assumption is that the behaviour collected under the legal definition contains a fairly small number of homogeneous sectors and comparatively large residue of heterogeneous items of behavior, items which don't fit into a comprehensive criminological typology, items which are essentially allergic to any such typology. (Mack et al., 1973, pp. 167-68.)

[b]*The U.S. President's Commission on Law Enforcement and Administration of Justice* set one Task Force to work on *Organized Crime* and a second group to study *The Professional Criminal*. The Task Force Report on Organized Crime was published in 1967. The second report was not published, but has been made available through the courtesy of the editor, Mr. Leroy Gould. The two working parties discussed their topics as separate and distinct criminal and criminological entities.

of crime are normally practiced by two distinct sets of criminals, what we might call the Bill Sykes set and the Al Capone set.[c]

But we ran into linguistic trouble at once. We found the situation to be one of almost complete terminological confusion. The two types of criminal process are distinct enough. But the labels are applied quite indiscriminately, not only by journalists but also by criminologists. "Professional" is used for *all* full-time, large-scale economically gainful crimes, irrespective of the Bill Sykes-Al Capone distinction (see for example McIntosh 1973: 66). "Organized" has the same general coverage. In the United States it carries the specialized meaning adopted to signify the Al Capone type of operation, which we shall from now on describe using the term "syndicated." But it is also good American practice to describe traditional forms of crime—burglary, robbery, fraud, etc.—as 'organized', given of course that the operation in question has been conducted with some degree of organization as defined in the dictionary.

European language habits are much the same. As a consequence of this initial booming and buzzing confusion it is impossible to go on to make the most elementary distinction in the subject matter itself. For example the distinction between the two modes of crime operates differently in the United States as compared with Europe. One of the two modes of crime, the traditional burglary kind, is pretty much the same in all the industrial countries; the European version of what we have just called syndicated crime performs only some of the criminal functions characteristic of the U.S. syndicates. In Europe the mobs make most of their money out of extortion, whereas in the United States supplying goods provides by far the greater part of syndicate income. Another American-European distinction concerns the relative status of the two types of crime and the two sets of criminal. In the United States the syndicates enjoy by far the higher status, and indeed appear to employ and to exploit the practioners of the older traditions. This does not appear to hold in Europe (for further discussion see Mack: 1973: 109-110). But a recent attempt to discuss these matters with two highly intelligent and highly literate colleagues, one American, one English, came to nothing, since both held that syndicated criminals were professionals.

There are the two kinds of criminal process. How should they be described and classified? One possible classification is implicit in many treatments; it is that between predatory and parasitical crime. This is a useful distinction so far as it goes. It is firmly founded in scientific zoological usage. But since the terminology and the distinction have been worked out for zoological purposes, it can apply to criminal behavior only by analogy, and by a broad analogy at that. Used in zoology the two types of animal, or organism, subdivide systematically into a varied and meaningful schema. But this subdivision is not so readily achieved in the criminal

---

[c]This second proposition is seldom explicitly discussed by serious writers in this field. Our own preliminary observation suggests that the two distinct kinds of crime are in fact usually practiced by two distinct groups of criminals (Mack 1973: 109).

analogy. Here it is the parasite concept at first sight attractively illuminating, which falls down really badly. It applies fairly straightforwardly to the extortion function. It doesn't make sense of the supply function. The U.S. Task Force report gave a succinct definition of this function. The core of organized crime activities, it says, is the supplying of goods and services which are prohibited or limited by law and for which there is a strong and lasting economic demand. One finds some difficulty in identifying the bootlegger, or the supplier of gambling facilities, as a parasite. It is possible to make the point, but only by working very hard at it. For example, since U.S. syndicates are in the position to charge high monopoly prices, higher than the price would be if the syndicates were open to lawful competition, they are to that extent parasitical on the public. But that is not what is meant when we apply the term to extortion rackets. Extortion rackets are obviously parasitical. In Europe, and to a large extent in the United States, they are parasitical on those classes and groups of people who for a variety of reasons are unwilling to call in the law to enable them to deal with threats or other intimidations—criminals and near-criminals, shady concerns and individuals operating in the no man's land between lawful and unlawful behavior. These people are made to pay continuing sums of money for permission to carry on activities which they could and would carry on if there were no extortion. That is the essence of the operation. The extortion racket also puts up the price of the commodity to the ultimate customer. Similarly the labor or business racket, which flourished in its most crude form in Capone's Chicago and continues nowadays in more sophisticated forms in different parts of the United States, is parasitical not only on the business concerns which suffer them but also on the public, which pays a higher price for the commodity. But the parasitism is primarily inflicted on the supplier or tradesman, not on the ultimate customer. But in the case of the supply function the criminal himself is the supplier. And in any case it is too difficult for even the most imaginative of typologists to class that considerable proportion of the U.S. population which sustains the demand for the goods and services so lavishly prohibited by U.S. state governments as the victim in a parasitical criminal process.

We have in fact gone well beyond the limits of the usefulness of the predator-parasite distinction. It cannot provide us with a typology. But it holds the germ of an idea which can, the idea of the role of the victim or victim-surrogate.

This idea provides the clearest statement of the distinction we started off with. Professional criminals strictly so-called, the professional criminals of the textbooks, operate within the traditional criminal-victim relationship. "Professional criminals usually work on victims who dislike being made victims. Syndicates sell their illicit goods to willing buyers. Abolish burglary and no one will complain except the burglars. Abolish the syndicates and you will have powerful unsupplied demands cruising around looking for new sources of supply" (Mack 1973: 110).

These are the two poles of a typological continuum: at one end the

traditional criminal-victim relationship; at the other end those victimless crimes
of which the clearest examples so far are certain of the supply activities of the
syndicates. These two ends of the spectrum are already well known and
generally accepted criminological common sense. But closer attention to recent
studies in a number of fields reveals a considerable differentiation between the
two extremes yielding a number of intermediate classifications; even more
important, it yields a pointer to what may be called the moving frontier of
crime, particularly in the field of business fraud. For it is a special obligation
on any attempt to elucidate a realistic limited typology such as that suggested
in this paper that it should *not* be limited to the existing corpus of crimes
defined and covered by statute, but should move with the times to incorporate
these activities which are in process of being designated as criminal, although
that process is only in mid-journey, still short of its definition-destination.

The following examples are to be taken as providing a tentative and incomplete indication of the range and sequence-order of the subdivisions of a notional
victim-role typology of crime. It is not yet possible, and indeed it may never be
possible, to achieve a completely systematic, schematic, theoretically significant
classification. We are not considering here the possibility of a dramaturgical
schema. If we were, considering the way in which victims behave, and have
behavior imposed on them, in situations where the victim role is clear—for
example burglary, confidence trickery, robbery, and other crimes in which the
criminal makes direct contact with the victim and/or his property—there
would be provided ample opportunities for ethno-methodological research.
But we are concerned here only with suggesting a typology of the social situation, emphasizing the interaction and interrelationship between the criminal,
the victim, the crime, and the law.

We begin by specifying the traditional criminal-victim relationship. This
is one in which the victim has no prior awareness of the crime, dislikes very
much being made a victim, and demonstrates his entire non-acceptance of
the transaction by notifying the police at the earliest possible moment.
The next gradation in the victim-role scale is one in which there is no prior
awareness of the crime, the victim dislikes being made a victim, but signifies
his acquiescence in the transaction by refraining from calling in the law. The
third gradation is like the second, with the exception only that there may be
some prior awareness of the intended crime, either because the criminals (front-
line or background operator) are sufficiently sure of their ground to intimate
their intentions; or because the victims learn of the intended crime from some
intermediate source of information.

The first of these categories might be termed victim non-acceptance. The
second and third might be described as victim-acquiescence, unwilling, with
or without prior awareness. These two cover a variety of social situations of
which four of the more frequent can be described here.

The first is where the victim himself is a criminal. Many examples of this could be regarded as simply a rough commercial settling of accounts in a continuing series of transactions, usually disputed. The second is where the victim is a near-criminal, in the sense that he has occasional transactions, amounting to a small proportion of his total business which is mostly law-abiding. He may, for example, be the occasional client of a fence (receiver), or he may do a little fencing on the side himself. A third situation is where there is no overt criminal association, but where the victim belongs to a minority group whose members enjoy full formal citizenship and protection from the law, but which prefers to accept informal sub-cultural sanctions over a wide range of activities. One special variation on this situation arises from the fact that these minority groups—the Jews are a fair example (where they are a small but homogeneous minority community in a well-established nation-state)—tend to do their best to protect their own, including their own villains. They may therefore strike a rough and ready bargain with criminals who make away with their property so as to avoid information being laid against in-group criminals whom they wish to protect. This kind of situation also favors those transactions with criminals whereby stolen property, usually jewelry, is brought back through some intermediary, by the owner or by arrangement with the insurance company, with or without police knowledge.

The fourth situation is one in which the victim belongs to an ethnic minority group, of which examples can readily be found among recent waves of immigrants. Here the criminal may well have a hold on the immigrants by threatening to inform the authorities of breaches of the immigration law on the part of relatives and friends who may be law breakers in no other sense.

These illustrative situations refer in the main to predatory crime. But the typology covers a parallel series of parasitical crimes of the kind conducted by the European-type syndicates. Various forms of extortion, already described as being inflicted on shady concerns, including gambling proprietors, are clear examples of victim-acquiescence strictly equivalent to the examples given above. The question of prior awareness is of course irrelevant as regards the parasitical factor. The essence of extortion and similar rackets is that they are business arrangements carried through over a period of time.

The next gradation or differentiation goes beyond victim-acquiescence, to victim-cooperation, in which the victim cooperates in the criminal process while still remaining a victim. He not only cooperates; he instigates, sustains, and defends the criminal process, while at the same time suffering from it and thoroughly disliking it. The prime example of this particular gradation is of course moneylending at exorbitant rates, or loan-sharking. One might define the clients of the loan shark as primarily customers. But they are also and mainly victims. Here a precise distinction must be made. Loan-sharking is not simply unlicensed moneylending at exorbitant rates of interest. If it were, it could not strictly and formally speaking be regarded as a crime, meaning by a crime that kind of offence which carries with it the liability to imprisonment of the offender. This is the case, at any rate, in Great Britain. But loan-sharking practically speaking is almost always accompanied by a lesser or greater degree of intimidation, involving the threat and the actuality of violence. The client-victim of the loan shark *instigates* the criminal process by asking for the loan; but the process does not become fully criminal until the borrower is submitted to and submits to the threat and sometimes the actuality of violence. It is at this point that the client-victim is described as not simply acquiescing in the crime but as sustaining and defending the continuing criminal transaction by refusing to cooperate in the legal processes which may be set in motion to defend him from intimidation and violence.

This is the clear lesson of a remarkable moneylending and intimidation trial in a British city in 1970. It followed two major trials in 1967 and 1968 in which a small, extremely violent group had been exposed and convicted; one member of the group being convicted of murder in the first of the trials, the other three members of the group being convicted of using violence and intimidation in an attempt to silence the witnesses whose evidence helped secure the murder conviction in the first trial.

Loan-sharking in England is of long standing. It antedates by fifty years and more the trials of the 1960s. It may well survive into the third millennium. But it operates in only a few of the more squalid industrial and residential areas, and affects only certain minority strata in these areas. The actual sums of money lent and borrowed are comparatively small—one pound, two pounds, five pounds, seldom more than twenty pounds—but the rates of interest are exceptionally high even by the standards of the classic American loan-sharking territories. For every 100p. (£1.00) borrowed, the interest charge in many and possibly the majority of transactions is no less than 40p. per week.

In the 1970 trial in Britain, the police saw the situation as one requiring a well-prepared intervention. The evidence showed that the moneylending was being conducted not as in the earlier part of the century by individuals and small groups unconnected with each other, but by a group of a dozen or more people, collectors and others, who could call on the service of three or four 'heavy men', sometimes called the team, sometimes called the Mafia, to beat up those who fell behind in their payments. The degree of beating up was on the whole minimal, but the borrowers, and particularly those who found it difficult to pay up, were obviously very frightened people.

The story in brief is that after an elaborate case had been prepared, in which a number of witnesses had expressed their readiness to give evidence, and to confirm in court evidence which they had already given in statements, the trial was initiated and was an almost complete failure. The witnesses retracted their written statements, and denied having any knowledge of intimidation or violence on the part of the accused men. As a consequence the twelve people charged were all found guilty of unlicensed moneylending, a minor offence; they were also found not guilty of intimidation. There was therefore no question of any sentence more weighty than a fine; none of the accused was sent to prison.

The next gradation in the victim-role continuum completes the dehydration of the term. The clients of the loan shark, as we have just seen, are cooperating victims, but they remain victims. But the people who take advantage of the illicit provision of gambling opportunities (mostly in the United States) and the people who bought the bootleg liquor (in the Prohibition era) are customers and clients and have nothing of the victim about them.

The next gradation takes us out of the sphere of traditional crime and of the equally well-established activity of the syndicates. It involves certain manifestations of company and business fraud. This field of study is doubly speculative. It combines activities which are clearly fraudulent and therefore clearly criminal with activities which are only questionably fraudulent and questionably criminal. The latter of these categories may, and probably will, be declared criminal when the process of the making of company law catches up with the ongoing activities of the ingenious people who make money by exploiting the deficiences of company law. A second obstacle confronting the mere criminologist is the difficulty of establishing firm propositions about large-scale company fraud, even in cases where the activities in question are clearly fraudulent and therefore clearly criminal. A recent British thesis on the subject calls attention to "the almost complete lack of accurate factual information, either on the incidence of the various offences or on the nature of the enforcement process" (Hadden 1967: 323). The general disposition among lawyers who are criminologically minded appears to be that the subject is best discussed inside the conceptual framework of company law, and in the context, understood only by specialist students of law, of the continual race between company law and the cohorts of company promoters, maneuverers, and outright fraudsters.

The main interest of the subject for our present purposes is that certain forms of company fraud which are indubitably criminal incorporate a role for the victim not covered by any of the above classifications. Here it is not simply a matter of victim-acquiescence, or victim-cooperation, or customer-cooperation. People who are defrauded, or who run the risk of being defrauded, tend in many cases to be not only willing but eager to share the risk. Insofar as there is any ground for calling them victims, they are victims who like being made victims. They are not so much victim-cooperators as positive participants in a criminal process which may have the result of depriving them of their property in the company.

The important special differentia in the case of criminal fraud, or of those species with which we are presently concerned, is that the shareholder's money is not stolen but is simply put at risk of loss. Hadden (1967) discusses those fraudulent company maneuvers where the offence lies more in the dishonesty of the methods employed than in the actual loss inflicted on shareholders or investors. Such dishonest methods include the use of forged documents, often in respect of collateral securities.

Thus the offenders may undertake to find sufficient capital to take

over another firm or company, and then finding themselves unable
to fulfil their commitments may turn to fabrication or falsification
in an attempt to 'bridge' the gap until the profits from the completed
deal may be employed to pay off the liabilities. Alternatively they
may set out to employ or 'borrow' money or credit which they have
no right to, in the hope that this temporary misuse will not come to
light. In either case, however, the crucial point is that the operation,
if successfully completed, will pay for itself. As a result the efficient
operator need have little to fear from the law since his 'victims' will
have no reason to complain: they too indeed may benefit substantially
from the skill of the offenders. It is equally very important, of course,
to understand the position in those cases where by ill-luck or bad
judgment the operation fails, for it is the failures which attract the
attention of the victims, of the public and eventually of the police.
Yet, though it is relatively well known that prosecutions follow
spectacular financial failures with sobering regularity, the identity
of interest of the offenders and of their 'victims' may often afford
an important and indeed a convincing defence. (Hadden 1967:
489-90).

The case just quoted could be said to be only marginally criminal. Certain
criminal acts are committed, but the objective of the operation, whether achieved
or unachieved, is not the transfer of the shareholder's money into the pockets
of the promoters. They stand to lose everything; the shareholders who support
them have a much more limited loss, in the majority of cases. But there are
many other forms of more extensive company fraud, particularly in the off-
shore area. The courts of Switzerland are at present in the process of deciding
whether the remarkable story of Investment Overseas Services will be regarded
in the future as the story of a gigantic swindle, or as simply the latest example
of the age-old bubble phenomenon. We are here just on or over the frontier
of crime. The frontier where certain practices have still to be pronounced on.
Will they eventually be defined as new types of crime, *or* simply age-old follies
refurbished, *or* business innovations and adaptations to changing circumstances?
One criticism of this paper so far might be that it tends to fall into the
old groove of discussing the different victim-roles in terms of types of victim
and types of victim motivation. This is only one side of the subject. A victim-
role typology must also include those situations in which the victim-role is
determined not so much by individual or group choices as by certain socio-
structural conditions. The point has already been well made that certain of
the so-called "victimless crimes," the peddling of bootleg alcohol, the provision
of gambling facilities, the traffic in soft drugs, are primarily to be considered
in terms of general social and political tensions, removable or irremovable. We
close this rather unsystematic list of victim-roles by drawing attention to an

example of victim-cooperation, combined with victim instigation, which can at least in part be explained as a direct outcome of economic and commercial processes, processes in which the motivation of the victims is broadly irrelevant. The crime concerned is that which is known in the United Kingdom as long-firm fraud. Long-firm fraud is the abuse of credit facilities in transactions between big suppliers and wholesale firms dealing in a wide range of goods of a kind which are easy to handle and move and hard to identify as to source.[d]

It is probable that there is a great many more long-firm frauds than are processed in the courts. The courts find it very difficult to distinguish between criminal activities and the consequence of incompetence or bad luck in business forecasting. As against this there is a good deal of effective prevention activity undertaken by trade security agencies. But one thing works in favor of the fraudsters: this is the tendency of many firms to give credit to doubtful propositions with doubtful references. They take the risk because in a highly competitive market they might otherwise lose business. This readiness to take risks is intensified when the market is not only highly competitive but is in a state of rapid movement. This structural weakness is intensified by the action of some very big firms, which give easy credit as a matter of policy, make no enquiries, and carry the consequent losses as a calculated wastage. In doing so they force the same policy on their smaller competitors. If these did not follow suit they would be crowded out of the market. It follows that long-firm fraudsters, particularly those who are already criminals *de grande envergure,* get away with a lot because of the nature of the market and of the behavior of the big fish.

References

Hadden, T. *The Development and Administration of the English Law of Criminal Fraud,* Institute of Criminology Library, 1967.

Jackson, R. *Occupied With Crime.* London: Harrap, 1967.

Mack, J.A. "The Organized and Professional Labels Criticised." *The International Journal of Criminology and Penology* 1, 2 (May 1973).

Mack, J.A.; Kerner, H.J.; and Susini, J. *The Crime Industry—Some Aspects of "Organized" and "Professional" Crime.* Strasbourg: Council of Europe, 1973.

McIntosh, M. "The Growth of Racketeering." In *Economy and Society,* Vol. 2 No. 1. London: Routledge, 1973.

---

[d]This crime has flourished in France for a long time as "carambouillage," and in Germany as "Stossbetrug." In the United States it is described officially as bankruptcy fraud, colloquially as "bust-out" and "scam" (Cressey 1969: 105).

In its simplest form it is described by Jackson as follows: ". . . it entails starting a business, ordering goods from the wholesalers, and paying for them almost at once. Then, once confidence has been established, the swindler starts giving larger orders and obtaining longer credit. Finally he sells the goods for cash and absconds with the proceeds" (Jackson 1967: 76).

13

The Offender's Perception of the Victim
Simha F. Landau

The role played by the victim in the criminal act was for long time neglected in both the theoretical and empirical work in criminology. However, since the late forties, the contributions of von Hentig (1948), Mendelsohn (1963), Nagel (1963), Ellenberger (1955), Schafer (1968), and others focused the attention of criminologists and other social scientists on this rather neglected aspect of the crime phenomenon. Nevertheless, most of the studies which did pay attention to the victim concentrated mainly on his demographic characteristics (sex, age, ethnic group, etc.), his objective contribution to the offense, and also on the victim-offender relationship (among others, see Wolfgang 1958; McClintock 1963; Amir 1971; Landau et al., forthcoming). The studies in this field did not pay attention to the offender's perception of the victim. How the victim is perceived by his offender is still an unanswered question.

Interestingly enough, this topic was somehow dealt with in experimental social psychology. These experiments, all done on non-delinquents (usually university students), investigated how harm-doers perceive or relate to their victims. Among the topics studied are: willingness to compensate the victim (Berscheid and Walster 1967; Berscheid et al. 1969), other strategies utilized by the harm-doer to restore psychological equity to his relationship with the victim (Walster and Prestholdt, 1966; Brock and Buss 1962; Davis and Jones, 1960), and the effect of the severity of the victim's suffering on his evaluation by an observer (Stokols and Schopler 1973).

In this context it is worth mentioning the well-known work of Sykes and Matza (1957) where among the "techniques of neutralization" we can find derogation of the victim, denial of responsibility and minimization of the victim's suffering. However, these rationalizations brought up by Sykes and Matza were part of their theory on delinquent behavior, in which formulation the victim played hardly any role at all.

The purpose of the present study is to fill the above-mentioned gap in victimological research. More specifically, besides the 'classical' variables examined in victimological studies (like victim-offender relationship, age, and

This study was supported by the Research Fund of the Faculty of Law, Hebrew University of Jerusalem. The author wishes to thank all those who assisted him in the various stages of the research. The willing cooperation of Mr. A. Nir, Prison Commissioner and the staff of Ramle, Ma'assiyahu and Tel-Mond Prisons made this research possible. Elja Akker, Karnit Kurtz, Shlomo Daniel, Ziva Zilka, and Norman Vagenberg were very helpful in the empirical work.

sex differences, etc.), we are interested here in finding out how the offender perceives the following factors relevant to the offense: the reason for committing the offense; the evaluation of the victim prior to the offense; suffering caused by the offender to the victim, to himself, and to their respective families; the offender's guilt feelings vs. blaming the victim and willingness to compensate the victim.

Needless to say, it would not be proper to view all offenders as one general group. By doing this we would be confusing the picture, because there are different types of offenders (according to various classifications), each with his specific characteristics and probably his specific type of victims. Therefore, the analysis of the variables in this study has to be done according to some typology of offenders. The typology chosen here is the most common, namely the legal one. Thus, our aim is to identify the specific profile of victim-perception in each type of offender included in this study. In addition, the relevance of our findings to the experimental work done on victim perception will be discussed.

The Study

Subjects

The total number of subjects is 104, all individually interviewed while serving their prison sentences. They were randomly chosen from among the total Jewish population in three Israeli prisons. Subjects were subdivided according to type of offense into the following four groups:

a.   Offenders against the person (hereinafter "violent offenders"): 37 subjects. The great majority among them are homicide offenders and the rest have been sentenced for bodily harm and assault.
b.   Offenders against property ("property offenders"): 26 subjects. This group includes offenders sentenced for robbery, house-breaking, theft, and receiving and possessing stolen property.
c.   Fraud and forgery offenders ("fraud offenders"): 18 subjects.
d.   Sex offenders: 23 subjects. The great majority of them were sentenced for rape, and the rest for sexual assault of minors, etc.

Before analysing the main findings of the study it is worth mentioning briefly some basic demographic and other characteristics of these groups of offenders. Not unexpectedly there are some significant differences between the groups as regards these variables.

1.   Country of origin. The great majority of sex offenders (83 percent), violent offenders (77 percent), and property offenders (68 percent)

stem from families of Oriental origin: the Middle East (apart from Israel) and North Africa. On the other hand most of the fraud offenders (56 percent) stem from families of European origin.

2. Age. The youngest group are the sex offenders (74 percent below the age of 25, and almost 50 percent below 20). Second come the property offenders (56 percent below 25). Among the violent offenders, about two-thirds (65 percent) are above 25 while the oldest group are the fraud offenders (all of them above 25).

3. Education. Here again, the two extreme groups are fraud offenders who are highest on education (52 percent continued their studies beyond elementary school), as opposed to sex offenders who are the lowest: 97 percent of them had either partial or up to full elementary education. The corresponding percentage among property offenders was 83 percent and among violent offenders 76 percent.

The Offence, the Offender, and the Victim

1. **Length of sentence.** In this variable the striking and significant differences between the groups are obvious, due to the different severity of the four types of offences. The group with the longest sentences were the violent offenders. About two-thirds of them (64 percent) got sentences above ten years of imprisonment (many sentenced for life). Almost three-quarters (72 percent) of the offenders in this group were sent to prison for periods above three years.

Second in severity of sentence are the sex offenders: 57 percent of them were sent to prison for periods above three years. Third in severity of sentences are the property offenders, the majority of whom (61 percent) were sentenced to periods below three years of imprisonment. The group with the shortest sentences are the fraud offenders: 89 percent of them were sentenced to periods below three years of imprisonment.

2. **Partnership in committing the offense.** As regards this variable there are only slight and non-significant differences between the four groups of offenders. Partnership in committing the offense is found mainly among property offenders (63 percent) and among sex offenders (52 percent). On the other hand more than half of the violent offenders (52 percent) and fraud offenders (56 percent) committed their offenses without partners.

3. **The number of victims in each offense.** Table 13-1 presents the findings as regards the number of victims, and shows that for the vast majority of violent and sex offenders there was only one victim in each case. On the other hand, in half of the cases of fraud and forgery there was more than one victim.

Table 13-1

The Number of Victims in Each Offence, by Type of Offender (In percentages)

	1. Violent Offenders	2. Property Offenders	3. Fraud Offenders	4. Sex Offenders	Total
1. One victim only	94.3	53.8	25.0	95.7	73.0
2. More than one victim	5.7	0	50.0	4.3	11.0
3. No specific personal victim	0	46.2	25.0	0	16.0
TOTAL	100.0	100.0	100.0	100.0	100.0
N	35	26	16	23	100

χ^2 = 33.3813
d.f. = 1 p < .001
(Columns combined: 1 and 4; 2 and 3)
(Rows combined: 2 and 3)

χ^2 = 26.3038
d.f. = 1 p < .001
(Columns combined: 1 and 4; 2 and 3)
(Rows combined: 1 and 2)

As to property offenders, we find there the highest proportion of cases without specific personal victims (cases like robbing a bank, breaking into a storehouse, etc.). These differences are statistically significant. These, together with some further findings, may have important implications as to different aspects of the offender's perceptions of the victim.

4. **Sex of victims.** The main findings in table 13-2, presenting the sex of the victims are, in the case of sex offenders, the great majority of victims are females (not surprising at all). On the other hand victims of property offenders are mainly males. The rate of males and females among victims of violent offenders is much more balanced (although males are a slight majority). As to fraud offenders, in most cases where there were specific personal victims, these were cases of multiple victims, comprising both males and females.

5. **Age of victim and victim-offender age gap.** These findings are presented in tables 13-3 and 13-4. Table 13-3 shows that the lowest age group of victims is in the category of sex offenders, while the oldest age group of victims is found among property offenders. These differences are not surprising at all and reflect the higher vulnerability of young women to sex offenses and of elderly persons to offenses against property. Victims of violence offenses are mainly in the age groups of 21-30 and 30 or above. However, about one-fifth of these victims are at the age of 20 or below. As to the age of victims of forgery and fraud, their numbers in tables 13-3 and 13-4 are too small to be analyzed separately. As to

Table 13-2
Sex of Victims by Type of Offender. (In percentages)

Sex	1. Violent Offenders	2. Property Offenders	3. Fraud Offenders	4. Sex Offenders	Total
1. Male	51.4	85.7	9.1	21.7	43.4
2. Female	42.9	14.3	27.3	73.9	44.6
3. Males and Females	5.7	0	63.6	4.3	12.0
Total	100.0	100.0	100.0	100.0	100.0
N	35	14	11	23	83*

*Here and in coming tables where only cases with specific and personal victims are analyzed, the total number of cases will be less than 104.

x^2 = 14.9530
d.f. = 2 $p < .001$
(Columns 3 and 4 combined)
(Row 3 excluded)

Table 13-3
Age of Victim by Type of Offender. (In percentages)

	1. Violent Offenders	2. Property Offenders	3. Fraud Offenders	4. Sex Offenders	Total
20 and below	19.4	0	0	69.6	30.6
21-30	32.3	21.4	50.0	21.7	27.8
31 and above	48.4	78.6	50.0	8.7	41.7
Total	100.0	100.0	100.0	100.0	100.0
N	31	14	4	23	72

x^2 = 29.1094
d.f. = 4 $p < .001$
(Columns 2 and 3 were combined)

the age-gap between victim and offender (table 13-4), we witness again consistent differences between our groups. In sex offenses, in more than half of the cases the age difference between victim and offender is less than five years (in either direction). In about one-third of the cases, the offender is five years or more older than the victim. Among property offenses, in nearly three-quarters

Table 13-4

Age Gap Between Victim and Offender by Type of Offenders (In percentages)

	1. *Violent Offenders*	2. *Property Offenders*	3. *Fraud Offenders*	4. *Sex Offenders*	*Total*
of .> vic. 5 years or more	32.3	0	25.0	34.8	26.4
age difference 1-5 years	29.0	28.6	25.0	56.5	37.5
of .< vic. 5 years or more	38.7	71.4	50.0	8.7	36.1
Total	100.0	100.0	100.0	100.0	100.0
N	31	14	4	23	72

x^2 =   16.7441
d.f.   =   4   p < .01
(Columns 2 and 3 were combined)

of the cases, the offender is five years or more younger than the victim, and in only less than 30 percent the age differences between victim and offender do not exceed five years (in either direction). As to violent offenses the figures seem to be more balanced. In about 40 percent of the cases the offender is five or more years younger than the victim; in about one-third of the cases the offender is five or more years older than the victim, and in about 30 percent of the cases age differences between them do not exceed five years (in either direction).

6. **Victim-offender relationship**. Table 13-5 shows in a clear way the specific patterns of relationship in each goup. Among violent offenses, in about 70 percent of the cases there were close relationships between victim and offender. The highest proportion of family relationship is found in this group. Among fraud offenses the proportion of close relationship is not much less (67 percent). On the other hand, as regards property and sex offenses, more than half of the victims were strangers to their offenders. Our findings as regards victim-offender relationship in sex offenses and offenses of violence, are in the general direction of the relevant literature summarized by Amir (1973). As to fraud and property offenses no available study for comparison could be located.

7. **The reason for committing the offense**. We are dealing here with reasons given by the offenders when asked why they committed their offenses. A quick glance at table 13-6 presenting these findings will explain why we are not dealing here with motives. In many instances the offender explained his behavior

Table 13-5
Victim-Offender Relationship by Type of Offender (In percentages)

	1. Violent Offenders	2. Property Offenders	3. Fraud Offenders	4. Sex Offenders	Total
1. Family Relationship	24.2	0	8.3	4.3	11.8
2. Acquaintance, Neighbour	45.5	41.2	58.3	43.5	45.9
3. Stranger	30.3	58.8	33.3	52.2	42.4
Total	100.0	100.0	100.0	100.0	100.0
N	33	17	12	23	85

x^2 = 7.3846
d.f. = 3 p < .05
(Rows 1 and 2 were combined)

Table 13-6
The Reason for Committing the Offence by Type of Offenders (In percentages)

	1. Violent Offenders	2. Property Offenders	3. Fraud Offenders	4. Sex Offenders	Total
1. Material Gain	11.5	70.0	86.7	0.0	40.0
2. Victim's Guilt	26.9	0.0	0.0	50.0	18.7
3. Drugs; Alcohol; State of Mind	7.7	25.0	13.3	42.9	20.0
4. Situational factors	53.8	5.0	0	7.1	21.3
Total	100.0	100.0	100.0	100.0	100.0
N	26	20	15	14	75

x^2 = 37.7232
d.f. = 1 p < .001
(Columns combined: 1 and 4; 2 and 3)
(Rows combined: 2, 3 and 4)

x^2 = 21.3368
d.f. = 1 p < .001
(Columns 1, 2 and 3 were combined)
(Rows combined: 1 and 4; 2 and 3)

x^2 = 25.0419
d.f. = 1 p < .001
(Columns 2, 3 and 4 were combined)
(Rows 1, 2 and 3 were combined)

towards the victim by blaming the victim, the situation, or his own special state of mind. Therefore, in many cases we are not dealing with motives of offenders but rather with some immediate situational factors and pressures which, according to the offender, played an important role in the occurrence of the offense. In order to analyze the specific reasons in each group of offenders, several chi-squares were computed, all of them significant (see table 13-6).

Rationalizations in explaining the offense is found least among property and fraud offenders. The great majority of offenders in these groups admit that the reason for their behavior was their wish for material gain. As to the other two groups the picture is completely different. More than half of the violent offenders blame situational factors for what happened (it was an accident; the partners initiated the assault, etc.). About one-quarter of these offenders blame the victim entirely for his victimization, when asked to give the reason for what happened. Sex offenders present quite a different picture. Half of them blame the victim (she wanted it, she has a bad reputation, etc.). Almost all the other offenders in this group claim a kind of diminished responsibility, either because of being under the influence of drugs or alcohol, or because of their impulsivity, depression or lack of control over their drives.

The fact that most of the offenders against property in our study do not make use of any rationalization seems to contradict Sykes and Matza's (1957) emphasis on these techniques among gang members who are (among other things) also heavily involved in property offenses. A possible explanation may be that in their theory, Sykes and Matza (1957) do not differentiate between different types of offender. Another possible explanation is that here we are dealing with offenders in prison and not with gang members in their natural setting. In any case we should bear in mind that the use of rationalizations by offenders as an explanation for their behavior is strongly connected with the type of offense.

8. **Would previous acquaintance with the victim have avoided the commission of the offense?** This question may be relevant only in those cases where the victim and offender were strangers to one another. As noted (see table 13-5), in most violence and fraud offenses the victim and the offender knew each other before the offense. Analyzing those cases where there was no such previous knowledge we found that among property offenders about 80 percent say they would not have committed the offense, and among sex offenders this proportion goes up to 100 percent. On the other hand, among violent offenders without previous knowledge of their victims, more than 40 percent would have committed the offense even if they had previously known their victims. Among fraud offenders this proportion is about one-third.

We have no on-the-spot interpretations for these differences, but they are quite interesting. However, in our opinion the answers to this question, especially those of property and sex offenders, should not be taken as very reliable.

9. **The estimation of the victim's strength prior to the offense.** In face-to-face encounters between the victim and the offender, the offender's estimation of his victim's strength may play an important role in his behavior. The highest proportion of cases where the victim was estimated as weaker than the offender was found among sex offenders (56 percent). Among violent offenders this proportion was only 38 percent, while among the other two groups only around 11 percent to 12 percent of the victims were estimated as weaker than the offender. One-third of the violent offenders estimated their victims as either equal or even stronger than themselves. In the other groups the frequency of this category was much lower (property and sex: 11 percent each; fraud— none). On the other hand the great majority of property and fraud offenders report that estimation of the victim's strength was not taken into consideration at all. This is understandable due to the fact that in many cases of offenses against property there is no direct contact with the victim, and as to fraud and forgery—physical strength does not play any role at all.

However, even among the other two types of offenders (sex and violence) a considerable number reply that they did not take into consideration the victim's strength (among violent offenders this proportion comprises about 30 percent and among sex offenders, one-third of the cases). These are cases where the offender acts under a strong impulse without any previous estimation of his ability to overcome his victim.

10. **Who chose the victim?** The question as regards the process and factors which influence the choice of the victim is an important topic in victimological study. Although this question is not investigated here extensively, table 13-7 does provide us with relevant information. From this table it can be seen that the tendency to point at a partner as the one who chose the victim, is highest among violent offenders (50 percent), while sex offenders are in the second place (30 percent). Among the other two groups this tendency is considerably lower. (It is worth reminding the reader that there was no significant difference between the groups as regards the number of offenders in each offense.)

The highest proportion of victims chosen by the offender himself is found among fraud offenders (89 percent) and then come sex offenders (65 percent), violent offenders (62 percent), and property offenders (36 percent). More than one-fourth of the violent offenders (27 percent) claim that the victim was chosen by chance, meaning there was some factors beyond the control of the offender or his partners which made the victim available. Among property and sex offenders, the proportion of this category is much lower (14 percent and 5 percent respectively), while among fraud offenders it does not appear at all.

Table 13-7
Who Chose the Victim? (In percentages)

	1. *Violent Offenders*	2. *Property Offenders*	3. *Fraud Offenders*	4. *Sex Offenders*	*Total*
1. The Offender	61.5	35.7	88.9	65.0	60.9
2. Some Partner(s)	11.5	50.0	11.1	30.0	24.6
3. Victim chosen by Chance	26.9	14.3	0.0	5.0	14.5
Total	100.0	100.0	100.0	100.0	100.0
N	26	14	9	20	69

x^2 = 4.6612
d.f. = 1 p $<$ .05
(Columns 1, 3 and 4 were combined)
(Rows 2 and 3 were combined)

11. **Suffering caused to the victim, to the offender, and to their respective families.** The findings as regards this topic are presented in tables 13-8 and 13-9, where salient differences between the groups are observed. The most striking findings in this respect is that the majority of property offenders (76 percent) and sex offenders (62 percent) claim that their behavior did not cause any suffering whatsoever to their victims. On the other hand most offenders in the other two groups (violence and fraud) do admit suffering on the part of their victims. However, even among these offenders about 40 percent deny any suffering caused to their victims. Those findings are particularly striking, bearing in mind that about three-quarters of the violent offenders *killed* their victims. It is clear that the mechanism of denial of the victim's suffering is very potent in the offender's cognitive system.

It is of interest to mention at this point that when asked as to their own suffering, an overwhelming majority of offenders said that they did suffer from their offense. It would appear that the offender perceives himself as the real victim of his behavior. The denial of the victim's suffering, together with the emphasis on his own suffering, served for the offender the important function of restoring psychological equity between him and his victim. We will further discuss this process in the coming pages.

As to suffering caused to the victim's family (table 13-9), the figures are quite similar to those on table 13-8, except for the group of fraud offenders. While most of these offenders admit that they caused suffering to their victims, they *all* report that no suffering was caused to the victim's family (similar to the reports of the property and sex offender). Only among violent offenders, most subjects admit that the victim's family also suffers as a result of their offense.

Table 13-8
Suffering Caused to the Victim by Type of Offender (In percentages)

	Violent Offenders	Property Offenders	Fraud Offenders	Sex Offenders	Total
Suffering Caused	60.9	23.8	60.0	38.1	45.0
No Suffering Caused	39.1	76.2	40.0	61.9	55.0
Total	100.0	100.0	100.0	100.0	100.0
N	23	21	15	21	80

x^2 = 7.9185
d.f. = 3 $p < .05$

Table 13-9
Suffering Caused to the Victim's Family by Type of Offender (In percentages)

	Violent Offenders	Property Offenders	Fraud Offenders	Sex Offenders	Total
Suffering Caused	56.0	9.5	0.0	4.8	21.0
No Suffering Caused	44.0	90.5	100.0	95.2	79.0
Total	100.0	100.0	100.0	100.0	100.0
N	25	21	14	21	81

x^2 = 27.1980
d.f. = 3 $p < .001$

As to the suffering of the offender's family, the figures are less unitary than as regards the offender's suffering. Although here, too, in all groups the majority of offenders claim that their family is suffering, this majority is especially high in the fraud and violent groups (100 percent and 80 percent respectively), while among property and sex offenders this majority is considerably smaller (67 percent and 52 percent respectively).

12. **The offender's victim's guilt.**   The findings as regards this important variable are presented in tables 13-10 and 13-11. Blaming the victim for the offense is a well-known argument used by offenders in court. However it is of interest to find out whether this defense is used with the same frequency by different types of offenders. The answer to this question is negative. From

Table 13-10

The Guilt of the Offender, by Type of Offender (In percentages)

	1. *Violent Offenders*	2. *Property Offenders*	3. *Fraud Offenders*	4. *Sex Offenders*	*Total*
1. Completely Guilty	33.3	76.2	75.0	33.3	52.4
2. Partially Guilty	20.8	4.8	25.0	23.8	18.3
3. Not Guilty	45.8	19.0	0.0	42.9	29.3
Total	100.0	100.0	100.0	100.0	100.0
N	24	21	16	21	82

x^2 = 10.5661
d.f. = 1 $p < .01$
(Columns combined: 1 and 4; 2 and 3)
(Rows 1 and 2 were combined)

Table 13-11

The Guilt of the Victim, by Type of Offender (In percentages)

Victim's Guilt	1. *Violent Offenders*	2. *Property Offenders*	3. *Fraud Offenders*	4. *Sex Offenders*	*Total*
1. Completely Guilty	52.0	11.8	0.0	26.3	27.0
2. Partially Guilty	32.0	5.9	30.8	42.1	28.4
3. Not Guilty	16.0	82.4	69.2	31.6	44.6
Total	100.0	100.0	100.0	100.0	100.0
N	25	17	13	19	74

x^2 = 20.9976
d.f. = 1 $p < .001$
(Columns combined: 1 and 4; 2 and 3)
(Rows 1 and 2 were combined)

table 13-10 it is seen in a very clear way that property and fraud offenders in most cases admit full guilt for their offense. On the other hand only one-third of the violent and sex offenders accept the full responsibility for their offense. Most of these offenders either admit to partial guilt or, even more frequently, claim complete innocence.

The figures as regards the guilt of the victim (table 13-11) are almost a mirror reflection of those in the previous table. Most of property and fraud offenders find the victim not guilty at all. On the other hand more than half of the violent offenders claim complete guilt on the victim's part. Among sex offenders this proportion is only about one-quarter of the cases: 42 percent of them see the victim as partially guilty and less than one-third in this group do not blame the victim at all for the offense.

Careful observation of the figures in tables 13-10 and 13-11 will reveal some inaccuracies and overlapping of the different categories in these tables. This means that there were cases in which the offender perceived one side as completely guilty and the other as partially guilty. However these minor overlaps do not distort the clear picture presented in tables 13-10 and 13-11.

13. **Willingness to compensate the victim.** Of all the offenders in this study only five did actually compensate their victims. Out of these, four were fraud offenders and one was a sex offender. Therefore, in table 13-12 we are dealing mainly with expressed willingness by the offender to compensate the victim, rather than with actual compensation.

The main difference as regards this variable is between fraud offenders and all the other offenders. While the majority of fraud offenders are willing to compensate the victim (and some even have done so), almost all other offenders are completely unwilling to do so. This unwillingness is the highest among violent offenders (91 percent) and sex offenders (88 percent) while among property offenders this proportion is a little bit lower (76.5 percent). (In cases of homicide it was made clear that compensation was meant for the victim's relatives.)

Table 13-12
Willingness to Compensate the Victim, by Type of Offender. (In percentages)

	1. Violent Offenders	2. Property Offenders	3. Fraud Offenders	4. Sex Offenders	Total
Compensated or Willing to Compensate	9.1	23.5	60.0	11.8	23.9
Unwilling to Compensate	90.9	76.5	40.0	88.2	76.1
Total	100.0	100.0	100.0	100.0	100.0
N	22	17	15	17	71

x^2 = 11.1921 (with Yates correction: Yates, 1934)
d.f. = 1 p < .001
(Columns 1, 2 and 4 were combined)

Summary and Discussion

The findings of this study revealed a distinct profile of victim-perception as well as other characteristic features in each group of offenders.

Violent offenders. Serving the longest prison sentences, these offenders usually committed their crime without partners on one victim only. A slight majority of their victims are males. The age range of the victims is mainly above 30 to 21-30. No specific trend as regards the victim-offender age gap was found. In most cases the victim was either a relative or an acquaintance of the offender. (The highest proportion of family relationship between them is in this group.) The great majority of these offenders blame situational factors or the victim as the reason for the offense. A considerable portion of those who were not previously acquainted with their victims would not have behaved differently if there had been a prior acquaintance between them. The proportion of cases where the victim was weaker, equal or stronger was evenly distributed. In most cases the offender chose the victim. However here we found the highest proportion of cases in which the victim was chosen by chance. Although in most cases the offender admitted causing suffering to the victim, in quite a considerable proportion of cases such suffering was denied. Most offenders perceived the victim as either completely or partially guilty for the offense. Almost all offenders were unwilling to compensate the victim (or his relatives).

Property Offenders. Usually, property offenders committed their crime with partners, and in many cases (more than in any other group) there was no specific personal victim. In cases of personal victims, these were mainly males. Victims of these offenders were older than those of other groups. In most cases the offender was at least five years younger than the victim. Usually they were strangers to each other. The reason for the offense was mainly material gain. Most offenders would not have committed the offense if they had known the victim previously. The victim's strength was not taken into consideration in the great majority of cases. In this group more than in any other the victim was chosen by a partner rather than by the offender. Most offenders in this group claim that the victim did not suffer. They perceive themselves as completely guilty, but are unwilling to compensate the victim.

Fraud and Forgery Offenders. These offenders are mainly of European origin (unlike the others who are mainly of Oriental origin). They are older, more educated, and were sentenced to shorter periods of imprisonment in comparison to the other three groups. Their offenses were mostly committed without partners, in many cases against more than one victim, of both sexes. In most cases victim and offender were acquaintances or relatives. The reason for the offense is mainly material gain. Of those who did not know their victims prior to the offense one-third would commit the offense even if they had not been acquainted with the victim. Here, as in the previous group, the strength of the victim was not considered at all by the offender. The victim was chosen mainly by the offender. Most offenders admit that they caused suffering to the victim, they perceive themselves as completely guilty and are willing to compensate the victim.

Sex Offenders. These offenders are the youngest and least educated. About half committed the offense with partners. Usually one female victim was involved. Most victims were below the age of twenty, and the victim-offender age-gap was usually less than five years (in either direction). Victims and offenders were usually strangers to each other. A great majority of the offenders see the victim or their own state of mind as the reason of the offense. All those who did not know the victim prior to the offense would not have committed it if such a knowledge had existed. In most cases the victim was perceived as weaker. However, in a considerable proportion of cases this was not taken in consideration. The victim was usually chosen by the offender. Most offenders deny causing any suffering to the victims, perceive the victims as completely or partially guilty, and are unwilling to compensate them.

Although our findings may have possible implications in several areas of victimological study, we will concentrate in the present discussion on those findings which are relevant to some experimental work done on victim-perception.

According to the equity theory (Macaulay and Walster 1971; Walster et al. 1973), one of the psychological consequences of doing harm is self-concept distress. There is a universally accepted moral code that one should be fair and equitable in dealings with others. Therefore harming another violates a normal individual's ethical principles and conflicts with self-expectations. While admitting that delinquents often seem to behave as if the exploitation of others was completely consonant with their self-expectation, the above-mentioned authors add that the evidence nevertheless suggests that even deviants do internalize standards of fairness, at least to some extent (Walster et al. 1973).

Our aim at this point is to find out whether some of our findings do fit a generalization made on the basis of experimental work in this field.

On the basis of the above mentioned and other works (like Stokols and Schopler 1973) our assumption is that the greater the actual suffering and harm caused to the victim, the greater is the harm-doer's distress, and therefore the greater will be his need to restore psychological equity. This will be done by blaming the victim for his misfortune, denying his suffering, and refusing to compensate him (based on Propositions III and IV of Walster et al. 1973).

The only way of objectively evaluating the damage and suffering caused to the victims in our study is by the severity of the punishment to the offender. By doing this we assume that when judging an offender, the severity of his offense is an important (although not the only) factor taken in consideration. According to this assumption the most severe cases in our study are those of the violent offenders and next come (in declining order) sex offenders, property offenders, and fraud offenders. Some of our findings are in almost exact accordance with this order of severity. The violent offenders, more than any other group, place full responsibility for the offense upon the victim. Next in this trend are the sex offenders, while property offenders are much lower in this respect, and none of the fraud offenders place the full guilt upon the victim. Similarly, violent offenders express the lowest willingness to compensate the victim; sex offenders are a bit higher (but still very low); property offenders are considerably more willing to compensate; and most fraud offenders, are willing to compensate the victim.

The findings as regards the guilt of the offender provide additional support to our above-mentioned assumption. Among the less severe groups, property and fraud offenders (where according to our assumption there was less damage and suffering caused to the victim and therefore less psychological distress), we find a much higher proportion of those who admit full guilt for the offense, while the other two groups mostly deny their guilt in order to restore equity.

In our interpretations we do not overlook the large empirical evidence on victim precipitation in violent and sex offences (Wolfgang 1958; Amir 1971; and others). Nevertheless, our basic assumption is that in spite of the actual contribution of the victim, in these offenses the offender finds himself in a state of strong self-concept distress. By derogating the victim and blaming him for the offense, these offenders are actually trying to restore the psychological equity between themselves and the victim.

However, as we have shown, our four groups of offenders did differ from each other in many other aspects as well, apart from the severity of sentence. Moreover, we are dealing here with different types of behavior, different personalities, etc. Therefore, what is needed is more controlled research on this topic with actual offenders.

An important aspect of such research with penalized offenders is that here we are dealing with harm-doers who were punished for their behavior, while in the experimental studies the harm-doers were not punished. Therefore in future studies these two aspects--degree of suffering caused to victim and severity of punishment to the offender—should be investigated and controlled in an adequate way.

These studies, besides their theoretical value, may also be of practical importance, especially in trying to find out in which types of offenders or situations compensation to the victim by the offender should be introduced

Our findings also have an implication as regards the interrelationship between the three important variables discussed in this paper: the offender's perception of his guilt, of the victim's suffering, and his willingness to compensate the victim. It is quite clear and not surprising that when the offender denies both his guilt and the suffering of the victim (like the sex offenders in our study) he will be unwilling to compensate his victim. However, what we have further shown in a clear way is that if only one of the first two variables exists, there will still be no willingness on the part of the offender to compensate the victim. Offenders who admit their guilt but deny suffering on the part of the victim (like property offenders), or those who deny their guilt but admit the victim's suffering (like violent offenders), are still unwilling to compensate the victim. It is only when the offender both perceives himself as guilty and the victim as suffering from his behavior, that his willingness to compensate the victim will be the greatest. On the basis of our findings we may conclude that from the point of view of the offender, his guilt or the victim's suffering, when appearing alone, are only necessary but not sufficient conditions for his willingness to compensate the victim. Only their joint appearance produces the maximal positive tendency on the part of the offender to compensate the victim.

These findings may have great relevance to some recent ideas according to which the offender should participate in the compensation of the victim. Therefore some more advanced research on these topics is also needed.

Research in the proposed direction will demand close cooperation of psychologists, criminologists, and lawyers in different positions in the administration of justice. The present study demonstrates the need and the importance of this type of research.

References

Amir, M. *Patterns in Forcible Rape* (Chicago: University of Chicago Press. 1971).

Amir, M. *Theoretical and Empirical Developments in Victimology* (Jerusalem: Academon, 1973), in Hebrew.

Berscheid, E., and Walster, E. "When does a harm-doer compensate a victim?" *Journal of Personality and Social Psychology* 6 (1967): 435-41.

Berscheid, E.; Walster, E.; and Barclay, A. "Effect of time on tendency to compensate a victim." *Psychological Reports* 25 (1969): 431-36.

Brock, T.C., and Buss, A.H. "Dissonance, aggression, and evaluation of pain." *Journal of Abnormal and Social Psychology* 65 (1962): 192-202.

Davis, K.E., and Jones, E.E. "Changes in interpersonal perception as a means of reducing cognitive dissonance." *Journal of Abnormal Psychology* 61 (1960): 402-410.

Ellenberger, H. "Psychological relationships between criminal and victim." *Archives of Criminal Psychodynamics* 1 (1955): 757-90.

Landau, S.F.; Drapkin, I.; and Arad, S. "Homicide victims." Unpublished manuscript.

Macaulay, S., and Walster, E. "Legal structures and restoring equity." *Journal of Social Issues* 27 (1971): 173-87.

McClintock, F.H. *Crimes of Violence* (London: Macmillan, 1963).

Mendelsohn, B. "The origin of the doctrine of Victimology." *Excerpta Criminologica* 3 (1964): 239-44.

Nagel, W.H. "The notion of victimology in criminology." *Excerpta Criminologica* 3 (1963): 245-52.

Schafer, S. *The Victim and His Criminal* (New York: Random House, 1968).

Siegel, S. *Nonparametric Statistics for the Behavioral Sciences* (New York: McGraw-Hill, 1956).

Stokols, D., and Schopler, J. "Reactions to victims under conditions of situational detachment: The effects of responsibility, severity, and expected future interaction." *Journal of Personality and Social Psychology* 25 (1973): 199-209.

Sykes, G.M., and Matza, D. "Techniques of neutralization: A theory of delinquency." *American Sociological Review* 22 (1957): 664-70.

von Hentig, H. *The Criminal and His Victim* (New Haven: Yale University Press, 1948).

Walster, E., and Prestholdt, P. "The effect of misjudging another: Overcompensation or dissonance reduction?" *Journal of Experimental Social Psychology* 2 (1966): 85-97.

Walster, E.; Berscheid, E.; and Walster, G.W. "New directions in equity research." *Journal of Personality and Social Psychology* 25 (1973): 151-76.

Wolfgang, M.E. *Patterns in Criminal Homicide* (Philadelphia: University of Pennsylvania Press, 1958).

Yates, F. "Contingency tables involving small numbers and the χ^2 test." Supplement to the *Journal of the Royal Statistical Society* 1 (1934): 217-35.

14

On the Psychodiagnosis of the Offender-Victim Relationship: An Approach to a Quantifying Description

Joachim Weber

The examination of the offender's personality has been an old tradition in everyday forensic judgment. Formerly this consisted only of psychiatric examinations, but nowadays it is usually complemented by psychological testings. This cooperation will often lead to a differentiated motivation analysis of the criminal act. The findings of victimology have decisively enlarged the increasing importance of the victim ("the other pole of criminogenesis," as Ellenberger[1] noted) in forensic judgment. This inclusion of the victim may aim at different points:

1. The general heuristic function. Scientific interest demands a study of the existing or supposed psychodynamic interaction between victim and offender.
2. The special case-oriented function. The criminal act in point is examined for possible projections and stereotypes. These are then analysed for their criminogenetic significance and ex post facto hypotheses are made.
3. The prognostic function. The predisposing variables (bio-psycho-sociological) have to be worked out and systematized for different crimes in order to contribute toward crime prevention.

In spite of these different aims research on the victim is still the exception for the following reasons:

1. The victim is no longer alive—often this is the fact in those very crimes where there has been antecedent to the act, a long interesting interaction between the parties.
2. There are real obstacles which make such an investigation impossible (e.g. the domicile of the victim is very remote; because of the victim's professional responsibilities, he can not take part in the investigation, or can not afford to give up the time).
3. The investigation would mean (understandably) a psychical stress; it would actualize the fears and feelings of guilt, which are connected with what has taken place and what has been suppressed or incompletely thought out.
   In comparison to the offender, the victim can't be compelled to take part in such an investigation. Therefore he often refuses to meet with the investigating team, because he does not wish to engage in the act any longer.

155

Moreover, a lot of offenses do not represent personal interaction, or in other words, a crime which engages offender and victim in a psychological interaction ("Beziehungsverbrechen"[2]). We are therefore only interested in two types of Fattah's victim system:[3]

1. the *latent victim*, whose psychological disposition consists for example of naïveté, superstition or greediness, and
2. the *provocative victim,* whose behavior in the precriminal situation is—in a conscious or unconscious way—an important criminogenetic contribution to the very crime.

It is understandable that, because of the difficulties described above, the number of suitable cases will only represent a small sample.

But even in those rare cases of forensic judgment when all necessary conditions are finally given, that is: (a) an Offender-Victim-Relationship (OVR) which occurred not only in a casual way and which includes at least a short prior communication; (b) a victim who can be found and who is able and willing to give evidence; and (c) a cooperative offender, there is still the problem of how this interaction can be psychodiagnostically instrumentalized. In other words: Which diagnostic procedures can be used to demonstrate the mutual projections and stereotypes?

The following scheme shows the two processes to be investigated:

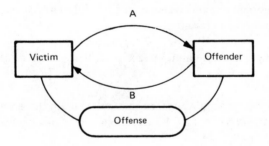

A = The victim develops a certain image of the offender (heterostereotype) and as a result behaves consciously or unconsciously in a crime-provocative fashion (e.g. the potential victim of rape, who flirts with the interesting and charming looking young man).

B = The offender also forms certain ideas about the victim which perhaps prove to be true in an ideal case (e.g. he interprets the behavior of the girl as desiring sexual adventure, only masked by current conventions).

These mutual expectations and attitudes could be easily revealed by a profound and detailed exploration of both participants in the crime. Often this is not only the best way; it is the only way. This is so because the behavior or the intelligence of the concerned person can disqualify the use of other procedures.

The disadvantage of this type of exploration, however, is that the information obtained doesn't represent standardized data, and will therefore permit only indirect comparisons. Nevertheless, if standardized tests are used a new dilemma is presented:

1. While some tests are objective, they are not always economic (e.g. the impatient victim will not complete the MMPI question).
2. Even though some tests are objective and economic, they are irrelevant; i.e., the score obtained is not interesting for the subject being studied (e.g. the IQ is not test).
3. Some other tests (Rorschach, TAT) may sometimes give us a fascinating insight into the individual way of perception. However, they do not explain the images which are mutually made by victim and offender, or they can not be quantified and controlled because their interpretation includes too many subjective parts.

Hence the proper procedure is to display standardized statements, which enable the parties concerned to demonstrate their autostereotype and heterostereotype in a quantitative way.

Semantic Differential

An appropriate method to reveal all the attitudes, expectations, bias, and projections which go into the make up of "social perception" may be the *Semantic Differential*[4] or *Polaritätenprofil*,[5] which is often used in social psychology research. It is this instrument which can limit the enormous number of possible characteristics and statements by which a person will describe another person or a certain topic, to a sample of standardized items. In other words: You take out a circumscribed, but arbitrarily defined sample from the universe of possible attributes, and represent the connotation field of a fixed subject (for instance the victim) as it relates to a fixed concept (offender).

Figure 14-1 is an example of a certain OVR, described with the Semantic Differential. The two profiles on the diagram show the offender-autostereotype (S_T) and his description of the victim (the victim-heterostereotype F_0). As you can see, this procedure delivers two profiles, and we can evaluate their similarity. This similarity may not only be described in an impressionistic way but also by

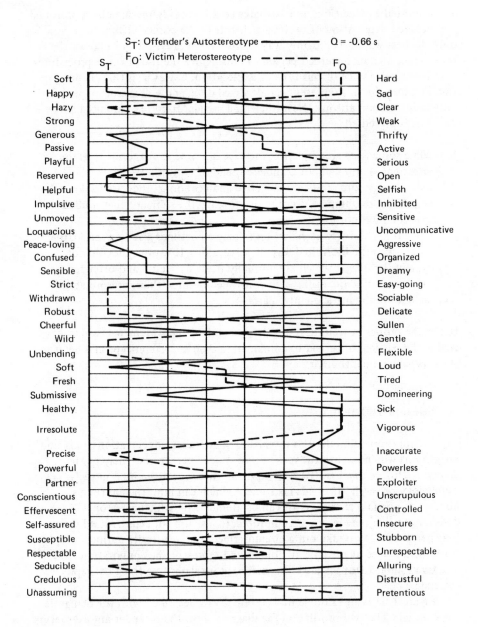

Figure 14-1. Semantic Differential*

---

*Unofficial translation from the German by Emilio C. Viano.

an exact mathematical operation. The Hofstätter formula gives us a coefficient of correlation:

$$Q_{xy} = 1 - \frac{D_{xy}^2 - k(M_x - M_y)^2 - (s_x - s_y)^2}{2\,s_x s_y},$$

which can vary from a maximum value + 1.00 (analogy) to a minimum value - 1.00 (contrast). Q = O means a partial contrast or an orthogonal-relation, because a zero-correlation is graphically represented by a 90° angle.

In the following example, fraud shall be used for an OVR to demonstrate in a general scheme the different kinds of possibilities auto-stereotype and heterostereotype may give to use for the pursuit of two victimological aims, the heuristic and prognostic. This scheme includes four topics, which have to be rated by means of the Semantic Differential:

1. The impostor in general.
2. The impostor in question.
3. The victim of fraud in general.
4. The victim of fraud in question.

These topics are rated by the offender, the victim, and an independent sample, which may stand for the population. This also will be used to characterize the impostor and the victim of fraud in general.

This scheme allows to form ten profiles, whose relationship could possibly display the expectations and distortions of perception which are connected with the criminal act and, moreover, the *victim's proneness* to the act (Figure 14-2).

Now we may ask: In what cases is there an *increased victim proneness*? Hypothetically, the following conditions come true:

1. $10 = 6$

   The similarity coefficient between the two profiles is significant: the victim fits exactly into the image the offender had of a victim of fraud in general.

2. $9 \neq 8$

   The victim has quite a different impression of the special offender than he does of impostors in general.

3. $6 = 2$ and $10 = 2$

   The offender's view of a victim of fraud in general is the same as the

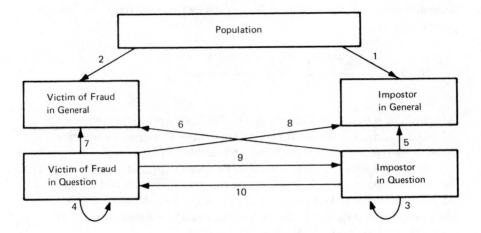

The numbers of the different rations signify:

1. The population's view of an impostor in general.
2. The population's view of a victim of fraud in general.
3. The offender's self-assessment.
4. The victim's self-assessment.
5. The offender's view of an impostor in general.
6. The offender's view of a victim of fraud in general.
7. The victim's view of a victim of fraud in general.
8. The victim's view of an impostor in general.
9. The victim's view of his special offender.
10. The offender's view of his special victim.

Figure 14-2.

population's view and the view that the offender has of the particular victim corresponds to the view which the general public has of the fraud victim in general.

4. $4 \neq 7$ but $4 = 2$

While the victim does not consider himself as a victim of fraud in general as this exists in his mind, his self-assessment contains just the same features which are regarded as typical for a victim of fraud in general.

If empirical studies could verify some of these hypotheses (for instance, that victims have quite a different perception of their offenders than they expect), it could be possible to prove assumptions about certain criminogenetic factors in a psychodiagnostical quantitative way.

Analysis of the mutual assessments, which are fixed in the Semantic

Differential, will give us as well interesting suggestions in the second-noted point, the *single case study*. A concrete instance of the Munich University Hospital's forensic-psychiatric department involves arson and may serve as an example:

A 55-year-old casual laborer W., who came from a wealthy worksman's family and who had been spoiled by his father as a youth, got a complete carpenter apprenticeship but had been working only as a driver and a representative. He described himself as a shirker and idler, but also as generous, good-humored, and of good nature. He had been twice divorced and in addition was responsible for two children born out of wedlock. He had been previously convicted at least four times, including among other things desertion, bodily injury, receiving stolen property, and neglecting his allowance for alimony. For the past ten years he has been living with the sixty-year-old waitress B., with whom he had had sexual intercourse only during their first months together. During this time he left her twice, but always returned soon for financial reasons. In the last months before the act, he always had the feeling of being taken advantage of and of being robbed by the woman. Moreover, he had been afraid that she will throw him out of the apartment, although he has contributed financially in the past from his pension. One day in autumn 1972, he once again thought he had been robbed by Mrs. B., who had left the house to go gambling, and in a sudden outburst of fury he set the apartment on fire.

The comparison of autostereotype and heterostereotype in this OVR by means of the Semantic Differential will lead to six similarity coefficients, which are shown in figure 14-3. Translated to a more comprehensible interpretation, the fifth coefficient in Figure 14-3, for instance, will reveal that the offender's favorable self-assessment (autostereotype) is significantly contrary to the unfavorable description of his victim (heterostereotype).

At this point we may resume the exploration, asking if Mr. W. consciously constructed this obvious distance from his partner in order to justify by this discrepancy his alienation and the quarrel between himself and the victim.

Giessen Test

A second method to quantify the autostereotype and heterostereotype in the OVR is shown by the comparison of profiles with the Giessen test.[6] This is a psychoanalytically planned questionnaire, which differs from other personality tests especially by including to a great extent social attitudes and reactions. Through the fact that this test can also be used for heterostereotyping, it gives us the ability to analyse the processes of transference in the OVR.

Figure 14-4 shows the autostereotype and heterostereotype of the already

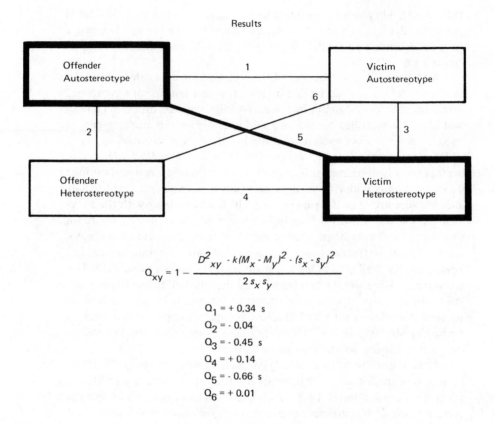

Figure 14-3. Case Study: Arson

noted example of arson. The interpretation can be done in a twofold manner:

1. The course of the two profiles is compared directly on the different scales of the data sheet. (For instance: neither the offender nor the victim thinks of himself as tyrannical; on the contrary, each describes the other as dominant.)
2. The similarity of profiles is calculated statistically.

The Spearman-Brown-correlation is not qualified, because it takes into account only the parallelism of the profiles, but not the value (position) of the actual scores. (It is possible to subtract a constant, which doesn't change the coefficient.)

New methods of single-case statistics, developed by Huber,[7] based on a generalization of Cattell's profile similarity coefficient—regarding the orthodox

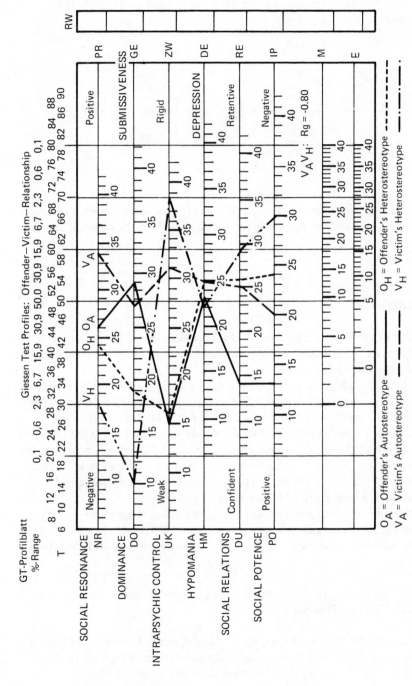

Figure 14-4. Giessen Test Profiles Offender-Victim-Relationship

theory of reliability—give us however the formula for a global similarity coefficient:

$$
R_g = \frac{2\sigma_x^2 \chi_{0.50}^2 - \displaystyle\sum_{j=1}^{m} \frac{D_j^2}{1 - r_{jj}}}{2\sigma_x^2 \chi_{0.50}^2 + \displaystyle\sum_{j=1}^{m} \frac{D_j^2}{1 - r_{jj}}}
$$

Referring to our concrete instance, a coefficient $R_g = -0.80$ between the auto-stereotype (V_A) and the heterostereotype (V_H) of the victim results. It shows that the victim is describing himself in exactly the opposite way than the offender does.

Rating Test

Another method to examine the OVR for analogies in the psychic structure is to elaborate the attitudes of both subjects toward an independent third topic, for instance, criminality.

Figure 14-5 shows a *rating* procedure for a sample of crimes, which are in fact not all identical with punishable offences, but are rated by general public opinion to a certain degree (and that is the psychological interesting fact!).

There is a scale, varying from 0 (no punishment) to 6 (severe punishment) which enables the rater to express his attitude. By this method one can get two profiles, reaching from liberality to dogmatic austerity, which allows us again to quantify by means of the product-moment-correlation the similarity or contrast of victim and offender attitudes.

Referring to our examples, there is a significant coefficient $r = +0.57$, expressing that victim and offender—in spite of all differences in their person-ality—produce a startling conformity in the condemnation of deviations by other persons.

TAT Matching Procedure

Finally a last procedure must be mentioned, which has still to be further developed and is planned to reveal unconscious correspondences in the OVR. It is a *TAT-Matching-Procedure*, which deals with ambiguous pictures

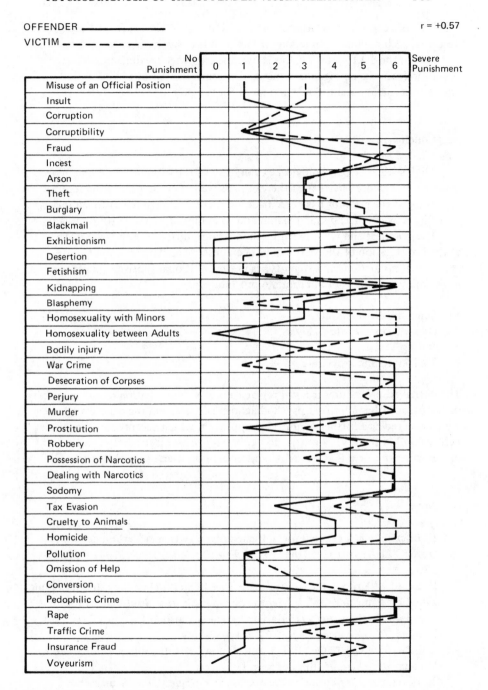

Figure 14-5. Criminality Rating

(15 TAT plates), whereby offender and victim have to choose from a pool of 15 cards, each naming a crime, one card which is to be matched with the pictures on the TAT plates. If this shows the existence of an identical interpretation from the ambiguous scenes and exceeds the law of probability, it would be a further quantifiable argument for the presence of an OVR.

Conclusion

The psychiatric-psychological exploration of the offender should be more often complemented by that of the victim as well. On the part of the forensic psychologist the attempt has been made to instrumentalize the assumed relationship between offender and victim and to exhibit it in a quantitative way.

The practical and test-related methodological difficulties, which appear at the investigation of the victim have been described. To also demonstrate the mutual projections and stereotypes in the OVR quantitatively, there are at the moment only four appropriate procedures:

1.   Semantic Differential
2.   Giessen Test Profile Analysis
3.   Rating Test
4.   TAT Matching Procedure

The described procedures can not replace a precise examination of the biography of the use of other approved psychodiagnostical tests. On the other hand, they are considered as a further quantifying approach, which accentuates the "social perception" in the OVR and tries to explore by these means the phenomenon of the conscious or unconscious attraction between these special "partners."

Notes

1.   H. Ellenberger "Psychologische Beziehungen zwischen Verbrecher and Opfer," *Zeitschrift f. Psychother. u. med. Psychol.*, 1954, (164), pp. 261-280.
2.   H. Schultz "Kriminolog. u. strafrechtliche Bemerkungen über die Beziehung zwischen Täter und Opfer," *Schweizer. Zeitschrift f. Strafrecht*, 1956, p. 171.
3.   A.E. Fattah "Towards a criminological classification of victims," *Internat. Criminal Police Review*, 1967, 22, pp. 162-163.
4.   C.E. Osgood, G.J. Tucci, P.H. Tannenbaum. *The Measurement of Meaning.* Urbana, Ill.: Univ. of Illinois Press, 1957.
5.   R. Hofstätter *Einführung in die Sozialpsychologie,* 1963, Stuttgart, p. 262.

6. D. Beckmann and H.E. Richter "Giessen-Test," 1972, Bern: Verlag Hans Huber, p. 9.

7. H. Huber "Verallgemeinerung des Cattellschen Profilähnlichkeitskoeffizienten r_p unter dem Aspekt der klassischen Reliabilitäts-theorie," *Zeitschrift f. exp. u. angew. Psychologie,* 1973, (1), XX, pp. 39-53.

15

Victimology: An Effect of Consciousness, Interpersonal Dynamics, and Human Physics

Joel M. Teutsch and Champion K. Teutsch

I. Introduction

A. Problem

The topic of victimology, as an aspect of human behavior and experience, has been generally considered up to now in a perspective that is neither consistent, scientific nor acceptable to every scientist, lawyer, theologian or layman. That the relationship between victim and victimizer should be governed by factors of whim or chance in a cosmos ruled by natural law appears unacceptable to us. Why, we ask, should man, who stands midway between macrocosm and microcosm, be an exception, apart from—instead of an integral part of—the rest of the univers? By the same token, if the concepts and equations of Newton, Einstein, and others have general validity, should they not also apply to man?

B. Investigation

1. Purpose. Our aim is to find useful answers to the preceding questions which serve as basic hypotheses for this study.

2. Scope. Our investigation includes the concepts and dynamics that apply to victimology with reference to practical examples from everyday life and finally to the assassination of President John F. Kennedy, an event that was and still is widely regarded as an accident stemming from the assassin's criminal intent and malice.

3. Method. By using a unique definition of consciousness, the interpersonal functional unit, and useful analogies, eight specific translations are made by us of concepts and formulae developed by Newton, Einstein, and others into what we have come to call Human Physics.

C. Most Specific Outcome

The most specific result of this investigation is that natural law as expressed by physics—and translated by us into Human Physics—has validity not only for victimology but for man's every form of activity. Therefore tragedies are predictable as well as preventable.

II. Method

A. Description

To establish a valid basis for the translation of the concepts and formulae of physics into their Human Physics equivalents, certain definitions had to be established. In addition, we had to develop new ways of looking at everyday phenomena encountered in interpersonal transactions. In doing so, we join the ranks of leading physicists. As Einstein said of Kepler's 'marvellous achievement,' '. . . knowledge cannot spring from experience alone but only from the comparison of the inventions of the intellect with observed fact." [1]

1. Victim. A victim, according to the dictionary, is a living creature sacrificed to some deity or as a religious rite, one who is killed, injured or subject to suffering, as well as one who is swindled or tricked. In most cultures he serves as an object of pity, of contempt, and for illustrating man's cruelty or injustice. There is one notable exception. It is the case, sanctioned by law, religion or popular opinion, where a malfeasant is punished by way of retribution for an illegal act. Such an event supposedly characterizes human or divine justice.

2. Consciousness. Victimization, like every form of human experience, is an effect of consciousness. Consciousness is a constant of life, an invisible attribute possessed by every human individual from—or even before—the moment of birth. To be conscious is to be alive. There exist as many variables or specific manifestations of consciousness as there are human individuals with their highly diversified and unique personal interpretations, interest, and experiences. We have found primary, secondary, tertiary, and even lower-order factors of consciousness that differ from individual to individual. At first consciousness is general or non-specific. As it is being built, it becomes structured or specific and then particularized. Subsequently, it will either enlarge or diminish in accordance with the prevailing circumstances.

For example, a baby may be only unconsciously aware of walking. However, as he focuses on the act, his consciousness, formerly nonspecific, becomes structured in that particular direction. As he builds a consciousness with respect to, say, walking, it is at first nonstatic or changeable. However, when he actually walks, the brain record gets involved. The structured and experienced consciousness of walking is recorded. Until modified, the brain remains static. Consciousness always substantiates the brain record, and the brain record substantiates consciousness.

Once the baby walks, he substantiates walking and forgets about his pre-vious non-walking state. Walking has become a constant for him. What he does with the newly acquired walking skill is a variable particularization that may manifest as a normal gait, pacing, hopping or running.

By the same process, the baby may build a consciousness of being a victim through appropriate interpretation or misinterpretation of parental abuse of the physical or oral type. His brother, though treated identically, may interpret the parental act in a more favorable light and emerge with a consciousness of being accepted or benefited. In the absence of modifying factors, the one who considers himself a victim will draw to himself as he matures victimizers in the form of teachers, classmates, employers, associates, a spouse, and even strangers in accordance with the undesirably structured consciousness. The brother will have considerably more pleasant interpersonal associations.

In each case, the brain as an impartial stimulus-response mechanism, spews out, without regard for sentiment, output only in accordance with the nature of the conceptual or empirical input it has been fed. The type of human behavior and mechanical performance encountered by any person is dictated, we have found, entirely by the individual consciousness factors that apply to him.

Actual experience of victimization is unnecessary for establishing a victim consciousness. Through fantasy, or identification with a victimized parent, as well as a victim depicted in a sermon, novel, motion picture, popular song, or a news report, an impressionable individual can become so conscious of the appropriate state that in due course he becomes an actual victim in his own life, realizing on a larger scale and on a basis modified by contemporary circum-stances the focused-upon fate of another or others in particular application to professional, marital or social situations. Conversely, by the same process, the consciousness of his victimizer can be acquired.

3. Functional Unit. The victim, it is apparent, cannot exist without the victimizer, who may be a human or nonhuman factor, such as an act of God or nature, sickness, accident or death. Victim and victimizer inevitably unite to form an interpersonal functional unit, in which the victimizer represents the positive or expectation-fulfilling factor while the victim is the negative or expec-tant factor. We have found that this functional unit operates in accordance with the same type of four-step cycle that characterizes the internal combustion engine. The process of interpersonal attraction, the pre-victimization activities, the actual victimization, and the subsequent inactivity or disassociation may be likened to the intake, compression, ignition, and exhaust strokes. At the same time, we have observed here a remarkable analogy to the childbirth process. Like a uterus that has just expelled one baby and gets ready for the conception of the next, the functional unit becomes active again in restructuring in appropriate environ-mental situation that permits the repetition of the same process, either on the same basis with the identical people or often on an entirely different basis and with totally different people. Nevertheless, the unit is based upon the same structure of consciousness which will and must produce the inevitable end result. It does not matter whether two, four, ten or one hundred million individuals constitute the complementary factors comprising the functional unit. The applicable dynamics and the outcome are the same.

Two facts stand out. There never is a victim who is not conscious of—and therefore does not identify with—the victimizer. Also, there never is a victimizer who is not conscious of—and therefore does not identify with—the victim. Consequently, as the victim's consciousness is modified, he will in due course become a positive factor who victimizes his former victimizer in the original functional unit or the positive factor in a new functional victimization unit. This principle is illustrated by Bruno Bettelheim's account of concentration camp inmates who abused other inmates in the same manner as their Nazi captors.[2] By the same token, as the victimizer's consciousness is modified, he will either become the negative or victimized factor in the original functional unit or in a new functional unit. This is precisely what happened to those in charge of concentration camps as well as their superiors.

In natural childbirth, the womb expels the mature fetus. By the same token, an environmental womb, once all human nurturing factors have made their necessary contributions, gives birth to the result that is natural for the particular ruling consciousness. With reference to our topic, victimology is the father, having intercourse with all that produces the victim and the victimizer as twins through an appropriate environmental womb. In terms of the applicable functional unit, the victimizer is the positive or male twin while the victim is the negative or female twin. To see whether a consciousness grows or diminishes, we must examine the appropriate results for the presence of essential nurturing factors.

4. **Interpersonal Dynamics.** It is noteworthy that those seemingly maltreating the victim often do so against their conscious intent. They may attempt to restrain themselves through will power or outside assistance. But invariably they will find themselves impelled by forces they as a rule cannot understand to play their critical or abusive rules. According to our findings, these forces are extrasensory, physiological, and electrical in nature.

a. **SSP.** The process by which the victim and the victimizer attract each other, often over great distances, is, we contend, supra-sensory—because it involves intra- as well as extrasensory processes—in nature. It originates in certain centers located in the victim's brain. There is stored learning about previous incidents in which he felt himself or others victimized. This learning actuates impulses on a frequency apparently located in the infrared range of the spectrum. Much like the carrier wave emitted by a radio station, these impulses are transmitted through space to the corresponding centers in the often totally unaware victimizer's brain. There they seem to instigate automatically the motivation, in terms of reasons that appear plausible or vital to him (but which usually are mere rationalizations), for contracting or encountering the victim so that he can interact with him in accordance with their complementary conceptual or empirical framework. The victimizer, we believe, also sends out complementary signals to attract the victim to himself. Children may be regarded as extensions of their parents because until they acquire a will of their own they act, react, and experience in accordance with the latters' consciousness.

Seen in this light *supra-sensory perception* (SSP) governs every type of interpersonal transaction, regardless of the end result. Every person, without exception, at all times uses SSP both consciously and unconsciously. But SSP is a faculty over which man has no monopoly. The female mosquito, for example, uses it to 'call' her male partner during the mating season. By rubbing her wings against the belly, she releases infrared signals that reach him over distances of up to thirty miles. All animals communicate in a similarly unique fashion.

b. **Physiology**. Once victim and victimizer have established contact, their respective nervous systems appear to dictate what takes place between them. We have already likened the victim's brain to a computer programmed by the conscious self. The same sort of stimulus that instigates the emanation of supra-sensory commands to the villain also triggers off nerve impulses flowing through the ganglia to the neurons. As these impulses reach the dendrites or nerve endings via the axones, centrons, and synapses, they cause the release of identical impulses in the dendrites of the individual who alone is capable, because of his unique preconditioning, to act as the expectation-fulfilling complementary human factor. By the same principle, the victimizer also induces, through the functions of his nervous system, complementary impulses in this victim's dendrites which flow to the cerebral hemispheres through the applicable neurons and ganglia.

c. **Electricity**. The preceding process may be likened to that involved in mutual induction. This well-known phenomenon occurs when an electrical current is increasing or decreasing in a circuit, and an electromotive force—and therefore also a current—are established in a neighboring circuit which shares the same field. The principle of self-induction may also be applied. We consider every human individual as a unique electrical circuit, electromagnet as well as modified transformer exercising an inductive effect upon other human individuals and vice versa. Therefore we can explain all interpersonal transactions in terms that are as precise and irrefutable as those evolved by Faraday, Maxwell, and Hertz.

The victim's every undesirable experience reinforces his already established plane of reference. Electrically speaking, the voltage and electromotive force applicable to his circuit is increased. So is the force of attraction which he exerts on other human factors contributing to his victimization. Consequently, they and others will tend to view him externally as a victim in precise accordance with his own concept.

5. Inheritance. Our studies have also revealed the powerful influence of inheritance. This is explicable in terms of the electromagnetic field—since a child acquires and initially functions in the brain-wave frequency range of his parents—as well as genetics. We have found undisputable evidence that ancestral attitudes and experiences are contained, together with information about physical characteristics, in the DNA in a unique molecular form that varies from family to family and, actually, from individual to individual. This explains why children given up for adoption sometimes reproduce the patterns of behavior and experience of their real, but to them unknown, parents and grandparents rather than of their adoptive parents.

From the viewpoint of electricity and genetics, the die is cast for the human fetus from the moment of conception. Were it not for the remarkable powers available to each individual to alter his DNA and therefore the course of his destiny (see III, C.), the outlook for the offspring of victimized families would be bleak indeed. Needless to say, the brain-wave pattern as well as DNA structure of victims who are related to each other bear a striking resemblance to each other. But, we assert, blood relationship is not a prerequisite for this sort of similarity. A potential victim from a family with a long history of persecution in, say, Poland probably does not differ drastically, as far as EEG and DNA are concerned, from a similar individual residing in South Africa or Vietnam, whose skin color is black or yellow, respectively. These people are closely related to each other because they came from the same mental though not physical family. As for the concept of victimology, mental relationship is more important than physical relationship.

6. Cosmology. The youngster in our example may also be regarded as the sun of a solar system in which those who victimize him, from his father on, constitute the planets. They are attracted to him by a centripetal force that is proportional to the strength of his self-concept as a victim. They revolve in their orbits around him because of this centripetal force and the centrifugal force resulting from their own consciousness. These human planets will remain in their fateful orbits as long as the conditions responsible for their linkup with the victim prevail. When he, through conscious effort, appropriate action or fortuitous experience, modifies or gives up his concept as a victim, the centripetal force holding them together diminishes and permits him to enter a new orbit or human solar system where he can victimize another human in a victim consciousness. Another alternative allowing for the dissolution of this unholy alliance occurs when a human planet, again through conscious effort or experience, gives up his victimizer role. This changes the centrifugal force holding him in the old orbit to the point where he can enter an orbit in another solar system that has a more beneficial purpose. On the other hand, such a human planet may also concentrate so greatly on his own abusive behavior and the victim's experience that he will leave his former orbit to become the sun or center of a new solar system in which he assumes the victim role. Conversely, the former victim may also identify with his oppressors and leave his position as the sun in his own system to emerge as a human planet revolving around a human sun that plays his former role as victim.

In any human solar system there can move and have their being only human factors and others that have the identical or at least complementary consciousness. This is another way of expressing the victim-victimizer relationship, which we have already described in terms of mutual induction.

In case two individuals with an overt or covert intent to harm another or others meet, they will reinforce each other in their capability to attract one or more potential victims. In terms of electricity, they will double—or, depending upon the nature of their association, multiply—the voltage powering their joint circuit. This will tend to induce an equally strong current in an adjacent or distant complementary circuit. Using the cosmological analogy, they may also be regarded as human double stars in a human solar system which, to remain in balance, requires the existence of a human planet or several such planets in a victim consciousness to assure the survival of the system. The same may happen even if the two individuals forming the system are conscious of others who have inflicted or are inflicting harm upon human victims.

Should two individuals be conscious of harm to themselves or others, there exist several possibilities. First, they may form a functional unit in which one becomes the harm-inflicting component while the other becomes the victim. Second, the two individuals could reinforce each other in their undesirable expectations until the emergence of one human factor or several such factors who will enable them to play their consciously or subconsciously preordained victim roles. Their expectation of harm must be as strong as the tendency to inflict harm of the one human factor or other human factors they attract. Conversely, the intent or fear to do harm by one person or more persons must be equivalent to the complementary expectation of harm latent in the victim or victims. The crucial factor is not the number of people involved but the strength of the applicable singular and collective consciousness. What matters is not quantity but quality or intensity.

It is obvious that the space occupied by any human solar system represents a unified field. From what we know about physics, perfect balance must prevail within this field. Whenever an old planet leaves or a new planet enters a system, there must be an appreciable change in the dynamics responsible for the perpetuation of the system. To avoid the vagaries of psychology, sociology, and other so-called humanistic fields, we looked for and found accurate explanations for all interpersonal phenomena only in physics.

B. Human Physics

1. **Newton's Laws.** The laws of Newton are still valid in the physical

universe, except when we approach considerations involving the speed of light
as covered by Einstein's Theory of General Relativity. Since man, according
to our reasoning, is an integral part of the universe, they must also apply to
Human Physics, provided we can succeed in translating Sir Isaac's discoveries
into their conceptual and mathematical equivalents with reference to man.
This is what we first learned to do with Newton's first law, the law of inertia.

    a. First Translation. A body moving with uniform velocity, Newton
showed, continues to move forever unless a force acts upon it. In physics,
a body is defined in terms of mass or m as follows: $m = W/g$, where W equals
weight and g equals gravity. To determine the strength of consciousness m_h
(or mass in application to man) as the equivalent of weight, we learned to
define consciousness as the product of interest or motivation M, attention
on—or identification with—one's own and others' efforts and experiences A,
interpretation as an aggregate of attitude and reaction R, and number of appropriate experiences N (i.e., $W = M \times A \times R \times N$). The Human Physics equivalent
for gravity we have learned to assume to be the product of the influence of
inheritance I, the degree of guilt G, the effect of adverse habit patterns H, and
the personal degree of confidence C. Consequently,

$$m_h = \frac{M \times A \times R \times N}{I \times G \times H \times C} \tag{1}$$

We have learned to use this formula with excellent results in computing consciousness of various types for human individuals. To establish a feasible
numerical rating scale, we have allowed the values for M, A, and R to range
from zero to ten. Obviously N can extend from zero to a number approaching
infinity. In similar fashion, the values for I, G, H, and C can vary from zero to
ten, depending upon the case.

    To simplify the task of computing consciousness, we have developed the
following rough equation for interest or motivation M:

$$M = i \times t \tag{1'}$$

where i is the intensity in degrees ranging from zero to ten and t the percentage of time devoted to a given object or task. For instance, a man spending 80
percent of his time on his job with only 2 degrees of interest will receive an M
score of 1.6 units (or $2 \times .80$). He could achieve the same score by devoting
only 20 percent of his total time available but by displaying 8 degrees of interest.

    b. Second Translation. As our previous discussion indicates, con-
sciousness never is static or has uniform motion. Therefore to tell us what
happens when outside forces act on the human consciousness, we must consider
Newton's second law. It states that if a force is applied to a body, the body

acquires an acceleration in the direction in which the force acts and proportional in magnitude to it, or $F = ma$, where F equals force, m the mass, and a the acceleration. The latter law is a mere corollary of the first law. The two laws point out that it is not a question of supplying a force to maintain a constant linear motion, but that a force is required to prevent it, once it is started.

In translating Newton's second law into Human Physics, we had to arrive at definitions for F and a that apply to all human individuals with the same universality as our definition for m. Accordingly, we have found F_h (force or effort in application to man) to be the product of m_h and a_h, the acceleration with which it, as it gathers momentum, produces an appropriate result, or:

$$F_h = m_h \times a_h \tag{2}$$

To compute the accurate value for a_h, it is necessary to determine the uniform motion or constant velocity (in terms of seconds, minutes or other units of time) with which a given consciousness produces incidents according to its nature. In case of uniformly accelerated motion where the velocity is not constant but changing uniformly, or even more complicated motions, special conceptual and mathematical considerations are necessary.

c. **Third Translation.** To simplify matters, we did not indicate so far a factor that must be considered when computing precisely the actual strength of the mass or consciousness. In case an individual striving for, say, freedom from victimization assists another or others who have the same goal, the effect for him is mathematically predictable. According to Newton's third law, to every force there is an equal and opposite reaction force. In terms of Human Physics:

$$F_h = R_h, \tag{3}$$

where F_h equals the human action or effort, while R_h is the appropriate reaction or reward. This means that the individual would benefit from his good deed in the form of greater freedom. Consequently, factor N in Equation (1) actually consists of the number of his own favorable experiences plus the number of similar experiences he helped produce for another or others. Mathematically speaking,

$$N = \sum Ex_p + \sum Ex_o, \tag{4}$$

where the suffix p equals personal experiences and the suffix o equals the experiences of others. For practical purposes, physical effort or support equals mental effort or support (see pp. 180 and 181).

The second part of our third translation pertains to an individual striving for freedom from victimization but opposing another or others in thought or deed, thus causing victimization for him or them. According to Newton's third law and Human Physics, he would suffer failure in return. This means that N in (1) would have to be reduced as follows:

$$N = \sum Ex_p - \sum Ex_o \tag{5}$$

Theoretically at least, this means that the latter sum could exceed the former. In that case, N—and therefore also m_h—would have a minus value.

Of course, factors M, A, and R with reference to another individual or others can differ drastically from the same factors with reference to the one under consideration. Consequently, the initial consciousness Equation (1) can be stated with greater accuracy as follows:

$$m_h = \frac{M \times A \times R \times N \pm M_1 \times A_1 \times R_1 \times N_1 \pm \ldots M_n \times A_n \times R_n \times N_n}{I \times G \times H \times C} \tag{6}$$

where the suffix 1 applies to the primary individual's motivation, attention, attitude, and contribution to appropriate experiences with regard to one person, while the suffix n applies to the same factors with regard to a number of persons ranging from two to infinity benefited or harmed by him. From this equation it is obvious that a person desirous of freedom from victimization enhances his chances by assisting another or others. At the same time, he assures his eventually becoming a victim by victimizing another or others. (We propose that the international unit of mental mass or consciousness be defined as:

$$m_h = 1 \text{ joel (pronounced: } j\bar{o}\ \partial 1), \tag{7}$$

where all factors from M to C have a unit value of one, while $\Sigma Ex_o = 0$. - CKT)

Not discussed so far, but worthy of mention, are the effects of thought and word patterns favoring or opposing a given result. For simplicity's sake, we will merely include them in the numerical values for M, A, and H. In many cases, they deserve special consideration and mathematical treatment because of their great influence on the end result.

d. **Fourth Translation.** The force of attraction between any two bodies in motion can be determined by Newton's fourth law, the law of universal gravitation: $F = m_1 \times m_2/d^2$, where F is the force of attraction, m_1 and m_2 are the masses of the bodies involved, and d^2 is the square of their distance. In terms of Human Physics, when one individual has a consciousness m_{h_1} and another a consciousness of m_{h_2} the force of human attraction F_h between them must be:

$$F_h = \frac{m_{h_1} \times m_{h_2}}{d_h^2} \tag{8}$$

where d_h^2 is the square of their difference of consciousness. This means that when two individuals have the identical consciousness with regard to one area of interest, such as victimization, $m_{h_1} = m_{h_2}$. At the same time, their difference of consciousness must be zero. Consequently, F_h equals ∞. This means the two will attract each other with a force of infinity. On the other hand, should the consciousness of two individuals differ drastically (i.e., infinitely from the viewpoint of mathematics), the force of attraction between them would be zero. In the first case, they are bound to meet and interact with each other until either one or both undergoes a change in consciousness. In the second case, they can never meet. On the basis of (8) it is easy to see why some persons from different parts of the earth—the members of this Symposium, for example—meet for relatively brief periods of time, why others marry or remain together for decades, and why still others, though living in the same building or city block, never come face to face. Of course, they share other consciousness factors that dictate their geographic though not mental proximity.

2. **Einstein's Theory of Relativity.** Newton's mechanics served a purpose typical for his day. It describes motions of objects that move much slower than light. For that matter, so does the special theory of relativity. But when we consider such phenomena as the electromagnetic field, interpersonal communication, thought, and light, we must resort to the general theory of relativity.[3] Einstein's mass-energy equation states that $E = mc^2$, where E is the energy, m the mass, and c the supposedly constant speed of light (i.e. approximately 299,792 kilometers per second).

a. **Fifth Translation.** We have learned to regard c not as a universal constant or the ultimate speed but as a variable depending upon the human consciousness. Einstein's prediction that light rays are influenced or bent under the influence of gravity has been confirmed experimentally by Eddington and others. Later, Heisenberg pronounced his Principle of Uncertainty, according to which the very act of observing disturbs the system.[4] The notion that the observer cannot be separated from the experiment was unacceptable even to Einstein. Our research has shown that even supposedly objective X-rays and photographs do not indicate the truth about physical phenomena but the human concept or misconcept. For instance, when photographers did not know that a certain woman was six months pregnant, their full-size pictures of her did not indicate her condition. After they had learned of it, their photographs, taken the same day two hours later, showed the appropriate enlargement of her usually slim figure.[5] In experiments conducted at the

Boeing Scientific Research Laboratories, and elsewhere, it was found that when the human factor was included in the observations, the quantum theory—or at least one of its axioms—does not apply.[6] Electron speed, we assert, depends not so much on the human individual's physical but on mental mass. The less influenced an individual or group constituting a human solar system is by a consciousness such as victimization, the more his 'light' or brain-wave emanations approach the speed of light. On the other hand, the more a human individual or group is controlled by undesirable (or 'grave') consciousness factors, the more 'depressed' he must be not only attitudinally but electrically. Consequently,

$$E_h = m_h c_h^2 \, , \tag{9}$$

where E_h is human energy, m_h consciousness and c_h the applicable 'light' or brain-wave pattern.

b. Sixth Translation. The assumption that there are speeds in the universe greater than 300,000 km/h, first pronounced by us in 1954 and later by George Sudarshan and Gerald Feinberg,[7] implies the existence of tachyons that always travel faster than light. Translated into Human Physics, this means that there must exist mental solar systems and galaxies governed by a consciousness higher than contemporary man can conceive. In practical terms, this merely confirms the accuracy of our assumptions leading to the establishment of Equation (9). This equation naturally must apply to thought, a unique energy form. Obviously it is capable of traveling at speeds much faster than light because we can transport our thoughts instantaneously to any point in the universe which light would take many years to reach. Electricity and magnetism are essentially the same phenomenon or different aspects of the same phenomenon. The union between the relativity theory and the quantum theory produced antiparticles into being, of which the positron is one. When it and the electron annihilate each other, they yield gamma rays or two light quanta, each of which carries away a minimum energy of mc^2. These are also obtained when a radioactive particle is converted into, say, light radiation.[8]

In nuclear fusion, a neutron and a proton can join to form a deuteron, losing as they do so a certain amount of energy, which is carried off as a light quantum. According to Einstein, this energy loss means that the deuteron must have less mass than the sum of its parts. This is indeed the case, and the difference in mass is called the 'binding energy' of the deuteron, since to break the deuteron up again we must supply this amount of energy. These facts make it feasible for us to suggest that mental emanations, especially the subconscious or unconscious sort, influence if not create matter and events. We have accumulated considerable evidence in support of this assumption. The energy loss encountered in the fusion process and the energy required to break up a deuteron by the photodisintegration process are, proportionately, equivalent to man's mental as well as, in most cases, physical effort required to produce a given result. Conscious thought is merely a contributor or an effect of the much stronger *basic inner direction* (B.I.D.) which we have found to be an aggregate, unique for every human individual, of genetic, unconscious, subconscious, as well as conscious factors, while functioning on a conscious as well as subconscious basis. This B.I.D. directs the flow of life so that all events, including personal and interpersonal human behavior and experience, as well as mechanical performance in the applicable functional unit or units, invariably cooperate to assure the appropriate outcome. Seen in this light, every human individual moves in accordance with his B.I.D., regardless of his or another's conscious reaction or interpretation.

Subconscious emanations represent a considerable force when we consider the mutual gravitational attraction among the energy particles involved. The excess energy that is available from gravity is converted into radiation. According to Helmholtz, the same principle, though later modified, pertains to the formation of the sun. This fact further justifies our reference to human solar systems. It is easy to see that the emanations or radiation from one individual interact with those of other humans in the same consciousness to reinforce each other to exercise a powerful synergistic effect upon all applicable human, material, and other environmental factors.[9]

c. **Seventh Translation.** As we reported in a previous publication,[10] the environment reflects man's consciousness. Einstein's theory of an expanding universe has its perfect analogy in Human Physics with respect to a consciousness as it is being built and produces appropriate experiences peculiar for it on a steadily expanding basis. The latter phenomenon is the Human Physics equivalent to the so-called red shift. Conversely, the fact that there are many cases of a diminishing consciousness, in accordance with our earlier observation, could explain the theory of a contracting universe advanced by some physicists. The gradual deceleration of appropriate events encountered in such cases is the Human Physics equivalent of the so-called blue shift that applies when objects approach the observer. This analogy coincides with the view of many experts who have come "to consider space, time and mass as illusions in the same way temperature is a sensory illusion."[11] According to philosophers and scientists from Democritus to Einstein and more recent authorities, " . . . the whole objective universe of matter and energy, atoms and stars, does not exist except as a construction of consciousness, an edifice of symbols shaped by the senses of man."[12]

The geometry of the universe appears to be a Friedmann geometry, with positive curvature, like a sphere, and with the property that light emitted at any given point will eventually come back to that point.[13] This idea, contained in Einstein's general theory of relativity, expresses Newton's third law (as expressed by our Third Translation) in an entirely different way. To us, this is a marvelous illustration of the unity of all scientific inquiry. Newton and

Einstein may have not been aware of it, but they both restated the Golden Rule in non-biblical terms.

d. **Eighth Translation.** The idea, already advanced by us, that man can move in several orbits in one human solar system or several such systems where he is the sun or planet as either victim or victimizer is perfectly analogous to findings by quantum physicists, reported by Arthur Koestler, who are unable to accept the atom as simply a miniature solar system. They discovered that the "electrons kept jumping from one orbit into a different orbit without passing through intervening space—as if the earth were suddenly transferred into the orbit of Mars without having to travel."[14]

III. Application

A. John F. Kennedy

We have selected the case of the late President of the United States to illustrate the preceding concepts and Human Physics equations.

1. **Consciousness.** Despite appearances and publicity to the contrary, JFK was conscious of being a victim of disease and in danger of death from early childhood on. Doctors, his family and he himself expected his premature end throughout his lifespan. As a young child he suffered several attacks of dangerous sickness. According to what he told Columnist Joseph Alsop, he had ". . . a sort of slow-motion leukemia . . ." (probably Addison's disease) and that he would ". . . probably last until . . . forty-five."[15] Besides, he was frequently his elder brother's victim. Joseph P. Jr. was the apple of their father's eye. Joseph P. Sr. groomed his first-born son early for the Presidency by discussing with him at table the issues of the day. But Joe Jr. won out over JFK not only in this important area but by taunting him in private as well as public and by beating him at sports. Once, in an around-the-block bicycle race, they collided head on. Typically, JFK lost. He required 28 stitches. Later, he was forced to quit Canterbury School because of a severe case of appendicitis. At Harvard University, while playing football, he injured his back. During World War II, a Japanese destroyer cut through JFK's small vessel, the PT 109, of which he was the captain. Two of his shipmates died, and for a moment he thought and felt the end had come as he was smashed across the deck with great force. Memorial services were held for him and his crew before their successful return.

In 1954 and again in 1955, he almost succumbed to serious disc operations on his back.[16] Further contributing to his consciousness of victimization were the deaths of his brother Joe Jr., in 1944, on a bombing mission over Europe, his brother-in-law, the Marquis of Hartington, in battle on Normandy a fortnight later, and the latter's wife and JFK's sister Kathleen in an air crash enroute to Cannes in 1948; his father's stroke and expected death in 1961; and the death of his son Patrick in 1963, an event that dashed forever his hopes of having another child from his wife. Another factor responsible for JFK's victimization was Joseph P. Kennedy's decree, based upon his own long-standing ambitions first for himself, then for his eldest son, that the reluctant JFK enter the political arena after Joe Jr.'s premature end.

Joe Sr. never stopped pushing his son ahead. He was already wearing a "Kennedy for President" tie while JFK was running for senator from Massachusetts against Henry Cabot Lodge. Rose Kennedy, JFK's mother, was also determined to boost her son's career. After all, her father, Boston Mayor John F. "Honey Fitz" Fitzgerald, had been beaten by the same Lodge's grandfather in the 1916 race for governor. In those days, Boston Irish Catholics considered themselves lucky to control City Hall.

JFK's victim consciousness was enhanced further by himself. On May 27, 1959, in reply to a letter from a friend of ours reminding him that no president elected in a year ending in zero had survived his stay in the White House, the future President wrote that he had never reflected on the matter, that it was "indeed, thought-provoking," and "should anyone take his phenomenon to heart . . . anyone, that is, who aspires to change his address to 1600 Pennsylvania Avenue . . . most probably the landlord would be left from 1960 to 1964 with a 'For Rent' sign hanging on the gatehouse door."[17]

Shortly after the 1960 election, his own father said, "Jack is the fellow who will give his life to this country."[18]

In his inaugural address, JFK said that "we shall pay *any* price . . . " On the same occasion, he referred to the time as one " . . . of maximum danger." His subconscious duly personalized these remarks.

Besides, JFK, as well as other members of the Kennedy clan, had acquired early a consciousness of futility or helplessness with regard to someone extremely close—his mentally ill sister Rosemary. Eventually, it applied to himself.

2. **Functional Unit.** The preceding facts make it evident that JFK was the negative factor in functional units in which sickness, his brother Joe Jr. (during their earlier years), the Japanese, his father, and eventually Lee Harvey Oswald represented the positive factors. Of course, in other areas and especially in politics he was the positive factor to several negative factors. Among them were Senator Lodge, Richard Nixon (whom he defeated in the 1960 presidential election), and Nikita Khrushchev (whom he out-maneuvered in the Cuban missile crisis).

3. **Identification.** During JFK's early years, President Abraham "Honest Abe" Lincoln had become his hero. He constantly read, talked, and dreamed about the Great Emancipator. For the young JFK, the life and death of Lincoln may be regarded as a tertiary consciousness factor. But when he entered the White House, it became primary for him. This was evident to the late Sam

Rayburn, Speaker of the House, and many others who commented on the Lincolnesque style of the new President's inaugural address. He spent his first night in the White House in Lincoln's room and bed and, on several evenings, together with his wife, read a book describing Lincoln's last days. JFK's Lincoln consciousness was further reinforced every time he saw, addressed, and thought of his secretary, Evelyn Lincoln (who feared for his safety and, like we and others, didn't want him to go to Dallas), as well as Lyndon B. Johnson, his vice president, whose surname was, because of the prevailing unconscious associations, the same as that of "Honest Abe's" successor. ("I'll give this damn job to Lyndon,"[19] he said prophetically upon finding himself criticized after the Bay of Pigs.) We see here the applicability of the principle of relative association.

To put it in a nutshell, JFK's brain record contained, first with regard to Lincoln, then with regard to himself, specific information pertaining to (a) being president, (b) being involved in Civil Rights, and (c) being assassinated. Mentally speaking, he had ceased to function as JFK but as a contemporary version, modified by contemporary circumstances, of his idol.

Jacqueline Kennedy made her husband's lying-in-state ceremonies and funeral arrangements conform to those for Lincoln. The coffin rested upon a catafalque duplicating Lincoln's. Later it was placed on the same catafalque in the Capitol rotunda that was used for President Lincoln on the same spot in April 1865. Next day, JFK's coffin was put on the caisson that had carried the body of FDR eighteen years before. Later in Arlington Cemetery, he was laid to rest in a grave on a little hill in front of the Custis-Lee mansion. Typically, it was a straight true line from the flag in front of this building across the grave to the center of the Lincoln Memorial. Earlier in the year, JFK had visited the cemetery, from where he enjoyed the magnificent view of Washington. "I could stay here forever," he told a friend. Mental law made sure that he—or at least his body—did.

4. Inheritance. This factor deserves only general mention here. Pat Kennedy, JFK's paternal great-grandfather, had been a victim of the Irish potato famine before succumbing to cholera at 35 in Boston. His son, P.J., a politically active saloonkeeper, and Mayor Fitzgerald, John's maternal grandfather, were successful up to a point. But eventually they became victims of James Michael Curley, their arch rival, who became Boston's mayor and fired and demoted all Fitzgerald appointees, as well as Yankee Protestantism, which controlled the state, and assured Fitzgerald's loss to Henry Cabot Lodge in the race for governor. P.J.'s son and JFK's father, Joe Sr., after becoming Ambassador to the Court of St. James, fell victim to his isolationism, which was in opposition to the anti-Hitler and pro-Allied policies of President Franklin D. Roosevelt (FDR).

5. B.I.D. Because of all the preceding factors, JFK's loyal subconscious had no choice but to interpret his B.I.D. to be death. This was especially true when he virtually assured the assassinations of South Vietnamese President Ngo Dinh Diem and his brother, Ngo Dinh Nhu, on November 1, 1963. Their fatal wounds were almost identical to the ones he sustained only three weeks later. On October 26, 1963, in a nationwide telecast, he had demanded ". . . changes in policy if not personnel" in the Diem government, which he also deprived of vital C.I.A. funds.[20] By the Saigon coup alone, JFK reduced the numerical value of N in Equation (5) and of m_h in Equation (6) to practically zero. Since the subconscious knows neither time, place nor person but only the one it serves, it may be regarded in JFK's case as a computer programmed by himself to assure his forceful removal from office.

As a result, JFK's consciousness was duly prepared. The environmental womb required for producing the appropriate event had to be in Dallas. Because there all the human nurturing factors, Oswald, Jacqueline Kennedy, Lyndon B. Johnson, and, later, Jack Ruby, contributed their personal backgrounds to enable JFK to play his preordained victim role. All principals were in their proper places according to their consciousness. The number of bullets and assassins does not really matter. A perfect baby, from the impartial viewpoint of consciousness, was born in the form of an assassination. (Human behavior, experience, and events, as we have previously shown, are no doubt directed by a collective consciousness or mind rather than by independent, consciously-directed, individual action. Otherwise, one would have to dismiss as accident or a fantastic coincidence the fact that the U.S. Army unit charged with conducting funeral ceremonies for deceased chiefs of state was well rehearsed for the JFK burial. The soldiers had prepared for a whole week for what they thought would be the death of the gravely ill former President Herbert Hoover. He lived almost another year.)

6. Table. Table 15-1 shows that similar mental factors were involved in the assassinations of Abraham Lincoln and JFK. A consciousness or patterns of success and accomplishment, short-period change, noncompletion and interruption, strong awareness of injustice pertinent to themselves and others, and mental illness, death and loss at the assassination site are found to apply, with minor deviations, for Abraham Lincoln, Joseph P. Kennedy, John F. Kennedy, Jacqueline Kennedy, John Wilkes Booth, Lee Harvey Oswald and his mother, Marguerite, Jack Ruby, and Lyndon B. Johnson.

As for mental illness, Abraham Lincoln was conscious of it, at least with regard to his wife Mary. He himself was often in melancholy moods, suffering states of deep depression. After their son Willie died in the White House, Mary Lincoln's prolonged agonizing prompted her husband to threaten to place her in an asylum. After his death, she was in fact institutionalized for a brief period. Joseph P. Kennedy, JFK, and Jacqueline Kennedy were conscious of mental illness and retardation because of Rosemary, the president's eldest sister. JFK's

Table 15-1
Mental Factors Involved in the Lincoln-Kennedy Assassinations

Consciousness (Patterns)	Lincoln	Joe, Sr.	JFK	Jackie	Booth	Mrs. O.	Oswald	Ruby	LBJ
Success & Accomplishment	Yes	Yes	Yes	Yes	Yes*	?	Yes*	Yes*	Yes
Short-period change (appr. every 3 yrs.)	Yes	Yes	Yes	Yes	Yes	Yes	Yes	Yes	Yes
Noncompletion & Interruption	Yes	Yes	Yes	Yes	Yes	Yes	Yes	Yes	Yes
Injustice	Yes	Yes	Yes	Yes	Yes	Yes	Yes	Yes	Yes
Mental Illness	Yes	Yes	Yes	Yes**	Yes	Yes	Yes	Yes	?
Death	Yes	Yes	Yes	Yes	Yes	Yes	Yes	Yes	Yes***
Loss at Assassination Site	Yes	?	Yes	Yes**	Yes	Yes	Yes	Yes	Yes
Assassination	Yes	?	Yes	Yes	Yes	?	Yes	Yes	Yes

*aspiration, fulfilled with murder
**probably acquired after marriage
***followed by political advance

©C.K. & J.M. Teutsch 1973, 1964

consciousness was open to an encounter with someone mentally imbalanced. "We are going into nut country today," he said to his wife, pointing at a black-bordered Texas newspaper advertisement that was extremely hostile to him.[21]

Evidence of mental instability if not illness is available about both Booth, Ruby, and Oswald. The latter had been found, at thirteen, to be "emotionally disturbed," but his mother ignored the psychiatrist's warning and removed her son from treatment.[22] Loss at the assassination applies to Lincoln, who lost a son while in office; to JFK, Lyndon B. Johnson, and the members of their families because they did not carry Dallas in the 1960 presidential election; to John Wilkes Booth, Lincoln's assassin, who was deeply affected by his victim's re-election, the victory of the North, and reverses in his acting career; and to Oswald and his mother who married and divorced in Dallas Edwin A. Ekdal, her son's stepfather, to whom he became attached. In the same city, Jack Ruby lost his manhood, according to medical records. He also experienced a sense of personal loss when JFK, whom he regarded as a friend, was murdered in Ruby's adopted city.

7. **Illustration**. Figure 15-1 shows that the assassination, in the center, was the result of the combined effects of each principal's conscious experiences as they filtered into the subconscious where they combined with the output of the other principals to produce the appropriate result. In every case, the applicable consciousness steadily enlarged itself until the crucial moment when it played its unique role contributing to the historic event. We have listed briefly the chief consciousness-building factors for Lee Harvey Oswald, Jacqueline Kennedy, Lyndon B. Johnson and Jack Ruby. Noteworthy is that Oswald had wanted to die, kill Major General Edwin A. Walker, and also identified with John Wilkes Booth, Lincoln's assassin. As his consciousness enlarged itself, he was virtually forced to play his tragic role, first as victimizer-assassin, then as victim. When he pulled the fateful trigger, his difference in consciousness from JFK was zero (in Equation [8]) because of the latter's role in the Saigon coup. Therefore F_h for them was infinite or inevitable. The same held true for Oswald and Ruby, when the latter, gun in hand, decided to murder the assassin. Eventually, Ruby, because of guilt, identification with other persecuted Jews, and the dynamics of Equation (3), became a victim whom even Attorney Belli's expertise could not save. The Dallas jury merely cooperated with Ruby's B.I.D.

Jacqueline Kennedy's consciousness had been prepared and built by her presence, at seventeen, when her beloved horse Donny had to be shot, her rejection, at twenty-one, by a man she loved, her experiences of a miscarriage, a still-born child, and the death of her son Patrick four months before the assassination. Besides, she had been deeply affected by her absence, in 1957, when her beloved father died a lonely death in a Manhattan hospital. She reportedly never forgave herself for not visiting him. Her consequent B.I.D.

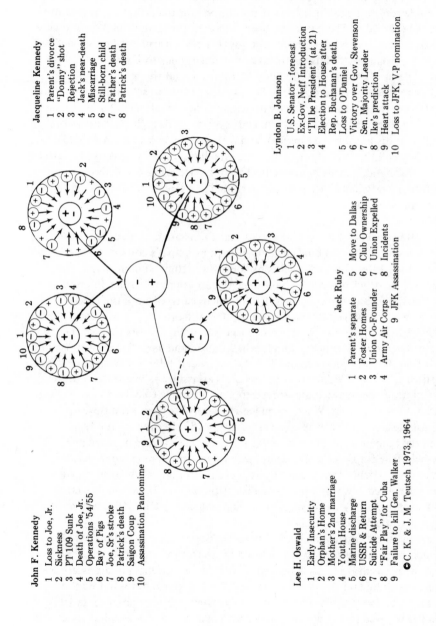

John F. Kennedy

1 Loss to Joe, Jr.
2 Sickness
3 PT 109 Sunk
4 Death of Joe, Jr.
5 Operations '54/55
6 Bay of Pigs
7 Joe, Sr's stroke
8 Patrick's death
9 Saigon Coup
10 Assassination Pantomime

Lee H. Oswald

1 Early Insecurity
2 Orphan's Home
3 Mother's 2nd marriage
4 Youth House
5 Marine discharge
6 USSR & Return
7 Suicide Attempt
8 "Fair Play" for Cuba
9 Failure to kill Gen. Walker

Jacqueline Kennedy

1 Parent's divorce
2 "Donny," shot
3 Rejection
4 Jack's near-death
5 Miscarriage
6 Still-born child
7 Father's death
8 Patrick's death

Lyndon B. Johnson

1 U.S. Senator - forecast
2 Ex-Gov. Neff Introduction
3 "I'll be President" (at 21)
4 Election to House after
   Rep. Buchanan's death
5 Loss to O'Daniel
6 Victory over Gov. Stevenson
7 Sen. Majority Leader
8 Ike's prediction
9 Heart attack
10 Loss to JFK, V-P nomination

Jack Ruby

1 Parent's separate   5 Move to Dallas
2 Foster Homes   6 Club Ownership
3 Union Co-Founder   7 Union Expelled
4 Army Air Corps   8 Incidents
                         9 JFK Assassination

● C. K. & J. M. Teutsch 1973, 1964

Figure 15-1. Principal Consciousness Factors Involved in Kennedy Assassinations

made as sure that she was physically present when her husband died as did his own B.I.D. It was strongly influenced by the fact that Mary Lincoln was also by her husband's side when he was shot.

Lyndon B. Johnson's consciousness played a powerful role in what happened at Dallas. He had become a U.S. congressman in 1937 after Representative Buchanan's death and a U.S. senator after Senator "Pappy" O'Daniel's death in 1948. Thus he was pre-conditioned to be first defeated in his quest for the presidency, for which he was mentally well prepared by many noteworthy factors, before succeeding at last upon JFK's demise. A thorough knowledge of life patterns by JFK and his advisers would have precluded the selection of the tall Texan. But LBJ's consciousness made him the logical aspirant to be JFK's running mate. When he was born in 1909 (exactly one hundred years after the birth of President Andrew Johnson), his father proudly announced, "A U.S. senator was born today."[23] Lyndon himself was less modest. He confidently predicted his becoming president while still a student at Southwestern State College. Decades later, Republican President "Ike" Eisenhower pointed to his seat when the able Democratic majority leader visited him in his office. "Some day," he said, "you'll be sitting in this chair."[24] Joe Cannon and other Democratic leaders had carefully groomed him for the nation's highest elective office. For a while, it looked like they had wasted their time. But JFK picked their man consciously to run with him and unconsciously to succeed him. He followed the example of Franklin D. Roosevelt, whom he had met and seen in the White House where his father, until his fall from grace, was a welcome and frequent visitor. FDR had insured his election to the presidency in 1932 by a political masterstroke—the selection as his running mate of John ("Cactus Jack") Vance Garner of Uvalde, Texas. (It is quite apparent that FDR exercised a strong mental influence on young JFK. With admiration, he focused upon the crippled leader his father had helped to reach the White House. By means of unconscious identification, JFK eventually suffered the back injury that was to give him trouble for the rest of his life. By the similar process of unconsciously associating physical handicap with the presidency, JFK's injury served as stimulus for Joseph P. Kennedy Sr. to initiate the sequence of events that propelled his son to the highest office in the land. Further proof of JFK's consciousness of FDR, who started the New Deal, was his decision to speak of the New Frontier.)

There were only two men JFK regarded as superior to himself. This first, in his younger years, was his brother Joe Jr. The second, after he came to Washington, was LBJ. After the already mentioned bicycle collision, Joe Jr. walked away seemingly without a scratch. JFK's face was a bloody mess. His brain at that time recorded that injury to himself meant no harm to the one he felt was superior to him. We can readily see why LBJ, subconsciously identified with Joe Jr. by JFK, was unharmed during the assassination. While the presidential jet stood, symbolically, on Texas soil, LBJ took the oath of office in the presence of the just widowed Jacqueline. Subsequently, in 1964, he was re-elected by a record margin before his victimization by his own Vietnam policies and a fatal heart attack.

8. **Human Physics.** In terms of Human Physics, JFK's consciousness m_h at the time of his inauguration can be calculated by use of Equation (6) to have been as follows:

$$m_h = \frac{9.6 \times 9.8 \times 9.1 \times 10 + 6(5.8 \times 6.1 \times 9.0 \times 2) - 2(3.8 \times 6.2 \times 8.2 \times 3 \times 7.4)}{2.3 \times 2.1 \times 3.8 \times 2.1} = 316 \text{ joels}$$

The numerical values used for the various factors in the equation are based upon mere assumptions. The space available here does not permit their detailed discussion.

At the time of his assassination, JFK's consciousness can be assumed to have been:

$$m_h = \frac{9.2 \times 2.1 \times 3.9 \times 14 + 6(3.2 \times 5.2 \times 6.8 \times 2) - 2(7.1 \times 6.8 \times 8.3 \times 2)}{9.3 \times 8.2 \times 8.8 \times 8.2} = .0014 \text{ joel}$$

The low values for A and R for himself stem from his growing identification with Abraham Lincoln and his awareness of conflict with Southern leaders of the Democratic Party. His purpose in coming to Dallas, in addition to building support for himself for the presidential election in 1964, was to give a boost to Senator Yarborough, who had been loyal to him for years. His active opposition had been to the leaders of South Vietnam. The effect of adverse inheritance factors is especially pronounced as long as the individual is unaware of it. The numerical value of his guilt, whether conscious or subconscious, was high. So was the adverse effect of his habit patterns as far as they related to undesirable aspects of his ideal (Lincoln).

His degree of confidence was low. While it was raining, the presidential party had arrived in Fort Worth and were jostled by the crowd in the dark. JFK was fond of mimicking others. For his wife, he acted out the would-be killer's role. Gesturing wildly, he pointed his index finger at the wall and jerked his thumb twice to show the action of the hammer. In pantomine, he dropped the gun and a briefcase, whirled in a deep crouch and "melted away in the crowd."[25]

Probably with the already mentioned hostile ad in mind he told the Fort Worth Chamber of Commerce, at what was to be his last breakfast, "This is a dangerous and uncertain world . . . " Before leaving the Texas Hotel for Dallas, he said to Kenneth P. O'Donnell and Mrs. Kennedy: "If anybody really wanted to shoot the President of the United States, it was not a very difficult job—all one had to do was to get on a high building some day with a telescopic rifle, and there was nothing anybody could do to defend against such an attempt."[26]

Further enlarging JFK's assassination consciousness was his call, a few hours before the final trip to Dallas, to "Cactus Jack" Garner, in Uvalde on his ninety-fourth birthday. It should be recalled that FDR almost fell victim to an assassination attempt in 1933, before starting his first term. In his place was killed Chicago Mayor Anton Cermak, who sat in the same car with him. Unconsciously at least, JFK's chat with Garner triggered off the associative memory of that tragedy, thus contributing to its modified repetition with reference to himself. (The same memory factor may have been at least partially responsible for the only near-tragic incident during JFK's quest for the presidency. When he was about to speak in the Windy City, police arrested an armed suspect who had boasted that he would kill the young candidate.)

B. Other Male Kennedys.

The consciousness of a family, business, athletic team, government or any collective unit does not depend upon personality as such. Like body cells, persons may die, only to be replaced by new ones. But the continuity of the flow of consciousness goes on. After the events in Dallas, the functional victimization unit in which John F. Kennedy had been the negative factor, became inactive and, technically, dissolved. The applicable dynamics decreed, in due course, the formation of a new functional unit with Senator Robert F. Kennedy as the negative factor and Sirhan Sirhan as the positive factor, once a suitable new environmental womb was formed, this time at the Ambassador Hotel in Los Angeles. In accordance with the global consciousness pertinent to the Kennedys, established on November 22, 1963, Joseph P. Kennedy's third son was not shot until a few minutes after it became known that he had won the California primary. This fact virtually assured him the Democratic nomination (since President Johnson had announced he would not seek a second term) and election to president. Robert F. Kennedy did not die until his older brother's widow, in accordance with her B.I.D., had reached his bedside after flying in from London. Again the functional victimization unit in the Kennedy consciousness became inactive and dissolved. Eventually, in accordance with the typical long-term rhythm, a new functional victimization unit involving a male Kennedy was formed, with Senator Edward A. "Ted" Kennedy as the only available candidate. This time, however, the environmental womb was located on Chappaquiddick Island, Massachusetts, with Mary Jo Kopechne instead of a Kennedy as the victim by a new variable of the fatal constant—drowning. Ted Kennedy was, evidently, the unwitting victimizer. He, in turn, was victimized by himself, the press, and the public for his involvement and evasiveness. In case Ted Kennedy should decide not to run in 1976, this would diminish the Kennedy consciousness of victimization. On the other hand, should he make his bid for the presidency, in accordance with the timetable supposedly established by his brother John, he would, in the absence of modifiers, embellish the appropriate consciousness. This, we predict, would assure his assassination immediately after the formation of a suitable environmental uterus.

Regardless of the senator's actions, however, the victimization consciousness pertaining to male members of the Kennedy family is already evident with regard to Joseph P. Kennedy Jr., Robert F. and Ethel Kennedy's eldest son. He was in the news last year as a passenger on a highjacked Air India plane. On February 24, 1973, Mayor Alioto reported that the young Kennedy had received threatening phone calls, alledgedly because he held down a post with the San Francisco Health Department from which he resigned a few weeks later. On March 27, 1973, he suffered a brain concussion in an auto accident. His reckless driving resulted in another accident on August 13, 1973.[27] A young woman was at least partially paralyzed and six other young passengers, among them his brother David, were injured. Joe Jr. received a $100 fine as well as a lecture from the judge.

His younger brother, Robert F. Kennedy Jr. also made news. In addition to a loitering and marijuana incident, he was mentioned as an intended kidnap victim of a group of Greek revolutionaries in August 1972. On July 19, 1973, a Chilean border guard supposedly fired a shot toward him and four companions in the Andes Mountains. "Even before the guy fired the shot, Buddy dived for the snow," reported Harvey Fleetwood, a freelance writer for *Harper's Magazine.*[28]

C. B.I.D. Modification

The B.I.D., we have found, can be modified through understanding and consciously directed, systematic action. As a result, we have learned to establish comprehensive improvement programs to enable potential or habitual victims in various aspects of experience to become de-victimized. By the same process, potential or habitual victimizers can be re-educated. The principle, by which we have learned to stop the growth of adverse environmental wombs, can be used for such commendable purposes as the facilitation of goal achievement as well as individual and collective improvement.

This presentation merely summarizes some of our extensive findings on this vital topic. We have prepared texts on the prevention of victimization and related subjects for future use.

IV. Discussion of Results

A. Main Principles

The facts presented here indicate that human behavior and experience in general and victimology in particular derive not from chance factors but from the operation of laws that are as precise and applicable as those governing the universe.

B. Evidence.

The concepts and equations developed by Newton, Einstein, and others were found to apply to man by means of eight translations into their Human Physics equivalents.

C. Opposing Theories

The evidence presented by us is so clear and irrefutable that it should dispel any doubts of expert and layman alike as to the validity of our assertion that man is subject to the same laws that govern his physical environment. If other researchers have arrived at different conclusions, the reasons do not lie in their lack of competence or effort but in our resort to conceptual inventions that enabled us to prove the accuracy of our hypotheses.

(Not directly opposed to our views but likely to solve only part of the problem is the view of authorities, such as Dr. Jack R. Ewalt, superintendent of the Massachusetts Mental Health Center, Bullard Professor of Psychiatry at Harvard, and president in 1964 of the American Psychiatric Association. At the APA's convention in Los Angeles he described as an unsolved challenge the question of what to do about people who are not "mentally ill" but who have little control over their aggressive urges. "In a social sense they are more deviant than many an ambulatory schizophrenic," he said. This problem, according to him, was highlighted by the attack on President Kennedy. He also mentioned the tendency of people who cannot control their aggressions competently to associate themselves with extreme causes of a patriotic or revolutionary nature or both.[29])

(If such persons require study and special treatment, we assert, so do those who are potential victims. Men do not function independently of each other. Although therapy no doubt would benefit the would-be aggressor, it could not prevent other, so far peaceful men from hurting or killing a fearful, harm-conscious or guilt-ridden person in accordance with his unspoken command or unconscious expectation. Murderers like Oswald usually do not appear to be potential assassins or potentially dangerous. In the presence of an examiner in a peaceful state of mind, they will tend to reflect his feelings. But they become dangerous when mentally or emotionally aroused by the overt or hidden hostility, fear, guilt or death wish of a potential victim. A dog will bite only one who is afraid, not the one who loves it. If animals respond to true human feelings, though covert, so do men.)

D. Conclusions

The results obtained by us should be studied with care. Specifically, they should instigate a modification of the generally still prevailing harsh judgment of the potential or habitual victimizer. He as well as the potential or habitual victim should be taught to modify his understanding and *modus operandi* so that he can escape his otherwise inexorable fate. As a result, he will benefit not only himself but the one or ones who would otherwise be forced to play the inevitable role or roles complementary to his own. Once the demand is stopped, the supply will cease automatically.

E. Qualification

The conclusions presented here apply to every aspect of interpersonal dynamics. Although we have specially studied the conditions that influence human behavior and experience only with reference to a relatively limited field of variables, our findings should prove valid also for the conditions representing the rest of the huge experimental complex or scope of human experience not considered here. We have found this to be true after nearly two decades of experimentation on ourselves and our large clientele. As a result we have found that human behavior and experience can be upgraded on the singular, collective, and universal scale. Specifically, the process of de-victimization is not only desirable but practical. So is the establishment of a worldwide climate favoring the elimination and prevention of victimization anywhere.

F. Application

Our experience has shown that the results of this study can be applied to psychiatry, psychology, medicine, law, sociology, business, industry, education, and religion as well as self-motivation and self-improvement.

G. Stimulation

We trust that the facts presented here will stimulate the reader to further thought and research on the subject of our investigation. In validating our findings, our emphasis had to be on quality rather than on their quantitative or large-scale application.

Notes

1. *Essays in Science,* by A. Einstein, New York: Wisdom Library, 1936.
2. *Social Change and Prejudice,* by B. Bettelheim & M. Janowitz, New York: Free Press of Glencoe, 1964.

3. *The Meaning of Relativity,* by A. Einstein, Princeton, N.J.: Princeton University Press, 1955.

4. *Physics and Philosophy,* by W. Heisenberg, New York: Harper, 1958.

5. *The Influence on Mental Factors on the Outcome of Law Cases,* by C.K. Teutsch, contained in Trial and Tort Trends of 1966, Vienna, Virginia: M. Coiner, 1967.

6. *Quantum Processes Predicted,* by H. Schmidt, *New Scientist,* October 16, 1969.

7. *The Prometheus Project,* by G. Feinberg, Garden City, N.J.: Doubleday, 1968.

8. *The Secrets of the Old One,* by Jeremy Bernstein, contained in *The New Yorker Magazine,* March 10 and 17, 1973.

9. Understand and Raise Your Consciousness—*From Here to Happiness,* by J.M. & C.K. Teutsch, Los Angeles, 1961, 1959 and New York: Cornerstone Library, 1967.

10. Ibid.

11. David Finkelstein, physicist, quoted in *Time Magazine,* April 23, 1973.

12. *The Universe and Dr. Einstein,* by L.K. Barnett, New York: William Sloane Associates, Inc., 1957.

13. J. Bernstein, *The Secrets of the Old One, supra.*

14. *The Roots of Coincidence,* by A. Koestler, New York: Random House, 1972.

15. *The Saturday Evening Post,* November 21, 1964.

16. *The Founding Father*, by R.J. Whalen, New York: The New American Library, 1964.

17. John F. Kennedy letter to Harry Squires of Granada Hills, California, May 27, 1959.

18. Hugh Sidey: *John F. Kennedy, President,* Greenwich, Conn.: Fawcett Publications, Inc., 1963, 1964.

19. Ibid.

20. Reported by M. Frankel, *New York Times,* November 2, 1963.

21. *Death of A President* by W. Manchester, New York: Harper Row, 1967.

22. *Life Magazine,* John F. Kennedy Memorial Edition.

23. *Life Magazine,* August 14, 1964.

24. Ibid.

25. W. Manchester, *Death of a President.*

26. *Life Magazine,* J.F.K. Memorial Edition.

27. *Los Angeles Times,* August 14, 1973.

28. *Los Angeles Times,* July 28, 1973.

29. *Los Angeles Times,* May 5, 1964.

16 The Victim in Contemporary Literature
Arthur Lapan

This paper is written wholly in the spirit of the amateur. It simply contains some thoughts about the victim in contemporary literature. But first I must clarify what I mean by the 'victim in contemporary literature'. I do not mean *analyses* of victims, as for example, Marx's analysis of what he took to be the victims of contemporary capitalism; nor anthropological and scholarly studies of the victim in sacrificial rites; nor diagnoses of the victims of guilt or repressed sexual passions, as in Freud; nor philosophical analyses of the victims of such things as contemporary nihilism, as in Camus' "The Myth of Sisyphus" and *The Rebel*. No, by 'the victim of contemporary literature' I mean simply the victim as we find him in contemporary drama and the novel. We will consider analyses of the victim only when they render intelligible the image of the victim as it appears in the contemporary drama and novel, and mainly in Kafka and Ionesco at that.

The distinction between books *about* the victim, and the victim in drama, etc., is of some significance. Books about the victim tend, as we said, to be analytical, their propositions have a logical relationship to one another, and an adequate interpretation of them would convey their meaning as well as they. The same is not true of the drama and novel. An interpretation of Kafka's *The Trial* is in no way a substitute for the novel itself. You have to read *The Trial* to get its meaning. In it the victim is not talked about, dissected, explained: he is present. And differences such as these have a different impact upon the reader. Camus' analysis of the absurd is lucid, rational, illuminating, but an absurd presence on the stage leaves us with anything but a sense of lucidity and rationality, although it may be equally illuminating and cathartic. Also it may produce a comic effect, which *theories* of the absurd rarely do.

Indeed, even in dramas and novels in which the victim is a central concern, there is a distinction between a lucid presentation of character and situation, and one which abandons rational forms. It is a matter of the congruity of form and content. In existentialist writers like Giraudoux, Anouilh, Silacrou, Sartre, and Camus, there is a pervasive sense of the meaninglessness of life, but this sense of irrationality, of dehumanization, of separateness, of helplessness, is conveyed by old, logically constructed meaningful conventions. In the Theatre of the Absurd, on the other hand, these rational conventions are abandoned, and the form of the drama, the relationships between the parts of the dialogue, and the character of the actions

themselves, become congruent with the sense of meaninglessness they communicate. This difference in form makes a crucial difference to the actual
image of the victim which emerges.

But this Symposium on Victimology is being held in Jerusalem, organized
by Jews, which tells us something about the literature, in whatever sense we
use the word 'literature'. For we ourselves are, or were, victims, or are identified
with them, and the same thing goes for the writers of the literature. It is a literature by victims, a literature of self-consciousness.

As for the value of this literature, we are all children of our time and culture,
even in reaction to them. The literature can therefore better help us understand
the minds of victims, so that we may better help them, and so that they can
understand themselves and better help themselves.

From the fact that so much of contemporary literature is written by victims
about victims, at least two things follow: first, that it is the victim who tends
to be the central character in much of contemporary literature, and secondly,
that in contemporary literature the victim is, in the language of the philosophers,
a subject, a center of value, and things are seen from his standpoint. Of course
the fact that the victim tends to be the central character of much of contemporary literature is also no doubt due to the fact that our century has been so
prolific in spawning victims.

Moreover, there are differences in contemporary literature in the way
in which he may see his suffering. In Brecht, victimization is wholly intelligible; it is embedded in a Marxist framework, in a capitalist process which
can be analyzed into its basic elements, which has an implicit, logical development which accounts for most forms of violence as well as exploitation, and
which also has an inherent redemptive goal. Violence is therefore meaningful in a moral as well as logical sense of the word. But in the Theatre of the
Absurd, as we have said, the victim finds his suffering altogether unintelligible.
He cannot explain it, it has no purpose, there is no redemption. And the
difference between these two attitudes of the victim towards his suffering
and towards violence necessarily affects the form in which the entire dramas
are cast. Brecht's 'epic' theatre is not the same as the Theatre of the
Absurd.

But precisely who is the victim in contemporary literature and what is he
a victim of? The moment we try to answer this question, we realize that in
contemporary literature the victim is not quite the same as the ordinary
common garden-variety victim: there is something unique about him, something which has to be understood in terms of the special character and predicament of contemporary Western culture. Ordinarily when we use the word
'victim', we mean a living being sacrificed to some deity or in the performance
of some religious ritual; or someone who is put to death, tortured or mutilated
by another; or a person who is subjected to oppression, deprivation, or suffering;
or again, someone who suffers death, loss or injury as a result of his own doing,

as a person who is a victim of his own neurosis; or someone who is tricked, duped, or subjected to hardship, someone badly taken advantage of, as a victim of propaganda, of chicanery in business, of advertisement, of brainwashing, etc. But when we use the word 'victim' in connection with contemporary literature, we mean something more.

This something more is that the victim in contemporary literature moves in a world in which God is dead, meaningless, without purpose. Perhaps we should say, in a nihilistic world. And perhaps this is due to the fact that in modern times natural science more and more came to be regarded as the source of truth about reality, about value, about the determinants of the solution of human problems, and to the fact that in the equations of modern science, of natural science that is, no reference to purpose is found, to values, to the good. Moreover, with the decline of the authority of revelation, the authority of traditional values also declined. Furthermore, many views arose which explained values as the results, as the products, of something else. Marx regarded them as conditioned by the means and methods of production and by the class struggle; Nietzsche, by the will-to-power; and Freud, by social needs. In these views, objective, rational, universally valid values were seen as but appearances. More often than not they were regarded as but appearances which masked men's more fundamental material drives and interests. Thus in Marx, objective, universal values are but the masks of the class interests of the bourgeoisie. In Nietzsche, the traditional Judeo-Christian values, humility, etc., are but masks for the resentment of the poor. Here, too, there are no universally valid and objective human values, only deceptions and self-deceptions.

The sense of meaninglessness which is so pervasive in contemporary literature also, no doubt, was an outcome of the loss of hope of ultimate redemption. We have already spoken of the death of God. But when the religious outlook declined, it did not disappear; it simply suffered a sea-change. Thus in Marxism you still have a sense of eventual redemption—this time by the proletarian revolution which is supposed to be implicit in the logical development of history. But the decline of Marxism among the intellectuals of the Western world was not so much due to a scrupulous methodological punctiliousness on their part; it was as much due to the actual experience of the Soviet Union itself, in which no withering away of the state was evident, but rather authority, terror, a resurgence of classes and bureaucracy.

All this is reflected in contemporary literature and in the image of the victim in contemporary literature. In Kafka's *The Castle* a surveyor looks for a castle—for a home—he cannot find, he does not even know exists. The uncertainty is built into the novel, it is part of its fabric. Man seems to be seeking for a meaning which escapes him; all the roads he takes culminate in dead-ends; what is present is his looking, but the meaning he seeks is not only inevitably undefined, its very existence is unreal. Thus his quest is absurd.

Waiting for Godot deals with the same theme. As Martin Esslin (1969)

points out in his excellent book *The Theatre of the Absurd*, to which I am
greatly indebted in this paper, the subject of the play is :

> the act of waiting as an essential and characteristic aspect of the
> human condition . . .[1] (The two tramps) live in hope; they wait
> for Godot, whose coming will bring the flow of time to a stop . . .
> (it is) the peace, the rest from waiting, the sense of having arrived
> in a haven, that Godot represents to the two tramps . . . Then they
> will no longer be tramps, homeless wanderers, but will have arrived
> home . . . (But) their appointment with him is by no means certain.
> (One tramp) does not remember it at all. (The other) is not quite
> sure what they asked Godot to do for them.[2] Indeed, according to
> Beckett himself the theme of the two thieves of the cross in the
> Christian Gospel, "the theme of the uncertainty of the hope of
> salvation and the fortuitousness of the bestowal of grace, (is the
> theme of the play) . . . Out of all the malefactors, out of the millions
> and millions of criminals that have been executed in the course of
> history, two, only two, had the chance of receiving absolution in
> the hour of their death in so uniquely effective a manner. One hap-
> pened to make a hostile remark; he was damned. One happened to
> contradict that hostile remark; he was saved . . . (But) these, after
> all, were not well-considered judgments, but chance exclamations
> uttered at a moment of supreme suffering and stress . . .[3] (And
> indeed in the play) Godot himself is unpredictable in bestowing
> kindness and punishment . . . His coming is not a source of pure
> joy, it can also mean damnation.[4]

What is the implication of all this for violence and for the victim of violence? It is, as we have said, that violence itself is felt to be senseless; it has
no policy, no rationale, no justification, and to the victim it appears wholly
incomprehensible and without consolation. (One is stimulated to ask whether
it is not precisely in this kind of climate that fascism is nurtured.) Time was
when the victim could be assured of an eventual just reward or punishment.
The world was a moral order (hence rational), his soul was immortal, and the
wicked were damned and those who maintained the law of the Lord in the
end sunned themselves in eternal blessedness. During the Englightenment
the religious picture of the world fell to the ground—among its adherents,
that is,—and the Idea of Progress took its place. But here the dedicated soul,
victimized by blind, brutal, self-interested men, still looked for justification
from the future. Condorcet, languishing in jail, is nonetheless confident that
his ideas will triumph in the future. And in Hegel and in Marxism that same
attitude prevails. Reality is not what is present but what is implicit in what
is present, and when that becomes explicit, today's violators will be confounded—
by history—and today's victim will prove true. We are all familiar with this
common-garden-variety attitude.

But in much of contemporary literature, violence simply has no significance, most often for the violator as well as for the victim. There is an episode that actually occurred to Beckett himself which illustrates this very well. He was stabbed in a Paris street by an underworld character who had accosted him for money, and had to be taken to the hospital with a perforated lung. Later, when his lung had healed, Beckett went to see his assailant in prison. He asked the apache why he had stabbed him, and received the answer: "Je ne sais pas, Monsieur." Or take Ionesco's play *Tueur Sans Gages—The Gratuitous Killer.*

Berenger, its hero, is a Chaplinesque little man, simple, awkward, but human. As the play opens, he is being shown round an ambitious new housing project by its creator, the municipal architect. This is a beautiful new quarter of the town, well-designed, with pleasant gardens and a pond. What is more, as the architect explains, permanent sun- shine is built into the project; however much it may rain in other parts of the city, the moment you cross the boundary of the *cité radieuse,* the radiant city, you enter a climate of perpetual spring. . .

But why, he asks, are the streets of this lovely quarter so deserted? He is shattered to hear that the inhabitants have either left or have locked themselves into their houses, because a mysterious killer is abroad in this happy place, who lures his victims to their death . . . Berenger is appalled. And when news comes that among the latest victims is Mlle. Dany, the architects's young secretary, whom he has just met and with whom he had fallen in love, he resolves to track down the killer.[5]

Berenger tells Edouard, a visitor of his, the horrible news about the killer, and is astonished to find that Edouard, in fact everybody, has long known about him, that everyone is used to the idea that such a killer is abroad.[6]

In the last act, Berenger is alone. He walks through the empty streets, the decor changing as he progresses. Suddenly he finds himself face to face with a grinning, giggling dwarf in shabby clothes. He knows that this is the killer. In a long speech Berenger tries to pursuade the killer, who is obviously a degenerate idiot, to desist from his murderous and senseless activity. He uses every known argument for philanthropy and goodness—patriotism, self-interest, social responsibility, Christianity, reason, the vanity of all activity, even that of murder. The killer never speaks a word, he merely giggles idiotically. In the end Berenger pulls out two old guns and tries to kill the killer but he cannot do it. He drops the guns and silently submits to the killer's raised knife.[7]

In Ionesco, too, violence is often seen as the real meaning behind activities which mask it and which are otherwise thought of as acts of communication and unity. Thus in his play *The Lesson*

Language is shown as an instrument of power. As the play proceeds,

the pupil who was eager, lively and alert, is gradually drained of her
vitality, while the professor, who was timid and nervous at the beginning, gradually gains in assurance and domination. It is clear that the
professor derives his progressive increase of power from his role as a
giver, a very arbitrary prescriber of meanings. Because words must
have the significance *he* decides to give them, the pupil comes under
his dominance . . . The discomfiture of the pupil announces itself
when she is suddenly overtaken by a violent toothache . . . In some
ways this toothache indicates the pupil's loss of the power to speak,
her loss of the gift of language . . . Progressively, all the parts of her
body begin to ache until, in an act of complete physical subjection,
she allows the professor to plunge the knife into her, accepting the
professor's final proposition, "The knife kills." The sexual connotation of this climactic moment of the play is quite openly indicated.
The pupil flops into a chair in an immodest position . . . her legs
spread wide and hanging over both sides of the chair. The professor
remains standing in front of her, his back to the audience. Murderer
and victim shout "Aaah" at the same . . . [8] The Lesson's main
proposition hinges on the sexual nature of all power and the relationship between language and power as the basis of all human
ties.[9]

Contemporary literature is not, of course, obsessed with power only.
Dehumanization, meaninglessness, irrationality, atomization, alienation,
isolation, separation, the failure to communicate, etc., are equally its themes.
But these are inseparable from violence and are caused by and are causes of
it. The question, however, is: How does contemporary literature respond to
violence and to its related phenomena? Does it consent to them, or does it
significantly negate them?

There is no doubt of the response in writers like Brecht. Here these things
are not only negated, his play is an open invitation to the audience to also
negate them. The primary intent of the plays is resistance, social resistance.
But in the case of men like Kafka, Ionesco, and Beckett, the case is somewhat
more complicated. *The characters in the play* do not always resist. Ionesco's
Berenger in his *Rhinoceros* finally succumbs to the plague of dehumanization,
fascism if you like. And in *The Gratuitous Killer*, as we saw, he consents to be
killed by the misshapen, anonymous idiot. But the *form* of the play, the play
itself, is another matter. The plays declare dehumanization, senseless violence,
to be absurd. Thereby they resist. The characters in the play may not always
resist, *but the play resists.*

What I am saying is that the play itself, its artistic form, generates in us
who see it the response 'absurd!' to the senseless victimization which appears
in the play. Absurdity is the significant form of a play like *Rhinoceros.* The
play itself, in other words, is a non-discursive, unique, esthetic symbol which

shows forth, exhibits absurdity. The play itself is to the absurd what Goethe says is true of the relationship between every symbol and what it symbolizes. "Goethe . . . defines a genuine symbol as a particular instance which is coalescent with a universal and which thereby plays a unique role by revealing, in a way that no other particular could quite do, the nature of that more general something."[10]

But the very word 'absurd', the very sentiment, the very form itself, is an implicit rejection and negation. Moreover, it is a saying 'No' which has resistance to such things as senseless violence and victimization implicit in it. Camus started off with "The Myth of Sisyphus" and ended up with *The Rebel.*

This sense of absurdity is often accompanied by the comic. The very senselessness of the violence and victimization, their very irrationality, are what arouse the comic. As Wylie Sypher says, "From earliest times the comic ritual has been presided over by a Lord of Misrule, and the improvisations of comedy have the aspect of a Feast of Unreason, a Revel of Fools."[11] Comedy here is also a form of negation.

In essence, it is meaninglessness itself which the plays declare to be absurd, which they thereby negate. In so doing they declare meaning to be a value, and rationality. The absurd is a response, an action, an affirmation of reason, of man, in the face of irrationality, dehumanization, violence, the loss of identity and, of course, meaninglessness.

The word 'victim', we said, referred to a living being sacrificed to some deity or in the performance of some religious ritual; and it is interesting to note that Aristotle, and many contemporary writers, also regard "comedy as a primal rite; a rite transformed to art." As F.M. Cornford puts it, "comedy is a scene of sacrifice and feast. Involved in this scene was the ancient rite of purging the tribe by expelling a scapegoat on whose head were heaped the sins of the past year. At this public purging or catharsis the scapegoat was often the divine man or animal, in the guise of a victim, to whom were transferred the sins and misfortunes of the worshippers. Eventually the divine character of the scapegoat was forgotten; as Fraser notes, he became an ordinary victim, a wretch who was a condemned criminal perhaps, actually as well as ritually guilty."[12]

Now in contemporary literature the 'heros' are also ordinary people, often wretches, certainly people of no consequence. They feel themselves to be victims, and what is more, they feel that they are being sacrificed, and that in the sacrificial process they are being reduced to utter nonentity, to utter nothingness. But a novel like *The Trial* or a play like *Waiting for Godot* differ, in what they make manifest, from an ancient sacrificial rite in that the sacrificial process is seen from the point of view of the victim. In writers like Brecht, of course, the sacrificial process is also seen from the point of view of the victim, but it is intrinsically meaningful, just as it is in Judaism or in Christianity. There is redemption in it. But in Kafka and Beckett it is an utterly senseless dead-end. It is this which, coupled with the implicit negation in it, gives it the sense of absurdity and makes it seem comic.

Where its form is consonant with its content, the Theatre of the Absurd, therefore, *is* a rite. If this is so, it reaches its culmination in Genet. In Genet, theatre is ritual, and deliberately, self-consciously so. "Genet strives for a theatre of ritual, but ritual is the regular repetition of mythical events and, as such, closely akin to sympathetic magic. . . A theatre as ritual and ceremonial as the theatre of ancient Greece presupposes a valid and vital body of beliefs and myths. And this is precisely what our own civilization lacks. Hence Genet is faced with the need to provide a plot structure that will furnish the rationale for his mock-liturgy and mock-ceremonial."[13]

" In *Les Négres* (*The Blacks*) he has found an extremely ingenious solution to this problem. Here he presents a play labeled a *clownerie* (a clown show), which is entirely ritual and therefore needs no plot devices at all. A group of blacks performs the ritual reenactment of its resentments and feelings of revenge before a white audience . . .[14] The central part of the ritual is a fantasy of the ritual murder of a white woman. . . Later, when the actual murder is lovingly reconstructed, the victim becomes a buxom white woman who has been so seduced by her black visitor's superior sexual attractions that she has invited him into her bedroom, where she is both violated and strangled. As an additional touch of irony, the black who has to enact the raped white woman is supposed in private life to be a black priest, Diouf. . .

"After the blacks have acted out their hatred and resentment, but also their feeling of guilt, the next phase follows—the fantasy of final liberation. The queen and her court descend, as though engaged on a punitive expedition to the colony. They are trapped and ignominiously put to death by the blacks, and the missionary bishop is castrated."[15] It is obvious that in this play, being a victim is part of a ritual, and an absurd ritual at that—a ritual of sacrifice and revenge, of murder and liberation.

I cannot forbear from mentioning another aspect of contemporary literature: its prophetic character, and this in novels and dramas whose subject is the victim. Here the meaninglessness and violence depicted in the literature prove prophetic. An excellent example is Kafka's *The Trial,* which was adapted for the Theatre de Marigny in Paris by Andre Gide and Jean-Louis Barrault, and which opened there on October 10, 1947. "Kafka's dream of guilt and the arbitrariness of the powers that rule the world was more for the French audience of 1947 than a mere fantasy. The author's private fears had become flesh, and had turned into the collective fear of nations; the vision of the world as absurd, arbitrary and irrational had proved a highly realistic assessment."

"Kafka's short stories and unfinished novels are essentially meticulously exact descriptions of nightmares and obsessions—the anxieties and guilt feelings of a sensitive human being lost in a world of convention and routine. The images of Kafka's own sense of loss of contact with reality, and his feelings of guilt at being unable to regain it—the nightmare of K. accused of a crime against a law he has never known; the predicament of that other K., the surveyor, who has been summoned to a castle he cannot penetrate—have become the supreme expression of the situation of modern man."[16] As Ionesco observes in a short but illuminating essay on Kafka: "This theme of man lost in a labyrith, without a guiding thread, is basic in Kafka's work. Yet if man no longer has a guiding thread, it is because he no longer wanted to have one. Hence his feeling of guilt, of anxiety, of the absurdity of history."[17]

Alfred Jarry's *UbuRoi* has also proved prophetically true. "Ubu is a savage caricature of a stupid, selfish bourgeois seen through the cruel eyes of a school-boy, but this Rabelaisian character, with his Falstaffian greed and cowardice, is more than mere social satire. He is a terrifying image of the animal nature of man, his cruelty and ruthlessness. Ubu makes himself king of Poland, kills and tortures all and sundry, and is finally chased out of the country. He is mean, vulgar and incredibly brutal, a monster that appeared ludicrously exaggerated in 1896, but was far surpassed by reality in 1945. Once again, an intuitive image of the dark side of human nature that a poet had projected onto the stage proved prophetically true."[18]

And again, two works by Ribemont-Dessaignes, *L'Empereur de Chine* (*The Emperor of China*), written in 1916, and *Le Bourreau du Peru* (*The Executioner of Peru*), published in 1928, assume a prophetic content through the free flow of imagination and the release of the subconscious fantasy of a poet. "*L'Empereur de Chine* is a powerful play that combines the elements of non-sense and violence which characterizes the Theatre of the Absurd. . . In *Le Bourreau du Peru* the government abdicates and hands the sacred seals of the state to the hangman, and a period of gratuitous murder and execution ensues. . . The outbreak of violence in the era of the Second World War is exactly forecast by *L'Empereur de Chine* and even more drastically by *Le Bourreau du Peru.* It is as though the destructiveness of the Dadaists—Ribemont-Dessaignes was a Dadaist—were a sublimated release of the same secular impulse toward aggression and violence that found expression in the mass murders of the totalitarian movements."[19]

This prophetic character of a work of literature is especially marked in Brecht's first real masterpiece *The Measures Taken*. Brecht, as already said, was a Communist, and in his play,

> . . . he now for the first time tackles the theme of Communism and
> Communist discipline itself. The moral conflict between ends and
> means is faced boldly and without fear of carrying it to its logical
> conclusion. The young comrade, whose heart has been too soft, who
> has failed to resist the temptation of helping the poor when the higher
> interests of the party lay in ignoring their suffering, must be killed.
> He sees the need for it himself and begs for death. The story is told
> and reenacted by a group of party workers after their return to head-
> quarters: each of them in turn plays the part of the young comrade,

for he represents a part of their own nature, the part they have to
suppress and kill in themselves. The 'control chorus', sitting in
judgment on the party workers, approves of their disciplinary measure and praises them for having been hard.[20]

In the end Brecht, who always considered himself a better Marxist
than the party pundits, was vindicated by history itself. *The Measures
Taken,* written in 1930, is an exact and horrifying anticipation of the
great confession trials of the Stalinist era. Many years before Bukharin
consented to his own execution in front of his judges, Brecht had given
that act of self-sacrifice for the sake of the party its great tragic expression.
With the intuition of the poet, he had grasped the real problem of Communist discipline with all its far-reaching implications. To this day
The Measures Taken remains the only great tragedy on the moral
dilemma of Soviet Communism.[21]

Again, in his comedy *Man Equals Man,* written by Brecht in the
middle twenties, "three greedy, wicked, and vulgar British colonial
soldiers completely transform a harmless little individual into a ferocious
fighting man by methods that foreshadow the brainwashing techniques
of totalitarian society with an accuracy as uncannily prophetic as that
with which *The Measures Taken* foreshadowed the Stalinist purge trials.
Little Galy Gay is accused of some crime till he feels an overwhelming
sense of guilt, condemned to death in a mock trial and is induced to
believe that he has been executed. Thereafter he willingly accepts his
new identity; and as Brecht says in the play:

> Mr. Bertholt Brecht will prove that one can
> Do whatever one wants with a man
> A man will be reassembled like a motor car in front of you
> And afterwards will be as good as new . . .[22]

Summary

This paper is about the victim in the contemporary drama and novel, and
particularly in Kafka, Ionesco, and Beckett. It is not about psychological,
political or anthropological analyses of victims. We are concerned with *presentations* of the victim. The novel or play is what Goethe called a genuine symbol,
i.e., a particular instance which is coalescent with a universal and which thereby
plays a unique role by revealing, in a way that no other particular could quite
do, the nature of that more general something.

In these presentations the victim tends to be the subject and central
character. There are two ways of presenting his victimization, however: either
as ultimately meaningful, as in Brecht, or as ultimately meaningless, as in Kafka,
Ionesco, and others. Where it is seen as ultimately meaningless, it is against the

background of a world in which God is dead, without purpose, in which values are unreal masks and in which there is no hope of ultimate redemption. All this is reflected in the very form of the literature. The violence which he suffers is therefore also felt by the victim to be senseless and inexplicable. Indeed, in such a world violence often has no significance for the violator as well.

Contemporary literature does not assent to victimization. Where victimization is seen as meaningful, as in Brecht, it is a literature of social resistance. Where it is seen as meaningless, the plays and novels *as symbols* negate it by presenting it as absurd, frequently comic. They are hereby a response to meaninglessness, an action, and an implicit affirmation of the value of reason and of man.

In the literature the 'heroes' are ordinary people, often wretches, who feel that they are being sacrificed, that they are scapegoats. Writers like Kafka and Beckett therefore present a sacrificial rite, but one which, unlike ancient sacrifices, is seen from the point of view of the victim. In Brecht, of course, the sacrifice is ultimately meaningful. But in Kafka, Beckett and others, it is a sacrificial rite which is utterly senseless, absurd, and often comic. In Genet the theatre as ritual is self-conscious.

Sometimes the meaninglessness and violence depicted in the literature prove prophetic, as in Kafka's *The Trial*. This is also true where the violence is thought to be meaningful, as in Brecht's play, *The Measures Taken*.

Notes

1. Martin Esslin, *The Theatre of the Absurd* (Garden City, New York: Anchor Books, Doubleday & Company, Inc., 1969), p. 29.
2. Ibid., p. 32.
3. Ibid., pp. 32-33.
4. Ibid., p. 33.
5. Ibid., p. 144.
6. Ibid., p. 145.
7. Ibid., pp. 145-146.
8. Ibid., pp. 117-118.
9. Ibid., p. 119.
10. Philip Wheelwright, *Heraclitus* (New York: Atheneum, 1971), p. 14.
11. Wylie Sypher, ed., *Comedy: with Introduction and Appendix: The Meanings of Comedy* (Garden City, New York: Doubleday and Company, Inc., 1956), p. 221.
12. Ibid., p. 225.
13. Esslin, *The Theatre of the Absurd*, p. 188.
14. Ibid., p. 188.
15. Ibid., p. 189.

16. Ibid., p. 307.

17. Ionesco, "Dans les armes de la ville," *Cahiers de la Compagnie Madelaine Renaud-Jean-Louis Barrault*, no. 20 (October 1957): 4.

18. Esslin, *The Theatre of the Absurd*, p. 310.

19. Ibid., p. 322.

20. Martin Esslin, *Brecht, the Man and his Work*, new rev. ed. (Garden City, New York: Doubleday and Company, Inc., 1971), pp. 162-163.

21. Ibid., p. 164.

22. Ibid., p. 261.

Conclusions and Recommendations Adopted by The First International Symposium on Victimology Held in Jerusalem, September 2-6, 1973

I. What Is Victimology?

1. a. Victimology may be defined as the scientific study of victims. Special attention, however, should be devoted to the problems of victims of crime, the primary concern of this Symposium.
   b. Criminology is enriched by a victimological orientation.
2. Individuals, groups, organizations, nations, and societies can be victimized.
3. Focus should be expanded from the 'two-dimensional' person-to-person interaction to the three or multidimensional one, thus including the bystander and other relevant persons.
4. Lack of concern by a bystander at the scene of a crime is objectionable and, whether or not a criminal act or omission, should be educationally counteracted.
5. The bystander who attempts to assist a victim should be granted immunity for his reasonable acts and compensation when injured.

II. Victimization

1. Research on hidden victimization is needed.
2. A subjective feeling of victimization may not be accompanied by a sufficiently objective basis for society to take responsive action.
3. Victimization of and by groups is no less serious than victimization on a person-to-person level.
4. Certain forms of inadvertence or negligence which occur in industrialized society are as great a cause of victimization as intentional acts.

III. Causes of Victimization

1. Just as certain persons are thought to have high probabilities for committing crime, so also others may have the same likelihood for being victimized.
2. The victim may precipitate the crime.
3. A victimizer may be a person who has himself previously been victimized.
4. The administration of justice may sometimes use excessive punishment and thereby victimize the former victimizer.

209

IV. Prevention, Treatment, and Research

1. a. Ineffective means of preventing and controlling crime may cause unnecessary suffering to victims, offenders and society.

   b. Legislators, courts, and other authorities responsible for crime prevention and control should evaluate and renovate the organizations and services in this field in order to increase their effectiveness and reduce unnecessary human suffering.

   c. Victimology can lead to improvement of legal procedures, including sentencing, and thereby reduce recidivism and the risks of victimization.

2. Institutional procedures should be provided to protect the victim against unintentional, harmful consequences of the judicial process. A balance should be reached between the needs and rights of the victim and the defendant.

3. a. Some governments and state organizations victimize vulnerable groups, causing a danger of escalation to mass violence. Such practices are condemned and an appeal is made to the conscience of mankind to maintain and enforce a restraining vigilance.

   b. International control of this type of victimization is necessary.

4. The right of asylum should be strengthened in order to assist the victim of the state.

5. Governmental and non-governmental bodies should provide both emergency and prolonged medical, psychiatric, psychological, and social services to victims of crime, without charge.

6. a. Research is needed on the extent to which victimization may lead victims to become offenders.

   b. Research into victim probabilities could help society to prevent the victimization of vulnerable persons.

V. Compensation

1. All nations should, as a matter of urgency, give consideration to the establishment of state systems of compensation for victims of crime and should seek to achieve maximum efficacy in the application of existing schemes and of those that may be established.

2. All available means should be employed to disseminate information about compensation schemes and the participation of all appropriate bodies—governmental and non-governmental—should be secured in their implementation.

3. All existing compensation schemes should be investigated and evaluated with a view to extending their application, bearing in mind the respective requirements of the various communities in which they operate.

It is suggested that the following questions be given full consideration by all nations intending to set up compensation schemes or intending to modify existing schemes:

1. Should there be a maximum and/or minimum level for compensation?
2. What is the nature of the losses that should be recompensed? e.g. direct damage, loss of earnings, pain and suffering.
3. Should consideration be given to the victim's conduct at the time of the offense and/or to his general character in determining the question of compensation?
4. Should payment be by right and denied only for stated reasons by the court?
5. Should present-day schemes be extended to include crimes against property?
6. Should the state be entitled to claim reimbursement from the criminal and/or should the state be empowered to compel criminals to give part of their earnings to the state?
7. Should states set up compulsory insurance schemes for certain professions whose exercise relies upon an element of fidelity and trust in order to cover damage caused by one of their members, e.g. doctors, lawyers, accountants, insurance companies, members of stock exchanges?
8. Should compensation schemes contain opportunities for appeal?
9. Should bystanders attempting to aid victims be entitled to compensation for damage or losses suffered?
10. Should the victim be entitled to immediate partial compensation in order to tide him over initial expenses, the determination of the final sum to be made subsequently by the compensation board?
11. Should an accused person who is found not guilty be entitled to compensation for court costs incurred and/or for other losses?
12. Should a judge in a criminal trial be entitled to order compensation by the state concurrently with his verdict?
13. Should the office of ombudsman be set up to provide direct focus on the needs of the victim, with special concern for mitigating immediate trauma, prevention of further stress at the hands of society, as well as for offering treatment for victim-recidivists?

This Symposium calls upon governmental and other national as well as international organizations to disseminate as widely as possible the conclusions and recommendations reached in the course of its deliberations, with the hope of achieving thereby the reduction and alleviation of victimization.

Name Index

Subject Index

Abortion, 68-69, 71

Bystander, 111; impact of laws on behavior of, 119-21; research questions, 121; role of, 119-20; typology, 112

Chronic drunkenness, 55-57
Compensation, 210; offender's willingness to compensate the victim, 149, 153
Criminalistics, 9
Criminology, 25-28, 39, 77-82

Einstein's theory of relativity, 179-82
Environments: and victimization, 13-14, 28-31
Europe, Council of, 127

Giessen test, 161-64

Harm, 83-84
Homosexuality, 64, 71

Iatrogenic disease, 61
Interpersonal dynamics, 172-75

Jurists, 9

Literature, contemporary, 197-207

Munchausen syndrome, 57
Mylonas law scale, 96

Nationalism, 39-41
Newton's laws, 175-79
Nomogenic disease, 61

Offender's perception of the victim, 137-53, 156-57, 159-61, 164
Organized crime, 127-35

Participant-as-victim, 68
Penal couple, 111
Physics, human, 169-82; and the case of President Kennedy, 182-91; and victimology, 192-94
Prevention, 210

Professional crime, 127-35
Prostitution, 69, 71
Psychiatry, 10
Psychoanalytic school, 58-59

Rape, 70
Rating test, 164
Refuse Act, 120
Research, 210; limits and risks, 7-8; major findings, 19-20; new perspectives, 3-7; questions, 211
Risk of victimization, 18-23
Rivers and Harbors Act, 120, 125
Rorschach test, 157

Semantic differential, 157-61
Sociology, 10

TAT matching procedure, 164-66
Tokugawa Administration, 115
Traffic offenses, 43-45
Traumatic neurosis, 57
Treatment, 210
Typology, 93-98, 129-35, 156-57

United Nations, 37, 38, 41-43, 120

Victim: definition, 15, 82-87, 170-72, 198-99, 203, 209; importance of in forensic judgments, 155; of governmental lawlessness, 45-51; in literature, 197-207; v.'s perception of the offender, 156-57, 159-61, 164
Victim-offender relationship, 12-14, 159-66, 169, 172-75, 200-204, 209
Victim-precipitation, 99-108
Victimity, 25-28
Victimization, 65-66; causes of, 209
Victimless crimes, 63-75, 130, 134
Victimology: and criminology, 25-28, 33-34; and the social sciences, 15-16; as a discipline, 17-19, 25-27, 77-87, 111; perspectives of, 31-35
Violence: and the victim in contemporary literature, 200-202, 206-207

List of Contributors

Inkeri Anttila, Ministry of Justice, Institute of Criminology, Helsinki, Finland.

Hugo A. Bedau, Department of Philosophy, Tufts University, Medford, Massachusetts.

Sung T. Cho, Department of Rehabilitation and Correction, Columbus, Ohio.

Hans Goeppinger, Institut fuer Kriminologie, Universitaet Tuebingen, Tuebingen, West Germany.

Stanley W. Johnston, Criminology Department, University of Melbourne, Parkville, Victoria, Australia.

Simha F. Landau, Institute of Criminology, Hebrew University, Jerusalem, Israel.

Arthur Lapan, Youth Services Agencies, The City of New York, New York.

John A. Mack, Criminology, University of Glasgow, Glasgow, Scotland.

Beniamin Mendelsohn, Lawyer, Jerusalem, Israel.

Jeffrey H. Reiman, Center for the Administration of Justice, The American University, Washington, D.C.

Zvonimir P. Separovic, Pravni Fakultet u Zagrebu, Zagreb, Yugoslavia.

Leon Sheleff, Institute of Criminology and Criminal Law, Tel Aviv University, Ramat Aviv, Israel.

Robert Silverman, Department of Sociology, University of Western Ontario, London, Ontario, Canada.

Joel M. Teutsch and Champion K. Teutsch, Consultants, Los Angeles, California.

Milo Tyndel, Department of Psychiatry, University of Toronto, Toronto, Canada.

Joachim Weber, Nervenklinik der Universitaet Muenchen, Muenchen, West Germany.

About the Editors

Israel Drapkin, M.D., has been Professor of Criminology and Director of the Institute of Criminology at the Hebrew University of Jerusalem since 1959. Previously, he was director of the Institute of Criminology of Chile (1936-59) and professor at the University of Chile (1950-59). He has served as correspondent to the United Nations Social Defence Section since 1950, and as a United Nations expert both in Israel and at the Asia and Far East Institute for the Prevention of Crime and Treatment of Offenders (UNAFEI). He has been visiting professor at the Haile Selassie I University (Addis Ababa), Central University of Venezuela, the University of Pennsylvania, and the American University (Washington, D.C.). Professor Drapkin was the chairman of the Organizing Committee of the First International Symposium on Victimology held in Jerusalem in 1973. He has contributed articles to professional journals and is the author or editor of several books, including coeditor (with Emilio Viano) of *Victimology* (Lexington Books, 1974).

Emilio Viano, Ph.D., is Associate Professor of Sociology and the Administration of Justice at The American University's Center for the Administration of Justice in Washington, D.C. He is also a faculty member in the Independent Study Program of the City University of New York, and, during 1974/75, at the Institute of Criminal Justice and Criminology of the University of Maryland. During 1973/74, Dr. Viano was the project director of the special project, "The Humanities and the Police," funded by the National Endowment for the Humanities. Previously, he was on the research staff of the National Council on Crime and Delinquency in New York City. Dr. Viano is the author of several articles which have appeared in professional journals, and is coauthor of *Social Problems and Criminal Justice* (Chicago: Nelson-Hall, 1974); coeditor (with Israel Drapkin) of *Victimology* (Lexington Books, 1974); coeditor of a volume on police-community relations to be published by J.B. Lippincott; and editor of a book on criminal justice research to be published by Lexington Books. He also coauthored *Management of Probation Services* (vols. I and II) and *Decision Making in Administration of Probation Services,* published by the National Council on Crime and Delinquency, and *Evaluation of Atlanta-Fulton County Correctional Agencies and Development of a Consolidation Plan* (McLean, Va.: PRC Public Management Services, Inc., 1973).